THE
Jesus
TRILOGY

THE Jesus TRILOGY

a paraphrase by

J. Daniel Small

A publication of Family Reclamation Project
ENJOYING GOD NEW TESTAMENT, VOLUME 1

DEDICATION

To my children and grandchildren,
and for the generations to come

It was for you he first set out to write this paraphrase before he died, to leave behind a legacy of far greater value than any monetary inheritance could ever have been. This is his lasting gift to you. Since he told me of his desire to do this for you, I have often been reminded of what Patrick Henry wrote in his last will and testament: "This is all the inheritance I give to my dear family. The religion of Christ will give them one which will make them rich indeed." To that I say, "Amen and amen." This was your dad's (grandpa's) heart for you — to make you rich indeed and to help you enjoy God as he did.

CONTENTS

FOREWORD

My wife and I first met Dan and Rebecca Small when they were interviewing for a leadership position at The Refuge, a retreat center on Washington's Olympic Peninsula. The Board was looking for a couple who could combine Christian discipleship with the practical skills required to maintain a wilderness retreat. Dan and Rebecca came with high recommendations and a lifetime of experience, together with an obvious love for that kind of work.

It didn't take long for us to discover another passion. We knew that both Dan and Rebecca had been nurtured in Plymouth Brethren circles, which guaranteed a certain exposure to Scripture, but camp leadership often squeezes out serious study of the Word of God. Not so with the Smalls; in addition to training kids in outdoor skills and the so-called "practical" virtues of the Christian life, they understood their mission to root disciples in biblical truth. In short, both Dan and Rebecca have a passion to see the Bible read, understood, and put into practice. What began with their own family and spread to camping and church ministry, has, in recent years, shaped Dan's dream of finding fresh ways to tell the biblical story. *The Jesus Trilogy* is the result.

Dan Small's book is a work of literature, but also of theology, with clear evidence of its author's lifelong study and reflection. *The Jesus Trilogy* stands in the best tradition of biblical paraphrasing, but it is much more than a paraphrase. The work is better described as a new way of telling the Jesus story. Like the New Testament, it begins with a form of the four Gospels, but doesn't end there. Luke's Book of Acts is presented as a second installment, entitled "The Sequel." Finally, the Jesus portrait reaches a climax in a grand finalé, John's Apocalypse (our Book of Revelation). The language of the *Trilogy* is paraphrastic, but the content is carefully selected texts of the New Testament. The primary selection principle is the story itself. In his acknowledgements, Dan credits Wyclif, Tyndale, and Luther, among classical translators, but special thanks is reserved for the modern works of J. B. Phillips, Eugene Peterson, and the New Living Translation (NLT).

Any serious reader who knows this genre will quickly place this volume within it. But to focus on the vocabulary of paraphrase is to miss what the work is all about. *The Jesus Trilogy* is not only a skillful paraphrase; it is a new way of organizing the essentials of the complete Jesus narrative. This, not the language by itself, is what makes this study unique. It is also what makes the story compelling.

The *Trilogy*, though taken from the New Testament, portrays a Jesus who comes from and returns to eternity. The author's goal is to tell the complete story, illuminating from the various texts the cosmic Christ. Although deeply and theologically selective, the text is drawn entirely from Scripture, and the narrative is faithful to the original "telling."

As might be expected from the title, the story is divided into three parts. An opening section, "The Story of Jesus," consists of what is called a "harmony" of all four Gospels. Anyone who has tried putting even the three "synoptic" Gospels together knows it is a task fraught with difficulties; adding the fourth Gospel (John) is an even greater challenge. Dan Small is, of course, not the first to attempt such a task; and, like those before him, he had to make difficult choices. The earliest known "harmony," the Diatessaron (literally, "through the four") by the second century Syrian apologist, Tatian, was both praised and criticized. Tragically, Tatian's work was mostly destroyed in the wake of heresy charges in his teaching. Whether, and how, his "Harmony" contributed to the controversy is not clear, but Tatian's fate reminds us that the endeavor carries its own risks.

All of this raises the question of how harmonizers, from Tatian to the present, select and collate their materials. Constructing a single narrative from four ideologically-charged Gospels follows no simple rules. The job requires theological as well as literary discernment. Our volume gives a prominent place to John's unique Gospel, weaving into its narrative the Synoptic (Matthew, Mark, Luke) tradition.

At times this means combining similar, but not identical, stories and paraphrasing the gist of a "Jesus saying" that may originally have been narrated in a variety of forms. An obvious example is found in the so-called "Sermon on the Mount," with clearly parallel, but distinctly different, forms in Matthew and Luke.

All of this makes the first section of the *Trilogy* potentially the most challenging. The second section, "The Sequel," is more straightforward. The Acts of the Apostles is, by Luke's own account, a sequel to his Gospel. *The Jesus Trilogy*, by including Acts as part of the Jesus story, makes it clear that the life and work of our Lord continues through His Spirit's presence in the Church. Dan Small's *Trilogy* intentionally blurs the distinction between "the Jesus Story" and "the Church Story." It is all the story of Jesus.

The volume comes to its grand conclusion with "The Finalé," and what a finalé it is! It begins with "God's revelation of things to come — a word from God regarding Jesus Christ." As in the first two sections, "The Finalé" begins and ends with Jesus. The "Mysterious Word," that at the start of the *Trilogy* "was with God and, in fact, was God," is about to be revealed, both in the seven churches and in the final conflict, as "the Word of God." When the dust settles and the City of God has become the dwelling place of the righteous, with the Lamb at its center, the narrative never loses its focus. Even as the book concludes, with both warning and invitation, we are reminded that all our world's darkness cannot survive the triumphal rising of One who is "The Bright Morning Star."

In "The Finalé," this drama is set out in eight acts, subdivided into various scenes. The last act is entitled "All Things New." From His eternal existence "with God" to his completion of the work of redemption, Jesus has left nothing unfinished. Part tragedy and part comedy, the drama achieves a glorious climax when the dwelling of God is truly with mankind. It would be a great story in any telling; in Dan Small's skillful re-telling, the Jesus Story is unforgettable and compelling.

A second, and future volume, *Letters to God's People*, will complete Dan's paraphrase of the New Testament. The genius of the *Trilogy* is its focus on "The Story." In good Jewish style, the format separates narrative from teaching, even knowing they ultimately come together in the life of God's people. *The Jesus Trilogy*, from beginning to end, by focusing on the narrative, concentrates the mind and heart in new and fresh ways.

One final note. Shortly after the completion of this work, Dan Small reached the end of a long battle with a bone marrow disease. Since then, Rebecca and the family have brought the work to the point of publication. For them, and us, Dan's loss is very real, but it is not the end of the story. His experience is well-described in the words with which C.S. Lewis closed *The Last Battle*: "Now at last they were beginning Chapter One of the Great Story which no one on earth has read: which goes on forever: in which every chapter is better than the one before."

Dan, you have captured the story of Jesus. Now you are reveling in the Great Story, and we can only imagine what that is like. Until then, thanks for leaving us *The Jesus Trilogy*. It has whetted our appetite for the next chapter!

Dr. Carl E. Armerding
Professor Emeritus and former President of Regent College

ACKNOWLEDGEMENTS

There are many to thank in a project like this; it's difficult to know where to begin, especially now that the author is no longer with us.

To Monty Mills, Dan and I will be forever indebted. Thank you for your mentoring in the Word those years ago, for your thorough study and research. The chronological rendering of "The Story of Jesus" (the consolidated Gospels) in the *Trilogy* is largely due to your previous work.

To Dennis Fuqua and Carl and Betsy Armerding, many thanks first of all for your support in bringing this work to completion and for your continual belief in its value. Thank you for the hours spent in helping to make some editorial decisions; I was grateful not to have to make all those judgment calls myself.

To all who read Dan's initial versions, thank you all for your helpful comments and critiques, for finding typos and other problems that needed fixing. I know the feedback was a great encouragement to Dan as he was working on it, and it kept him connected with all of you.

To Mattaniah, many thanks for designing the cover and for spending many long hours with us on formatting.

Finally, to our daughters Keren and Tirzah, thank you for the hours spent reading it with me as we walked together through the editing process, helping with a few syntax decisions and the grammatical mechanics. Thank you, Tirzah, for taking the final draft and working your formatting magic. It would not have gotten done without you.

I'm sure that I have missed some whom I am unaware of but who would have been acknowledged had Dan still been here to write this. For that I apologize, yet I am grateful to know the God who knows all the details and never misses an opportunity to reward the smallest act done in His Name: your acknowledgement will yet come, and from One far greater than I. To Him, the real Author of this *Trilogy* whose loving genius designed this time-space story from beginning to end before He had spoken the first word of creative power, to Him be glory and praise for eternal ages to come.

-RPS

PREFACE

Taken from Dan's last blog entry:
April 29, 2015

It's been almost two years since I started this blog with this entry:

Just a word about the "Finally, then . . ." title for my blog. I don't mean for it to sound ominous. It's somewhat tongue-in-cheek as I recall several places in the New Testament where the author invokes this "concluding statement" and then proceeds to write page after page. The fact is, we don't know (most of us) when FINALLY will happen to our earthsuit. But, we don't walk around with our head in the sand when symptoms appear suggesting major life-threatening conditions. So, this blog may last a few weeks, months, or years — as the Lord wills! Meanwhile, I'll pass on some "concluding statements" you might find helpful as you run the race (or crawl the path).

Oh, and a word about HOME. I like how C. S. Lewis put it: "If we find ourselves with a desire that nothing in this world can satisfy, the most probable explanation is that we were made for another world." I really like his use of the word DESIRE because I'm coming to believe that what we DESIRE is the most important thing about us!

And what a two years it has been. [But] the time has come, as it does for everyone, to face the fact that the meds surrendered the fight. So, what happens next? I don't have a clue. I am eternally grateful for a heritage that includes a deeply embedded confidence that "The Lord is my Helper, what shall I fear?"

We'll hope to get the rest of *The Jesus Trilogy* scheduled on the blog and then, maybe, someday, in print. At the end of the day, when it's all been said and done, "Just give me Jesus!"[†]

Editor's note:

When Dan was diagnosed with a rare bone marrow disease in the summer of 2013, his life changed dramatically. He went from being a very high-energy, highly productive person who was indefatigable to having to sit in a recliner or lie in bed most of the time. In December of that year he almost died. We both thought it was the end, and I began making some initial funeral arrangements. The night he was at his lowest, he told the Lord he was ready to go Home; but if he were to live on, he wanted to spend the rest of his life helping others "enjoy God." He had meditated much on the first catechism question and answer. Q: "What is the chief end of man?" A: "The chief end of man is to glorify God and to enjoy him forever." That night his health made a rather dramatic turn-around — far from being fully healed, mind you, for it was a continual roller coaster of ups and downs, of high hopes and shattered hopes; but God gave him an additional year and a half.

Dan wanted first of all to leave a legacy for his grandchildren that would lead them to an eternal inheritance — something far greater than a financial inheritance. And secondly, he wanted others to come to know the joy he was finding in God, regardless of the circumstances that may be swirling around them. He couldn't do much, but he could write. So he set out to write his own paraphrase of the New Testament, beginning with what he called *The Jesus Trilogy*.

[†] He died on the morning of May 8, 2015. His wife and children finished posting the last seven days of the daily readings of *The Jesus Trilogy* paraphrase..

Dan had always wanted to be able to hand people a very readable biblical account of Jesus, one that told the full story of Jesus. Using a consolidated Gospel put together by his mentor, Monty Mills, in Dallas, TX, Dan set out to merge all four Gospels into a single chronological story that could be read as one composite book. His style is easy and down to earth, fresh and stimulating.

As he got further along in this writing endeavor, he realized that though we often stop Jesus' story at the end of the Gospel of John, the story doesn't stop there. It continues on in the lives of the apostles through the person of the Holy Spirit, the same Spirit who lived in Jesus. Nor does it stop there. The full story has yet to be completed, and its completion is foretold in the final book of the New Testament, the Revelation of Jesus Christ. Even then, the story does not end. No, Revelation simply tells the beginning of the next chapter. Eternity alone will be sufficient to write of the magnificence and glory and wonder of Jesus.

As he was finishing up the paraphrase of Revelation, Dan shared this insight with me: The first two chapters of Genesis and the last two chapters of Revelation are like mirror images of each other. Genesis tells of the original creation, perfect and beautiful in every way; God pronounced it "very good." Revelation tells of the new creation, again restored to its perfect and beautiful state as God had originally designed it to be. With Adam and Eve's choice in the Garden to believe satan's word over God's word, the beauty and perfection were marred — but not permanently. Everything in between the first two chapters and the last two chapters of the Bible tells of God's redemptive plan to restore all things to His original design. One day all things will be as God intended, as He, in His goodness and love, envisioned with that first spoken Word, "Let there be light."

Jesus is the fulcrum upon which this redemptive plan tilts. Through Him the plan will be fully accomplished. And for eternal ages we will sing and declare the wonders of Him who loved us enough to die for us so that the great evil of sin and all its consequences could be rolled back.

By God's grace, *The Jesus Trilogy* has at last been completed and made ready for publication. It has been my privilege, along with the help of my daughters and son, to complete the editing and formatting of this paraphrase. As he said in one of his blog entries, he had started four books altogether. This is the first.

It is my prayer, as it was Dan's, that this paraphrase will be used to bring many into a true enjoyment of the God who made them and calls them, yes, longs for them to be His own. May you come to know the greatness of His love for you, and may you come to enjoy fellowship with God as Dan did and so glorify Him forever. I also pray that this volume will bear greater fruit in his death than that which was produced during his life.

-RPS

THE STORY OF JESUS
(GOSPELS)

In addition to adapting the grammar and structure to make the text more readable, I have consolidated the various stories and events from all four Gospels, Matthew, Mark, Luke, & John, into one continuous biography.[†]

Read the life of Jesus as He lived it.

[†] For the order of the chronology of "The Story of Jesus," Dan has relied heavily on *The Consolidated Gospel.* Copyright © 1984, Montague Stephen Mills; distributed by 3E Ministries.

THE PROLOGUE:
JESUS' PRE-EARTHLY LIFE

Many have already written about the life of Jesus Christ. Relying on eye-witnesses and reputable sources, this record is offered to you as an orderly account of the events as they occurred.

In the beginning God spoke. He expressed who He was using words. We begin our story with The Word. Mysteriously, this "Word" was with God and, in fact, was God. We are told that this "Word" created everything that exists, so we recognize Him as the Source of all LIFE. That LIFE is light-filled. He can diffuse the darkness (ignorance and evil) that permeates our world.

Even more mysterious is the fact that this God-Word became a human child and grew up, living right here in our neighborhoods. This light-source shone into the world He'd made, but the darkened human race didn't recognize Him. But whoever did take hold of Him was given the gift of a lifetime: a new identity as one of God's own children, not based on their credentials or efforts but just because that's what God desired for them.

John, the one who baptized, came on the scene before Jesus went public. He prepared the way by announcing Jesus' arrival and encouraging everyone to "see the light" of who He was. John was quick to acknowledge that he himself was not the Light, but that Someone was coming who had existed long before John had been born. (More will be said shortly about John's miracle birth.)

In his introduction, John made it clear that although no human had ever seen God, Jesus had; and coming from the heart of the Godhead, Jesus would make it possible for mankind to get to know God. John also hinted at the major shift in how humans would relate to God. "This Jesus," he declared "is not bringing laws like Moses did. He is bringing something called grace." Grace and truth would be the hallmarks of Jesus' message.

In case some might mistake Jesus, the God-man, for an alien or think of Him as other-than-human, we have the genealogies of His mother Mary, as well as His earthly father (not biological, but that will be explained in a few pages, too), showing that He can trace His human blood-line through King David, the Patriarchs, and all the way back to Adam.[†]

---

† See Appendices A and B for the genealogical records found in Matthew and Luke.

Jesus' Birth and Early Life

During the reign of Herod over Judea, the Jewish temple duties were handled by a rotation of authorized priests. Among the duties was the burning of incense in the Holy Place day after day. Our story begins when this routine was interrupted by a supernatural visitor who startled a priest named Zacharias. Zacharias and his wife Elizabeth were up in years and had prayed in vain for a child, an heir, which was so important in their culture. They had lived as faithful God-followers even though their prayers had gone unanswered.

So on this day when it was Zacharias' turn to do the temple chores, he was working inside the sacred room, putting the daily incense on the altar. Suddenly an angel was standing in front of him beside the altar. Naturally, he was struck with fear, which the angel perceived. "Nothing to be afraid of, Zacharias. I'm here to tell you that your many prayers have been heard and your dear wife Elizabeth will become pregnant. You are going to have a son!"

The angel went on to explain that his name would be John; he would have a special assignment, some dietary restrictions, and the tremendous privilege of preparing the entrance of the long-awaited Messiah. He also noted that this miracle baby would experience the infusion of God's Spirit even while in the womb. "He will turn many of Israel's children toward the Lord their God," he went on to say, "and in the spirit and power of Elijah he will turn the hearts of fathers to their children and cause rebels to listen to the wisdom of those who are godly."

I'm sure you can appreciate Zacharias' skepticism, knowing that both he and his wife were way beyond childbearing years. He asked, rather doubtfully, how this could possibly happen.

Now, the angel Gabriel wasn't used to anyone questioning his word, especially when he knew it had been given him by the Sovereign Ruler of the universe. You can almost hear the edge in his voice as he answers, "I am Gabriel who stands in the very presence of God Almighty! He sent me with this exciting news; but since you doubt my words, I'm going to strike your tongue so that from this hour until all this takes place you won't be able to say a word."

Meanwhile, the crowd outside was wondering why Zacharias' routine tasks were taking so long. As he emerged and they saw that he couldn't speak, they realized through his gestures that something out of the ordinary had taken place. Once his term of service was completed, Zacharias returned home to Elizabeth. And she conceived. For the next five months she stayed out of the public eye, astonished that the Lord had "looked on her" in this special way.

Six months later Gabriel was given another assignment, this time to the humble village of Nazareth in northern Israel. There a young girl named Mary, who was probably in her teens, was awaiting her upcoming marriage to a man named Joseph. The angel appeared to her in her house with this announcement: "Good news! The Lord is about to give you the highest honor any woman could have!"

Needless to say, Mary was as unprepared for this as Zacharias had been in the temple. Seeing the stunned look on her face, Gabriel continued, "God is so pleased with you that He's chosen you to become the mother of the promised Messiah! When He is born, you'll name Him Jesus; and someday He will take the throne of David and rule forever!"

Mary's response wasn't the same as Zacharias' had been. Yes, she had questions about how this would take place since she wasn't yet married, but there was an obvious willingness in her voice when she asked, "How will this happen since I'm not married yet?"

Patiently, Gabriel filled in a few more details for her. "God's Spirit will come upon you and the Power of the Highest will overshadow you so that, in fact, your son will be the Son of God. And," he went on, "God said to tell you that your Aunt Elizabeth down in Judah is six months along in her miracle pregnancy. He wanted you to know that with Him nothing is impossible."

From her heart, Mary spoke these precious words, "I am the humble servant of the Lord. I am willing for this to happen just as you have said." Then the angel departed.

Mary took the news about her elderly aunt as a hint from God that she should go to visit her. She made the long, lonely trip south. When Mary arrived at her aunt's home, Elizabeth, hearing Mary's voice at the door, felt the child in her womb jump. God's Spirit filled Elizabeth's heart and voice with this amazing tribute:

"What a blessing! You are truly the most blessed woman in history! And bless that little child in your womb! How is it that the mother of my Lord should grace my humble home? The moment I heard your voice, my baby leaped for joy inside. Bless you, child, for believing what the Lord has told you."

Mary responded with her own words of thanks:

"My inmost soul is overwhelmed by the Lord. My spirit overflows with joy! He has reached out to a simple village girl like me and has given me the greatest place any woman could hope for. He is so mighty, so holy, and so merciful. This shows that He brings down all those who are proud and raises up the humble who fear Him. Those who have nothing, He has filled with good things; those who are focused on their wealth have been sent away empty. He hasn't forgotten His chosen people but has remembered His promise to Abraham, and He will bring it to pass."

Mary stayed on with Elizabeth for about three months until it was time for Elizabeth's child to be born. At his birth the whole community came to celebrate along with her.

Meanwhile, Zacharias remained unable to speak. It was when the baby was eight days old, the traditional age for the circumcision of male babies, that he was given his official name. Everyone was sure they would name this firstborn after his father Zacharias. But no, Elizabeth was insisting on naming him "John" even though there were no men in their family line with that name. So naturally they turned to Zacharias to settle the issue. He took a writing tablet and spelled out the name, "J-O-H-N." Everyone was shocked.

But they were even more surprised when Zacharias began speaking out loud for the first time in over nine months. He praised God, and the Holy Spirit filled his heart and lips with these prophetic words:

> "Look what God has done! He has visited His people and is raising up Someone to save us from our enemies. For generations prophets have said this day would come, a Day when we could be set free to live for Him every day of our lives!
>
> And you, my own son, will be the forerunner, proclaiming a message of sins taken away. This promised Deliverer will visit us from heaven; and, like the rising sun, He will give light to all who have been sitting in darkness and the shadow of death, and will guide our feet into the way of peace."

As you can imagine, the story about these strange events rippled through the hill country for a long time, causing everyone to wonder, "What kind of child is this going to be?"

John grew up in the southern desert area of Israel, and the supernatural hand of God in his life was evident as he became strong in spirit.

Mary returned home to Nazareth; and being over three months along, there was no hiding that she was pregnant. Joseph, a God-fearing man, realized that it would be wrong for him to marry someone who was immoral. Because he was gracious and wanted to spare Mary public humiliation, he began looking for a way to deal with her sin privately.

Wrestling with this late into the night, he fell asleep and had a dream. An angel was there calling his name. "Joseph, heir of David's line, do not hesitate to take Mary as your own wife. The child in her was not conceived in sin but by the infusion of God's Spirit. It's a boy and you'll name Him 'Jesus.' (In their mother-tongue, this name is 'Yeshua,' which means 'the Lord saves.') He will, in fact, save His people from their sins."

Isaiah had prophesied this seven hundred years earlier when he wrote, "A virgin will conceive and give birth to a son. People will call His name 'Immanuel.'" (Immanuel means "God with us.")

Once Joseph was fully awake, he made arrangements to immediately take her as his wife. However, respecting her unique condition, they did not consummate their relationship until after Jesus was born.

Meanwhile in Rome, Caesar Augustus decreed that everyone in the Empire should be registered for tax purposes. So throughout the Middle East, everyone had to travel to their home city. That meant Joseph and Mary would have to go to Bethlehem, about 80 miles south of Nazareth. As they approached the village, Mary realized the birth was imminent; so they looked for a suitable room but were unsuccessful. The best they could do was to turn an animal shelter into a make-shift birthing center.

That night some shepherds doing night watch were shaken out of their slumber by a burst of light. The whole sky was ablaze with light! An angel of the Lord was standing before them and said, "Don't be afraid! I have exciting news for you and for people everywhere! Just now, over in Bethlehem, a Savior has been born! He is the long-promised Messiah! Look for a newborn child, wrapped up snugly and lying in a manger."

No sooner had the angel made this announcement than the bright sky was filled with thousands of angels, like a choir, saying, "Glory to God on high! Peace and blessing to mankind on earth!"

And then the scene was over. The angels had gone and the night sky returned to normal. Quite motivated by this, they said, "Let's go NOW! We've got to see what the Lord has just announced!" They ran toward the village and found everything just like they'd been told. With hearts full of worship, they exuberantly shared their story with everyone they met before returning to their flocks. The townsfolk marveled, but Mary cherished these stories in her heart.

On the eighth day, when the baby was circumcised, they gave Him the name Jesus just as the angel had instructed Mary before He was conceived.

After forty days (the Jewish purification period following the birth of a son), they took Jesus to the temple in Jerusalem. The Old Testament Law prescribed that firstborn sons, who technically "belong to the Lord," be redeemed by presenting an animal sacrifice. Poorer folks could substitute a pair of turtledoves or young pigeons. This is what Jesus' parents brought with them.

As they approached the temple, an elderly man named Simeon introduced himself to them, explaining that God had revealed to him that he wouldn't die before seeing the promised Messiah. That very morning the Holy Spirit had urged him to come to the temple, and he'd arrived about the same time as Joseph and Mary with their infant Son.

Tenderly, Simeon took the baby from His mother and held Him. As he gazed at the infant face, he prayed, "Lord, now You can take me Home. Just as You promised, my eyes have seen the One whom You have prepared to bring salvation to the whole world!" As he handed the Child back to Mary, Simeon prophesied, saying, "Your Child will shake things up as He exposes the hearts of many. He will face strong opposition, and deep suffering will be your lot as His mother."

As they stood there, Anna, an eighty-four-year-old widow approached them. In recent years she had stayed at the temple, often fasting and praying night and day, longing for God to deliver Jerusalem from its oppressors. Upon seeing the young Child, she burst out in thanksgiving and began telling others about Him — those who, like her, had been looking for a deliverer.

Joseph and Mary wondered at these unusual events as they completed the prescribed rituals and returned home.

Sometime later, maybe as much as two years, a group of scholar-astronomers from the East, known in the region as "king-makers," arrived in Jerusalem. It caused quite a stir when they entered the city, announcing that they'd come to pay homage to the newborn "king of the Jews." Herod, who was king of the region, gathered the religious leaders and scribes and asked if the archives had any information about this. Sure enough, they found an obscure passage in the book of Micah predicting that Bethlehem, a small village of Judea, would someday be the birthplace of a Ruler who would shepherd the nation.

So Herod gave the visitors directions. In a private consultation he asked them when they had first seen the star. Feigning a desire to worship this new king, he urged them to report back once they'd found Him. As they were leaving the city, the star they'd seen previously appeared again and led them right to the door of the home where Jesus was living with His parents. They were so overjoyed! Seeing the Child, they bowed low and worshiped Him. Then they presented Him with rich gifts of gold, frankincense, and myrrh.

However, when they left Bethlehem, they did not return through Jerusalem because they had been warned in a dream NOT to go back to Herod. So they took an alternate route to their own country.

At about the same time, an angel appeared to Joseph in a dream, instructing him to take the family to Egypt because Herod was out to destroy their Child. Though this hadn't been in their plans, God had foretold it centuries before through the prophet who said, "I have called My Son out of Egypt."

It was a good thing that they left Bethlehem immediately. The angel was right. Herod was so furious about being slighted by the mysterious "king-makers" that he ordered every male child in the region to be killed. Based on the timing of events described by the visitors, the order was directed at all boys who had been born in the previous two years. Jeremiah the prophet had written about this tragic event some 600 years earlier: "A voice was heard in Ramah: crying, weeping, and loud groaning; Rachel weeping for her children and refusing to be comforted because they are taken from her."

In time, Herod died; and an angel of the Lord again appeared in a dream to Joseph, telling him that it was safe to return home to Israel. Along the way Joseph learned that Herod's son Archelaus had been named king. In another dream an angel directed Joseph not to return to Bethlehem but to his home in Galilee. They ended up settling in their hometown of Nazareth, and the ancient prophecy that declared "He will be called a Nazarene" was fulfilled.

Jesus' childhood was marked by extraordinary wisdom, and He became strong in both spirit and body. The only story recorded from His early years took place when He was twelve years old. His parents took Him to Jerusalem to celebrate Passover. As was the custom, crowds of people made the pilgrimage for this feast. When the time came for returning to their homes, Jesus' parents naturally assumed He was in the company of all the youth. After a long day's travel, they looked for Jesus and discovered the fact that He was not among the travelers. So they returned to Jerusalem to find Him.

Meanwhile, Jesus had been occupied with the teachers in the temple. He participated in their discussions, listening and asking questions. These religious leaders were quite astonished at how informed and insightful Jesus was.

When Joseph and Mary finally located Jesus, they were amazed at what He had been doing. Mary, who was quite overcome with worry, chided Him for causing them this distress. Jesus' reply (which they didn't understand at the time) was that they ought to have expected Him to be "doing My Father's business." Jesus returned with them to Nazareth, submitting Himself to them. God's blessing was upon Him, and He was loved and respected by all who knew Him.

Mary treasured all this in her heart.

Jesus' Preparation for Ministry

It wasn't until Jesus was about thirty years old that the details of His life have been more fully recorded. The historical context was Tiberius Caesar's fifteenth year as emperor. Pontius Pilate was the Roman governor in Judea; Herod, Philip, and Lysanias were Jewish tetrarchs over different regions of Israel; the Jewish high priests at the time were Annas and his son-in-law, Caiaphas.

It was at this time that John the Baptizer began his public ministry, calling the nation to repent and be baptized and saying that the kingdom of heaven had arrived on earth. Dressed in an unusual outfit of a camel's hair tunic and leather belt, and known for a strange diet of locusts and wild honey, he was remarkably effective in attracting large numbers of people from miles around. They came to the Jordan River to confess their sins and to be baptized by him.

It's worth noting that several prophets had predicted John's ministry centuries earlier. They said of him, "Behold, I send My messenger before Your face, who will prepare Your way for You;" and, "the voice of one crying in the wilderness, 'Prepare the way of the Lord. Make His paths straight. Every valley shall be filled and every mountain and hill brought low, the crooked places shall be made straight and the rough ways made smooth, and all flesh shall see the salvation of God.'"

John attracted large crowds, but it wasn't because his message made them feel good. He confronted their hypocrisy and nationalistic ego when he said, "You brood of poisonous snakes, who warned you that you were headed for God's wrath? If you're serious about repentance, it has to change the way you live. No hiding behind this empty claim of being 'Abraham's descendants' as if your bloodline is all that matters. If God wanted to, He could start a whole new set of Abraham's children out of these rocks. Every tree that fails to bear good fruit gets chopped down and thrown into the fire. I'm telling you, the axe is about to strike the root of the tree! You'd better make sure that your repentance isn't just words but that it produces the fruit of real changed character!"

The people were shaken by this, asking, "What do we need to do?"

"For example," John said, "if you've got two coats, give one to someone who needs it. The same goes with your food. Look out for others' needs, not just your own."

A few of the tax collectors in the crowd asked what they should do. John replied, "Only collect what you're required to. Stop padding the bill and siphoning off excess for your own pockets."

Then some soldiers wanted to know what "fruits of repentance" meant for them. "Stop intimidating and taking advantage of others. And stop complaining about your wages" was John's response.

John's message and methods caused the people to wonder if perhaps he was the promised Messiah for whom they had been waiting. He silenced that rumor when he declared, "There is One coming who is so much greater than I am that I'm not worthy even to unfasten His sandals. Yes, I've been baptizing you with water, but He will baptize with the Holy Spirit and with fire. Not only that, He also comes ready to separate wheat from chaff, gathering the wheat into His barn, but burning the chaff with unquenchable fire."

It wasn't long before Jesus went from His hometown of Nazareth in Galilee down to the Jordan River to be baptized by John. John was incredulous. "You should be baptizing me! Surely You don't need to be baptized."

Jesus simply explained that this was part of God's process of making all things right. In identifying with those being baptized, Jesus was affirming both His humanness as well as the call to a Kingdom way of life. So Jesus was baptized by John in the Jordan. As He came up out of the water, the skies opened. God the Spirit came out of the clouds in the form of a dove and landed on Jesus. Then, coming out of heaven in a voice all could hear were these words: "You are My precious Son; I'm so proud of You. You are the joy of My life."

Immediately following his public baptism, Jesus, being filled with the Spirit, was driven by the Spirit into the desert to be tempted by the devil, Satan. He was alone except for the wild beasts that inhabited the region. Having fasted for forty days, he was very hungry.

That was when the devil tempted Him by suggesting that He command the stones to become bread, adding derisively, "If You are the Son of God."

Jesus, not taking His cues from the Tempter, quoted Scripture in replying, "It is written, 'Man shall not live by bread alone, but by every word that proceeds from the mouth of God.'"

Next, the devil took Him to the pinnacle of the temple in Jerusalem. Satan, following suit, quoted Scripture to add weight to his temptation, saying, "If you are the Son of God, throw yourself down from here; for it is written, 'He shall give His angels charge over You to keep You,' and 'In their hands they shall bear You up lest You dash Your foot against a stone.'"

Jesus responded with another Scripture, saying to him, "It is also written, 'You shall not tempt the Lord your God.'"

For his final attempt to get Jesus to submit to his counsel, Satan took Him to a very high mountain from which they could see all the kingdoms of the world and their glory at once. From there he offered Jesus rule over it all, saying, "All this authority and the honors and privileges that come with it will be Yours. Since it has been handed over to me, I can give it to whomever I choose. All You have to do is fall down and worship me, and it's Yours!"

Jesus' terse and unequivocal reply was, "Away with you, Satan! For it is written, 'You shall worship the Lord your God and Him only shall you serve.'"

Having failed to win Jesus over, Satan left Him until a more opportune time. Then angels came to strengthen Jesus.

Jesus' First Two Years of Ministry

Meanwhile, John continued baptizing along the Jordan River. Some of the Jewish religious leaders were sent from Jerusalem to investigate. They asked whether he considered himself to be the Messiah, a reincarnation of Elijah, or perhaps the Prophet predicted in their ancient writings. John flatly denied those roles, saying that the One they were describing was, in fact, among them. He went on to state that the Messiah, although yet to be revealed, had existed long before he had.

It was the very next day that John saw Jesus coming toward him and said, "Look, the Lamb of God who takes away the sin of the world! This is the One of whom I said, 'He is greater than I am because He existed before I did.'" John also reminded the crowd that just a few weeks before he had seen the Spirit descend upon Him from heaven in the form of a dove. "God had revealed to me," he went on to say, "that this would be the visible confirmation of the arrival of the One who baptizes with the Holy Spirit. I saw it and I'm testifying: here He is, the Son of God."

The next day Jesus passed the place where John and two of his disciples were standing. John again told them, "There is the Lamb of God."

Immediately the two disciples of John left him and began to follow Jesus. Jesus turned and saw them coming and asked what they were looking for.

"Where are you staying, Teacher?" they asked.

"Come and see" was Jesus' reply. So they went along and spent the day with Him. One of them, whose name was Andrew, quickly found his brother, Simon Peter, and told him, "We have found the Messiah!" He brought him to Jesus.

When Jesus met Simon, He said, "So you are Simon, son of Jonah. I will change your name to Cephas" (which means stone).

The next day Jesus decided to return to Galilee. He found Philip and invited him to come along. Philip was from Bethsaida, the same city as Andrew and Peter. He found his friend Nathanael and told him about Jesus, saying, "We've met the One whom Moses and the Prophets said would come — the Messiah! His name is Jesus. He's from Nazareth, son of a carpenter by the name of Joseph."

Nathanael responded by saying, "Can anything good come out of Nazareth?"

To which Philip said simply, "Come and see."

As Nathanael approached, Jesus said to him, "Now here is an Israelite whose life is above reproach!"

Nathanael was taken aback. "How do You know me?"

Jesus told him that He'd seen him sitting under a fig tree before Philip had come up to him.

Nathanael was convinced. "Teacher, You are the Son of God, rightful king of Israel."

Commending him, Jesus went on to say, "So you believe who I am just because I said I saw you under the fig tree? You will most certainly see greater proofs in the days to come: the heavens opening and angels going back and forth between heaven and the Son of Man."

A few days later Jesus and His disciples were invited to a wedding in Cana. Jesus' mother also attended; and when she heard that the hosts had run out of wine for the feast, she approached her Son about the situation. He let her know it was not time to publicly reveal that He was the Messiah.

Nevertheless, in a few minutes He instructed the servants to fill six large stone water pots with water. No sooner had they filled them with water than Jesus told them to take a cupful to the master of ceremonies.

The servants knew where the wine had come from, but the host had no idea. So he called to the bridegroom, saying, "This is remarkable! At most celebrations they serve the good wine first and save the lower quality for later. Instead, you have saved the best for last!"

And so it was that Jesus demonstrated His unique power. This was his first miracle. It increased the disciples' faith in Him.

From there, Jesus, His family, and His disciples went to Capernaum for a few days. Then He made His way to Jerusalem for the Passover.

When He arrived at the temple, He saw the courtyard filled with animals and with people conducting business. Jesus found some scraps of rope and wove them into a whip which He then used to drive all the animals out of the sacred space. He also dumped out the money boxes and declared loudly, "Get these things out of here! Do not turn My Father's house into a public market!"

Needless to say, this caused quite a commotion. The disciples recalled the Scripture that says, "Zeal for the sacredness of Your house overwhelmed Me."

Some of the leaders approached Jesus and asked, "Who gave You the right to do this? Give us some sign that You have this kind of authority."

Jesus said cryptically, "Destroy this temple and three days later I'll raise it back up."

The Jews were incredulous, "We've been working on rebuilding this for forty-six years. How can You talk about doing it in just three days?"

Of course, He was referring to His body; but it wasn't until three years later, after His resurrection, that the disciples put this all together and more fully believed the Scriptures and what Jesus had told them.

The people were astonished at the reports of His miraculous powers, and many believed what had been claimed about Him; but

Jesus didn't put too much stock in their support, knowing how fickle people can be.

One evening a Pharisee named Nicodemus approached Jesus privately. "Teacher, we've been talking about You and recognize that You must have come from God because no one could do the signs and wonders You're doing unless God was empowering him."

"Listen to Me," Jesus answered, "no one can possibly know what God is doing unless they have been reborn from Above."

Nicodemus was confused. "Surely You're not suggesting that a grown man like me has to get back into my mother's womb to be born all over again."

Jesus explained further, saying, "You are thinking strictly from a physical perspective. You have been born physically; but to see the Kingdom of God, you must have a life conceived by the Spirit in your spirit. This is something that happens invisibly, like wind. You can't see the wind, but you can hear it and see when it is blowing."

Nicodemus couldn't wrap his mind around this concept. "I just don't understand," he told Jesus.

Jesus rebuked him, saying, "Aren't you a prominent teacher in Israel? How is it that you don't already know this? I can tell that you don't trust My testimony. This is so basic. If you don't grasp this, how can you hope to understand the larger message God is speaking? There is only One who came from heaven and can truly explain the truths of heaven — that is, the Son of Man.

"Nicodemus, do you recall the story of Moses putting the brass serpent on a pole in the desert? That was a foreshadow of how the Son of Man must be lifted up for the healing and deliverance of all who look to Him in faith. Trusting God's heart is at the center of the message. It was out of His exceedingly great love for mankind that God gave His Son to deliver them from death and to impart to them His very own eternal life. The Son was not sent as Judge to condemn but as Savior to rescue from condemnation.

"Those who accept the Son for who He is and receive His message have escaped judgment. Unfortunately, because most prefer living in darkness where they can get away with doing evil, hating the light that exposes their misdeeds, they remain condemned.

"Those with nothing to hide, whose actions originate in God, have no problem being transparent, letting their deeds be seen for what they are: Truth!"

From Jerusalem Jesus and His disciples went to a town called Aenon near Salim where John was baptizing. As Jesus taught, His disciples baptized. Some of the people went to John with the report that Jesus was drawing bigger crowds than he was.

John replied with sincerity and humility, "What we have is from God. My message is not something I made up to attract a following. You recall how clearly I stated that I am not the Messiah; I was just sent to prepare the way for Him, like the best man introducing the bridegroom at a wedding. As 'best man' I'm not jealous but elated for Him. He will be the focus of attention; I must fade into the background.

"This is only right since He has come from heaven and I am from the earth. He is explaining life from heaven's perspective, but most folks won't accept it. Those who do believe Him discover God's truth. He speaks God's words, and everything He says and does is by the Spirit of God.

"It is evident that the Father loves the Son and has put Him in charge of everything. Everyone who accepts and trusts the Son gets in on everything He is and has . . . forever! Conversely, those who reject Him miss out on His life and can only look forward to God's holy judgment."

John was imprisoned for publicly exposing Herod's many misconducts, which included adultery with his sister-in-law Herodias. When Jesus learned about John's incarceration and also of the Pharisees' awareness that His popularity was eclipsing that of John the Baptizer, He left Judea to return to Galilee.

Ordinarily, Jews traveling between Judea and Galilee took the long way around, avoiding Samaria because they despised Samaritans. But leading His disciples north, Jesus explained that He needed to go through Samaria. Around noon they approached the city of Sychar, the site of Jacob's well. This was an area bequeathed to Joseph by the patriarch Jacob.

Jesus was quite tired so He rested by the well while the disciples went into the city for some lunch. When a woman approached the well, Jesus asked her if she would give Him a cup of water. Knowing that Jews normally wouldn't have any dealings with Samaritans, she asked Him, "How is it that You, a Jew, are willing to ask a Samaritan for a drink — and a woman, no less?"

Jesus said, "Ma'am, if you only knew what God wants to give you and who it is you're speaking with, you would be asking Me for a drink of living water!"

The woman didn't know what to say to that. She couldn't imagine what He was talking about. "Sir, I see that You don't have anything to draw water with," she said. "Where would You get this 'living water'? Surely You're not claiming to be greater than our forefather Jacob, who watered his flocks and drank from this well himself, are You?"

Jesus replied, "Everyone who drinks from this well will have to come back again and again, but whoever drinks of the water I give will never thirst again. The water I give will spring up inside him, bringing God's kind of life."

That sounded great to the woman. She told Him, "I'd like some of that water! That way I won't have to keep coming out here to this well."

Jesus' response was rather unusual. He asked her to get her husband, to which she replied, "I don't have a husband."

Then Jesus told her, "You are right when you say you don't have a husband right now. You have had five husbands, and you're not married to the man with whom you're currently living."

No doubt embarrassed by the course of this conversation, she changed the subject. "Sir, you're obviously a prophet with special insights. Our fathers have worshiped for generations on this mountain while the Jews say Jerusalem is the only proper place God has ordained for worship." The question inferred was, "Who is right?"

Jesus used her diversion to announce the very essence of His message. "Ma'am," He said to her, "although the emphasis has for centuries been about where we worship, that's about to change forever. The Jews do have an advantage because the message explaining all this does come through their bloodline. However, regardless of heritage, God is looking for those who worship Him genuinely from the core of their being. God is spirit, you know, so what matters is whether we live authentically out of our spirits."

Eager to end this conversation, as it was getting a little deep, she said, "I'm sure that when the promised Messiah comes, He'll be able to explain all this."

Jesus smiled and replied, "Here I am." Before they could continue the discussion, the disciples returned from the town. It was obvious from the look on their faces that they were shocked to see their Master openly conversing with a Samaritan woman.

She took this interruption as an opportunity to hurry back to the city, forgetting to take her waterpot with her. Going immediately to some of the men, she said, "You've got to come see this Man I met, who, never having seen me before, told me everything I've ever done. Do you think He could be the Messiah?"

This piqued their curiosity and a crowd headed for the well. Meanwhile, Jesus' disciples urged Him to join in their meal. "You go ahead," He said, "I'm feeling pretty full right now Myself." The disciples looked at each other, wondering if someone else had brought by some food. Jesus explained, "What satisfies Me most is doing the work the Father has assigned Me. Look around; the harvest is ready! Obviously I'm not talking about the physical fields of grain you can see; they won't be ready for another four months. No, I'm talking about a spiritual crop that produces eternal life. Some have the task of planting the seeds; others get to reap the fruit. In this work others have been planting seeds for a long time, and you get to be part of their hard work by gathering the harvest."

The disciples were about to see this come true. The crowd came out to meet Him and were so taken with His message that they urged Him to stay on in Sychar. Jesus and His disciples stayed for two days. The testimony of the villagers was, "We first believed because of what the woman told us about You; but now, having heard for ourselves, we know that You are the Messiah, the One sent to save the world."

Then Jesus, empowered by the Spirit, returned to Galilee. Many of the people had been to Jerusalem and news of His activities had spread quickly. He was welcomed in the region and He taught regularly in their synagogues.

One of the towns in Galilee was Cana where He had turned water into wine. An influential leader from Cana found Jesus and begged Him to come to his home to heal his son who lay at the point of death. Jesus rebuked him, saying, "Why won't you believe in Me unless I do a miracle?"

But the official persisted, "Sir, come quickly or he will surely die."

To which Jesus stated simply, "You may return home; your son is healed." The man took Jesus at His word and headed home.

Along the way, some of his servants ran to meet him and joyfully announced that his son was better. The man asked when the change had occurred, and they told him it had been around one o'clock in the afternoon. The official realized that this was the very hour he had met with Jesus. Then he and his entire household believed in Jesus. This was the second miracle Jesus performed in Galilee.

From there Jesus made His way to His hometown of Nazareth. On the Sabbath He went to the synagogue as usual. He stood up to read the Scripture of the day. When He was given the scroll, He opened to the prophet Isaiah and read these words: "The Spirit of the Lord is upon Me, because He has anointed Me to preach the gospel to the poor. He has sent Me to heal the brokenhearted, to preach deliverance to the captives and recovery of sight to the blind, to set at liberty those who are oppressed, to preach the acceptable year of the Lord."

After handing the scroll back to the attendant, He sat down. Everyone was watching and waiting to see if He would comment on the passage. He spoke to them and said, "Today this Scripture has been fulfilled before your very eyes!"

The congregation was amazed at how simply yet profoundly He spoke. They couldn't get over the fact that this was "Joseph's son," who had grown up in their neighborhood.

He rebuked them, saying, "I know you're waiting to see Me perform the miracles you've been hearing about; but, as the saying goes, 'no prophet is honored by those he grew up with.' No, as history records, back in the days of Elijah there was a great famine. There were plenty of widows in Israel, but he was sent to help a Sidonian widow. And in Elisha's day, while there were many lepers in Israel, none of them was healed — only Naaman, the Syrian."

Suddenly the mood in the synagogue changed and everyone became furious. They dragged Him toward a cliff at the edge of town, intending to throw Him off; but mysteriously, He walked right through the crowd and got away.

Jesus moved to Capernaum and established that as His home. Capernaum is at the north end of the Sea of Galilee in the regions originally parceled out to Zebulun and Naphtali, two of the original tribes of Israel. Once again, a prophecy from centuries before was being fulfilled: "The land of Zebulun and the land of Naphtali, the way of the sea, beyond the Jordan, Galilee of the Gentiles: the people who sat in darkness saw a great light; and upon those who sat in the region and shadow of death, light has dawned."

From that time on Jesus' message was, "Get serious about your life and turn from your sinful ways: God's Kingdom is here."

One day as He walked near the Sea of Galilee, He noticed Simon Peter and Andrew whom He had met previously. They were fisherman, but Jesus invited them to follow Him, saying, "I will teach you to fish for the souls of men." Without hesitation they left their nets and followed Him. Further down the beach they came upon James and John along with their father Zebedee. They were busy mending nets, but Jesus also invited them to become His followers. They quickly left everything with their father and his hired hands.

Together they went to Capernaum and entered the synagogue on the Sabbath. Jesus taught the people and they were amazed at how He spoke with such authority, unlike their usual teachers.

On one Sabbath a man who had a demon was in attendance. He shouted at Jesus, saying, "Leave us alone! What do we have to do with You, Jesus of Nazareth? Have You come to destroy us? I know who You are: the Holy One from God!"

Jesus rebuked the spirit, telling it to be quiet and to come out of the man. Then the man's body shook violently. The spirit shrieked and came out of him. After this, Jesus' teaching and authority were the topic of much conversation throughout Galilee. The people wondered how He could command evil spirits and get them to obey Him with a word.

After the synagogue service Jesus and His followers went to the home of Simon Peter and Andrew, where Simon's mother-in-law was sick with a high fever. They told Jesus about it and asked Him to help. He went to her side, took her hand, and rebuked the fever. Immediately she was healed, got out of bed, and began serving them.

That same evening the whole community showed up at the house where Jesus was staying. They brought all kinds of sick and demon-possessed to Him. He healed them all, laying hands on them and casting out demons with a command. The demons kept shouting, "You are the Messiah, the Son of God!" But Jesus silenced them.

The prophet Isaiah had predicted Jesus' healing work when he wrote, "He Himself took our infirmities and removed our diseases."

Jesus got up very early the next morning and went out to a quiet place away from the city where He could pray. Before long, Simon and the others found Him and told Him that everyone was looking for Him. The crowd didn't want Him to leave, but He explained that He had to preach the message of God's Kingdom to the other cities.

He went throughout Galilee preaching, healing, and casting out demons. His fame spread and they kept bringing Him all who had various afflictions. People also came from Syria, Decapolis, Jerusalem, Judea, and beyond the Jordan. Soon the crowds were so large He had to get in a boat and teach them from there.

After a while He told Simon to take the boat out farther and put in their nets for a catch. Simon retorted with the complaint that they'd been fishing all night and had caught nothing. "But, Master, since You say so, we'll try it," he rather begrudgingly assented.

No sooner had they dropped their nets in than they were teeming with so many fish the nets began to break. They signaled to their partners in the other boat to come and help them. The catch was so great that when they loaded them into the boats they began to sink.

Simon, who had been fishing that lake all his life, had never seen anything like it. He knew Jesus had caused this. He fell down in front of Him and said, "O Lord, I'm not worthy to have You in my boat. I am too much of a sinner to be around You."

Jesus reassured him, saying, "Don't be afraid. From now on you'll be in the business of catching men." So as soon as they reached the shore, they left their fishing boats to follow Him.

Jesus took His disciples away from the city and began to explain to them how God's Kingdom differed from life as they'd known it.

"God's blessing is on all who recognize their poverty without Him. Heaven's Kingdom is prepared for people like that.

"All who have known deep sorrow over their sin will experience great comfort.

"In God's plan the earth belongs not to the power brokers but to the humble.

"All who long for God's way of life will find full satisfaction in Him.

"Those who show mercy to others will themselves be shown mercy.

"Only those whose hearts are pure will see God.

"Those who are truly God's children will work peace in the world.

"Along the way, as you live like this, you will suffer persecution, slander, and false accusations; but you can rejoice anyway because God is saving up a huge reward for you in His Kingdom. Know that you're in good company with the holy prophets of old who were similarly mistreated.

"On the other hand, what troubles and heartaches await you who revel in your prosperity! What desperate hunger lies in store for all who boast of their affluence! The ones who spend their days in frivolity and pleasure will discover what mourning and grief feel like, and all who are given places of honor by the crowds will find out how worthless that praise is. For generations, people like them cheered on the false teachers and prophets.

"While you are in the world, you serve as salt, preserving and enhancing — unless you lose your 'saltiness,' in which case you've lost your value. While you are in the world, you are like lights, doing good things that can be seen by others to help them recognize and honor your Father in heaven. Let your life be a beacon of light in the darkness.

"I am not bringing you a new teaching that does away with the Old Testament. No, I have come to demonstrate how all that it teaches can be lived to the full. Those who minimize the importance of God's revealed will won't amount to much in His Kingdom, while those who live it and teach it will be great. My message is this: unless and until you are living better than the scribes and Pharisees, you won't even get into the Kingdom of Heaven. Surely a blind person can't provide assistance to others who are blind; they'll both fall into the ditch. Those who truly learn from their teachers eventually become like them.

"Let me explain what I mean. The letter of the Law, to which the scribes and Pharisees proudly adhere, says, 'You must not murder.' They are quick to bring murderers to justice. But I'm here to tell you that if you even get angry with your brother, call him a fool, or curse him in your heart, you are in danger of the fiery judgment of hell.

"Once you understand the tremendous value God places on human souls, you'll make reconciliation and restitution a priority, even to the point of interrupting your worship. If, while you are worshiping, you remember that you have offended someone, drop what you're doing and go make peace with them. Only then will your offering be pleasing to the Lord.

"Here's another example: The commandment literally says, 'You must not commit adultery.' I'm telling you that if you even look twice at a woman to satisfy your sexual appetite, you have broken this law. Once you recognize the sacredness of human sexuality, you'll see why it would be better to pluck out your eyes and go through life blind or handicapped than to be led astray by your senses and end up in hell.

"The scribes and Pharisees have declared: 'Whoever divorces his wife, let him give her a certificate of divorce;' but I say that whoever divorces his wife (unless she has been unfaithful) is making her an adulteress, because whoever marries a divorced woman is committing adultery.

"They have also made up elaborate rules about the right way to make promises or swear oaths. Supposedly, if you swear by heaven or earth or Jerusalem, your word is more binding. My word to you is that everyone should speak forthrightly, honestly, and plainly: 'yes' means yes, 'no' means no; and if you say you'll do something, be sure you follow through. After all, what good is it to swear by something over which you have no control? Heaven, after all, is God's throne; the earth, His footstool; and Jerusalem belongs to the great King. Why, you can't even stop your hair from turning gray, so what good is it to 'swear by your own head'?

"The Law, as understood by the scribes and Pharisees, exacts meticulous retribution — that is, 'an eye for an eye and a tooth for a tooth'; but let Me describe God's heart in this matter: If someone hits you, don't hit him back. If he wins a case against you and demands your shirt as payment, give him your jacket as well. And if anyone forces you to go a mile with him (as soldiers often did in those days, requiring citizens to carry their packs), offer to go a second mile. In God's Kingdom if someone has a need and asks for help, we don't turn our backs on him.

"Your religious teachers take the command to 'love your neighbor' and add 'hate your enemy.' On the contrary, I encourage you to love your enemies and to pray for those who abuse you; do good things for those who hate you and even bless the ones who curse you. That will demonstrate that you are like your Heavenly Father who equally dispenses sunlight and rain upon those who are honest and good as well as upon the evildoers. Only loving those who are nice to you is no great accomplishment. Anyone can do that! Treat others the way you want to be treated. If you only greet the folks you like, you're acting just like the pagans. No, your lives must reflect the heart of your Heavenly Father: perfectly loving.

"Earlier I explained that when you do good deeds it gives the world a chance to see what a life connected with God can look like. Having said that, you have to be careful that you don't end up living for the attention and praise of the people around you. If you do that, you'll miss out on getting the reward only God can give.

"Here are a few examples:

1. Don't broadcast when you help the poor. You've seen the type. They hire a trumpeter to march in front of them, calling attention to their act of mercy. What a sham! Instead, if you do these acts in secret, your Father who sees everything will reward you in His time.

2. Don't make a show of praying to God. Again, the guys that stand and give long prayers in church may impress the people, but they don't have God's attention. He loves to meet with you in private and hear your heart rather than hearing a bunch of fancy words. After all, He knows what you need before you even ask Him.

"This is how you should pray:

Our Heavenly Father,
may Your name be honored in our lives,
may You govern our lives
and may Your heart's desire be accomplished
here on earth the way it is in heaven.
We recognize You as our Source
and ask only for what we need for this day.
We know we need Your forgiveness,
and we need You to help us
forgive others who wrong us.
Protect us from the tempter;
and when we are tempted,
help us to never choose evil.
The Kingdom, the power, and the glory
belong to You forever. Amen.

"Only if you are willing to forgive those who have wronged you, will your Heavenly Father forgive you. If you refuse to forgive, the Father cannot extend forgiveness to you.

3. Finally, if you decide to fast by denying yourself some food or pleasure in order to draw near to God, don't let others know about it. Again, your Father who looks on the heart

will reward you far better than the praise you might get from friends for being 'so spiritual.'

"Probably one of the biggest areas in which God's Kingdom contrasts with our normal thinking has to do with money. What you treasure will run your life, so don't waste it piling up all kinds of earthly possessions. There is a way to stockpile treasures in Heaven where they can't get stolen or lose their value. Do that instead.

"Don't you see that what you think is most important will color all the rest of your desires? If you're focused on earthly delights, your whole life will be characterized by darkness. If you look at things the way God designed you to, then your whole body will be full of light.

"So when it comes to money, you can't love money and God. You'll always end up loving one and hating the other because it interferes with what you want.

"In practical terms, this means you should never worry about temporal things like food, clothing, or housing. Instead, if you really believe God is your Source and that He cares for you, focus your desires on the things He loves and He'll take care of the details. Look how well He provides for the birds. Look how magnificently He clothes the flowers which are 'here today and gone tomorrow.' Keep reminding yourself how much more valuable you are to Him than these things. The pagans who don't know the Father fuss over these things. But what profit is there in worrying about the future — especially when we know the God who has everything under control.

"Be careful, too, how you think and talk about others. On the one hand, you dare not be judgmental because you realize how many flaws there are in your own character. Deal honestly with your own issues first, then you can help others with theirs. Treat others the way you want to be treated. On the other hand, I'm not saying that you shouldn't be discerning. Some people are simply not ready for Kingdom truth; and if you waste your time trying to convince them, they'll make you sorry you did. They are like pigs trampling precious pearls and then turning to attack you.

"The great thing about living in the Kingdom is that your Heavenly Father is so much better than the very best dad this world can imagine. No loving father would let his son down by giving him a stone to eat when he asked for bread or by handing him a snake when he wanted fish, would he? So when you come to the Father, ask and you will receive. Lacking wisdom? Seek it from Him and you'll find what you're looking for. Needing doors to be opened? Knock on His door and watch what He opens.

"My final point is that life will offer you many choices and lots of decisions. Don't go with the crowd. They're taking the easy way, not realizing that it leads to disaster. Choose the right path even though it may be lonely and hard going at times.

"Along the way you'll find plenty of folks ready to tell you which way to go. There are a lot of greedy wolves out there who cover themselves in sheepskin and try to make you think they are like you. Watch their lives; you can tell a tree by the fruit it produces. Evil people can only hope to produce trouble because of what they store in their hearts. They could no more produce good works than a clump of thistles can sprout figs. Listening to people's words will reveal what is in their hearts. Upright men have a lot to offer because of the good treasure they've invested in their hearts. If a person consistently exhibits good character, you can be sure he or she is a 'good tree.'

"How is it that you call me 'Lord' but aren't interested in doing the things I say to do? You see, it's not what someone says that matters. On the Day of Judgment a whole lot of folks will claim to have served Me, saying, 'Lord, Lord, didn't we do all these things in Your name?' I'll have to tell them outright, 'Away from Me. I never knew you. You were actually working against Me.' It makes sense, doesn't it, that only those who live the way My Heavenly Father wants them to will enter His Kingdom?

"You can picture it like this: Everyone who hears what I've just said and takes action on it is like a sensible man who builds his house on a rock. No matter what storms come against that house, it can't be destroyed because it's attached to a secure foundation.

"On the other hand, if you listen to My teaching and go on living life the way you always have, you're building your life on sand. When the hard times come, you'll come crashing down."

As Jesus finished speaking, the people just sat there in awe. In all their lives they hadn't heard anyone teach with such authority; He knew what He was talking about and meant every word.

The first thing that happened as Jesus and the crowd came toward the town was an encounter with a leper. The man knelt in front of Jesus and said, "Sir, I know You could heal me if You wanted to."

Jesus laid His hand on the man's head and said, "Of course I want to. Be clean!" The man's disease disappeared. Nothing like this had ever happened before, so Jesus instructed him to go to the priest and follow the instructions Moses had prescribed. Jesus knew that this would be startling evidence to the priests. "Oh, and don't say anything to anyone before you do this," Jesus told him.

Instead, the man went all over the region spreading his good news. As a result the crowds became so huge that Jesus could rarely go into the cities. He had to stay out in the rural areas, and the people came to Him for healing. But Jesus would often escape to the desert to pray.

One day a Roman centurion who lived in Capernaum heard that Jesus was nearby. He sent some of the influential Jewish leaders to appeal to Him for help; his servant was paralyzed and desperately ill. They approached Jesus, explaining that, even though this was a Roman soldier, he had been very helpful in the community, having built them a synagogue, and was worthy of Jesus' attention.

Jesus was more than willing to help, so He went with them. He wasn't far from the house when the centurion sent some friends to convey a message. "Sir," they explained, "our friend, the centurion, wants You to know that he's not important enough to have You come into his home or even to personally approach You. He said to tell You that he knows if You would just give the command, his servant would recover. You see, he's very familiar with how authority works. He's got men under him who instantly do whatever he tells them to, and he knows You have the authority to do this."

When Jesus heard this, He was amazed. "This man gets it," He said to the crowd, "and he's a Gentile! Take note! When I sit down in the Kingdom of Heaven to feast with Abraham, Isaac, and Jacob, there will be a lot of folks there who aren't Jewish, while many who ought to have understood who I am will be banished to outer darkness and filled with regret."

Having issued that warning, Jesus told the friends that when they went back, they would find that what the centurion believed could happen did happen. Yes, as it turns out, the servant had been healed at the very moment Jesus said that.

Some days later when Jesus was at home in Capernaum, a crowd gathered. Soon there were so many in and around the place that no one else could possibly get to Him. Among those who were present were many Pharisees and teachers of the Law from nearby towns and from as far away as Jerusalem. Again, Jesus displayed His power and many were being healed.

It so happened that some men brought their friend who was paralyzed to see Jesus, carrying him on a stretcher; but because of the crowd, they couldn't get in. That didn't stop them. Since the houses had flat roofs with stairs on the side leading up, they took their friend onto the roof and proceeded to remove some of the ceiling tiles. Once they had a large enough opening, they lowered their friend on his stretcher right in front of Jesus. Amazed at the determination and faith of the friends, Jesus looked at the paralytic and said, "This is your day, son; your sins are forgiven!"

That wasn't what anyone was expecting to hear, and the scribes were thinking to themselves, "That's blasphemy! Only God can forgive sins."

Jesus perceived by the Spirit what they were thinking, so He rebuked them, saying, "Why are you thinking that? Is it easier to say, 'Your sins are forgiven' or 'Get up and walk'? To show that the Son of Man has authority to forgive sins, I'll now tell him to get up and walk.

"Rise up," Jesus commanded. "Take your bedding and be on your way."

Immediately the man got up. He was overjoyed, the crowd was awestruck, and all were thanking God for imparting such power to this unusual Man.

Later on, Jesus left the house and was heading down to the sea with the massive crowd at His heels. Along the way He saw a man named Levi (also called Matthew) sitting at his desk in the tax-collector's office. Jesus invited him to come along as one of His disciples. Matthew jumped to his feet, left his books, and followed Him.

Not long afterward, Matthew hosted a great party at his estate for his friends and fellow tax-collectors (not the most respected folk in the community) to meet Jesus.

The Pharisees apparently weren't invited, but they heard about it and confronted some of His disciples, asking, "Does your Master know the kind of people He's eating with?"

Jesus overheard the question and retorted with this question: "Now, who goes to see the doctor — the healthy or the sick? I didn't come to help the people who think they're just fine; I'm here for those who know they need My help. You should go back and study the phrase 'I desire mercy and not sacrifice' until you understand what God meant by it."

Later some of John's disciples and orthodox Jews asked Jesus why He and His disciples seemed to spend more time feasting than fasting. Jesus explained using the analogy of a wedding. "Surely you wouldn't expect the wedding guests to fast when the bridegroom is with them. A time will come — after the bridegroom leaves — when there will be plenty of time to fast."

He went on to illustrate that their problem lay in trying to fit His message into their religious system. He gave the example of patching torn clothing, saying, "A tailor knows better than to patch with unshrunken material. If he did, the first time it got laundered the material would shrink and make the tear even bigger." He gave them another example of a vintner making good wine. "If he put new wine into weathered, used containers, they'd burst as the wine aged. That's why they always use new wineskins when making wine. Your problem is that you're satisfied with the old and don't want the 'new wine' I'm offering."

Sometime later during one of the feasts, Jesus went back to Jerusalem. Near one of the city gates called the Sheep Gate was a public pool that had five levels of deck surrounding it. There was a legend that from time to time an angel would "stir the waters" and whoever got to the water first was healed. Jesus saw a man lying there who had obviously been there for a long time; he'd been disabled for thirty-eight years. So He asked the man, "Would you like to be healed?"

Rather than answering directly, the man explained that he couldn't be healed because someone else always beat him to the water when it was stirred. Jesus said, "Just get up and take your bedroll home." The man stood to his feet, rolled up his mat, and began making his way home.

You'd think everyone would have been thrilled, but there was a problem. Some orthodox Jews saw the man and confronted him. "Don't you know it's the Sabbath? You shouldn't be doing work like carrying your bedding." The man explained that he'd just been healed, and whoever healed him had told him to take his bedroll home.

"Who told you that?" they demanded. But the man had no idea who Jesus was; He had disappeared into the crowd by then.

Later that day Jesus found him in the temple and warned him, "Now that you've been healed, be careful not to make wrong choices again, lest something worse happen to you."

The next time the man saw the legalistic Jews, he told them that it had been Jesus who healed him. This infuriated them, and they looked for a way to kill Jesus because He was desecrating the Sabbath. To make matters worse, Jesus told the crowds, "My Father is the One doing this work through Me — even though it's the Sabbath." So now, on top of Sabbath-breaking, Jesus was claiming to be equal with God, like a son with his father. That was blasphemy in the minds of the Jewish leaders.

Jesus didn't shy away from the subject. He went on at length, explaining His relationship with the Father. "The truth is I don't do anything of My own initiative. My Father loves Me and shows Me what He's doing, and I work alongside Him. He plans to do even greater things that are sure to amaze you: the Father can raise the dead, and I likewise give life to the dead. The fact is that the Father has turned over the judgment of mankind to Me. If you won't honor Me for who I am, then it reveals you aren't honoring the Father who sent Me.

"Speaking of judgment, whoever takes Me at My word and embraces My message as being God's truth has already escaped death and judgment and has begun really living. This isn't some future resurrection I'm describing; it's for anyone here and now who will listen to Me. The Father and I have this life in Us, and We can give it to whomever We choose.

"Yes, there will be a future resurrection and some will enter eternity with Our life in them, while others will face an eternity of separation from Us. I'm not making this up. The Father has established this and I am speaking for Him. My life isn't about doing the things I want to do but about always pursuing the desires My Father has.

"You may not feel that you can take My word about this, but I have witnesses to confirm that I speak the truth. John the Baptist testified about Me and you respected his ministry (at least for a while), but I have a far greater witness: the miracles I've already done. They are proof that God is working through Me. Yes, the Father who sent Me here has also testified about Me.

"Unfortunately, you wouldn't be able to recognize His voice. The way you're responding to Me shows that you don't have a clue what He's saying even though you study the Scriptures diligently. You think that the more you learn about the Law the better off you are; when the truth of the matter is that all those Scriptures point to Me, yet you won't come to Me for life.

"I don't need approval from you. I've seen your circles of approval; it's more important to you to get men's praise than to be honored by God. You clearly haven't experienced the love of God for yourselves. And don't tell Me you're Moses' disciples. Everything Moses wrote pointed to Me, so you really don't believe his words or you'd be receiving Mine."

A week later on the Sabbath, Jesus and the disciples were walking through some fields and they picked a few heads of grain. After rubbing them in their hands to remove the chaff, they ate them. The Pharisees were right there accusing them of working on the Sabbath again. Jesus decided to give them a lesson on Sabbath-keeping.

"Have you read about the time when David and his men were famished, and the only food they could find was the showbread from the temple? Don't you remember how Abiathar, the high priest, gave them some even though it was against the Law?

"How about the fact that every Saturday your own priests break the Sabbath just doing their jobs? God doesn't hold that against them. You don't understand the heart of God or you'd appreciate His preference for 'mercy over sacrifice,' and you wouldn't be so quick to condemn people whom He doesn't. You would also realize that One greater than the temple is here and that God created the Sabbath as a blessing for mankind, not as a way to oppress them."

The Sabbath controversy wasn't going to go away. On yet another Sabbath day while Jesus was teaching in the synagogue, a man with a withered hand showed up. Of course, the scribes and Pharisees were all eyes, waiting to see if Jesus would heal him. Jesus knew what they were thinking so He asked them, "Is it against the Law to heal on the Sabbath?" Then He called for the man to come down to the front where everyone could see what He was about to do. Jesus repeated the question, "Which is against the Law, doing good by saving lives even though it's the Sabbath or doing evil by destroying them?"

The crowd remained silent. "Tell me none of you has ever had to go out and rescue a sheep that fell into a pit on the Sabbath. Be honest, did you think twice about lifting the helpless creature out? Now which is of greater value, a sheep or a human being? So we're agreed then: it's okay to do good on the Sabbath."

Jesus could see that the Pharisees were hardened in their rejection of Him and He was angry. He told the man to stretch out his hand, which, when he did, became instantly as healthy as his other hand. That made the Pharisees so furious that they left and began plotting with the Herodians† to destroy Him.

Jesus, knowing what they were up to, headed back to Galilee with His disciples. A crowd made up of folks from Galilee, Judea, Jerusalem, Idumea, the other side of the Jordan, and Tyre and Sidon all

†A radical group that was normally at odds with the Pharisees' agenda because they wanted a political coup to restore Herod's dynasty.

converged around Him. He asked His disciples to prepare a boat in case He needed to get away before being crushed by the multitude. Once again He healed all who were afflicted and cast out the demons. Whenever the unclean spirits cried out, "You are the Son of God," He warned them to stop revealing His identity.

God had spoken about His coming Messiah through Isaiah the prophet: "Look at My Servant, whom I have chosen. He is My Beloved, who pleases Me. I will put My Spirit upon Him, and He will proclaim justice to the nations. He will not fight or shout or raise His voice in public. He will not crush the weakest reed or put out a flickering candle. Ultimately, He will cause justice to be victorious and His name will be the hope of all the world."

One evening Jesus went alone to a mountain and He spent the whole night in prayer. The next morning He called His followers together and chose twelve from among them to be His apostles. Their names were Simon (whom He named Peter), James and John (the sons of Zebedee, whom Jesus affectionately called the "Sons of Thunder"), Andrew, Philip, Bartholomew, Matthew, Thomas, James (Alphaeus' son), Thaddaeus, Simon (the political activist), and Judas Iscariot (who later betrayed Him). In commissioning them He endowed them with the power to heal and cast out demons just as He had.

The next day as they came into the town of Nain, they encountered a funeral procession. A large crowd accompanied the grieving widow who had just lost her only son. They were carrying his body to the cemetery. Jesus approached the woman with deep compassion and encouraged her to stop weeping. As He said this, He touched the open coffin and the crowd came to a standstill. "Young man," Jesus said, "get up."

Instantly the boy sat up and began talking. Jesus reunited him with his mother, and a wave of fear and awe swept through the crowd. One and then another exclaimed, "God has come to help us! What a prophet He has sent us! Glory to God!" This amazing miracle got reported far and wide, as you can imagine.

All this time John the Baptist had been languishing in prison. When he heard reports of the great miracles Jesus was doing, he sent some of his disciples to ask Him whether, in fact, He was the promised Messiah or if they should be looking for someone else to come and deliver them.

They brought the question to Jesus even as He was healing many who were sick, blind, and oppressed with demons. Jesus told them to reassure John that He was doing the work of the Messiah: there were blind who could see, lame who could walk, dead who were alive, and masses of poor who had heard the Good News. Even though all this hadn't resulted in deliverance for John the Baptist, Jesus wanted John's disciples to be sure and convey this message. "And tell John," He went on to say, "blessed are those who don't get offended when My actions don't fit with their expectations."

After John's disciples left, Jesus used the occasion to talk with the crowd about John and his ministry. "Speaking of expectations, what did you think you would find when you first went to meet John? A wimpy hermit? Or maybe a flashy grandstander? Those of you who expected a prophet found what you were looking for — and much more! In the honorable trail of God's spokespersons, John had the prime assignment as the messenger predicted by Isaiah who would 'prepare the way' before Me.

"However, as great as John was, being the last of the old order, those who now respond to the Kingdom message are in a greater position than he was. Yes, tax-collectors accepted God's message by submitting to John's baptism, while the Pharisees and experts in the Law refused his baptism, rejecting God's plan for them. From the beginning of John's preaching till now, the Kingdom has been making progress in spite of the violent attacks against it. And before John came, all the prophets of old and even the Law of Moses pointed forward to this time. For those willing to hear My message, John is obviously the promised forerunner, the one coming 'in the spirit of Elijah' to herald the new Kingdom as Malachi foretold.

"But how can I describe this fickle generation? It reminds Me of the children's rhyme you hear in the market, 'We play happy songs and you won't dance; so we play sad songs and you don't want that either.' What I mean is, John showed up with an austere, restrictive diet, and folks said he was possessed; but I come feasting and enjoying the good things of life, and they reject me as a glutton and drunkard, a low-life. Well, time will tell. In the end all will see what's right."

Jesus then turned the focus on the cities of Galilee where He had done most of His miracles. "What a golden opportunity this generation is missing! Why, if Tyre and Sidon had seen and heard the things you have, they would have repented long ago. And as for you, Capernaum, who think you're so great, Sodom and Gomorrah will get off easier on Judgment Day than you will; because if I had shown up and done there the miracles you've seen, those cities would still be around today."

As He often did, Jesus looked up right in the middle of talking to the people and began talking to God: "Thank You, Father, Supreme Lord of heaven and earth; I love how You work. You've hidden these things from all who think they're so smart, while revealing them to any who receive it with childlike simplicity."

Turning again to the crowd, He explained, "Everything I say and do comes from the Father. No one knows Me as He does and no one knows Him as I do, unless I choose to reveal Him to them. Come, all of you who are worn out with trying to get it right; experience My rest. Walk with Me and work with Me — watch how I do it. Learn the unforced rhythms of grace. I won't lay anything heavy or ill-fitting on you. Keep company with Me and you'll learn to live freely and lightly."[†]

One of the Pharisees invited Jesus to come to his home for a meal. During the meal a woman of ill-repute came in. Weeping, she approached Jesus. Because they usually ate their dinners reclining, she came up behind Jesus and knelt at His feet. She washed His feet with her tears, wiped them with her hair, and kissed them. Then she anointed them with a fragrant oil.

Of course, the Pharisee was appalled at this and thought to himself, *If He were really a man of God, He'd know what kind of woman this is; and He would have stopped her.*

Jesus said to him, "Simon, let Me tell you a story."

[†]As paraphrased by Eugene Peterson in *The Message*, Matthew 11:29-30

Simon, the host, replied, "Do tell."

And so Jesus began, "Once upon a time there was a banker who had made loans to two individuals. As time went on, it turned out that neither one could afford to pay back their debt. The banker, kind fellow that he was, forgave them both. Now, a question for you, Simon: If one of them owed fifty dollars and the other one ten times that, which one would love the banker more?"

Simon said, "No doubt it would be the one with the larger debt."

Jesus answered, "You got that right! Now, about this woman: whereas you didn't offer Me the common courtesy of a foot-rinsing and a towel to dry them when I arrived, she, on the other hand, has washed My feet with her tears and dried them with her hair. Some hosts greet their guests with a friendly kiss on the cheek — which you didn't; she hasn't stopped kissing My feet since she got here. And some hosts bless their guests with a token anointing of perfume upon entering the house — again, not something you were inclined to do for Me; but the fragrant aroma of the oil she rubbed on my feet now fills the room. In other words, she, who may have sinned greatly in your eyes, has loved much. As for those who don't feel the need for forgiveness, there's not too much gratitude in their hearts."

Then Jesus turned to the woman and said, "Your many sins are all forgiven." While the other guests were trying to wrap their minds around how He could claim to forgive sins, Jesus went on to tell her, "Your trusting response to God has set you free. Go in peace."

Jesus continued His ministry to the towns and cities throughout Israel, spreading the liberating and exciting message of what God's Kingdom was like and how to be part of it. The twelve apostles went everywhere with Him, as well as a few women whose lives had been touched by Jesus. Among the women were Mary from Magdala, whom Jesus had rescued from seven demons; Joanna, wife of one of Herod's personal assistants; and another named Susanna. Many women who had the means saw to the provisions Jesus and His disciples needed from day to day.

In one place they entered a house, but the crowd pressed in so tightly there wasn't even room to sit down and eat. Not everyone was so impressed, however. Even some of his own family were saying that He was "out of His mind." Nevertheless, a steady flow of blind, mute, and demon-possessed came and received their healing. The phenomenon was causing people to wonder if, in fact, this was the "Son of David" who would become their great deliverer and king.

The Pharisees would have none of it. Instead, they started explaining away Jesus' activities as being energized by Beelzebub, another name for Satan, the ruler of the demons.

Jesus knew what they were thinking and spoke up, using some stories to make His point. "Really now, why would Satan be in the business of casting out demons? Everyone knows that a kingdom divided from within can't stand long. That's no way to take dominion. Besides, if My exorcism is authored by Beelzebub, as you suggest, where do your sons get their power to do the same thing? If, on the other hand, I am doing this by the power of God, then the Kingdom of God has come here and now.

"Who would ever think of breaking into the home of a strong man to rob him without first tying him up? Once that's taken care of, he can plunder the whole place.

"I'm here to tell you that anyone who isn't actively working with Me is working against Me; and worse than that, if anyone attributes My message or the work that I'm doing to the devil, they have committed an unpardonable sin — not because of what they're saying about Me but because of what they're saying about God's Holy Spirit who is behind everything I do.

"It's easy to tell what kind of tree you have by the fruit it produces. Some of you are like poisonous snakes spitting out your venom. What should we expect? What comes out of a man's mouth is whatever his heart is full of. Your own words, even the most insignificant ones, will testify against you in the Great Judgment. But those who have stored up good treasure in their hearts will speak good things, and their testimony will acquit them on that Day. Words have consequences."

The scribes and Pharisees shifted the subject matter by suggesting they just needed some clear sign or evidence that He was who He claimed to be.

Jesus didn't change the subject but continued His scathing exposé: "It's an adulterous, unbelieving generation that requires more signs. Here's a sign for you: Jonah was in the belly of a great fish for three long days and nights; in the same way, the Son of Man will spend three days in the heart of the earth.

"Need another sign? The men of Nineveh will shake their heads at your unbelief since they repented when Jonah preached judgment to them, and I'm greater than Jonah.

"Or this one? The queen of Sheba will testify against you at the judgment since she traveled a long distance to hear what Solomon had to say, and I'm greater than Solomon.

"We've been talking about unclean spirits. Listen to this: suppose an evil spirit leaves a man and goes out looking for a better victim but, after searching far and wide, finds nothing. That spirit will not only return to the cleaned-up yet empty soul, but he will also bring seven more treacherous spirits with him. Without question, the man is worse off at the end than he was at first. That's a warning for this wicked generation."

While He was teaching the multitude, His mother and brothers came to talk with Him; but they couldn't get anywhere near Him. Someone noticed them and let Him know they were there.

Jesus' response was unexpected. "You want to meet My family?" He asked. "It's you. Any of you who loves My Father and is anxious to hear what He says and to do what He wants you to do is a member of My real family."

Later that day He left the house and the crowd followed Him down to the lake where He got into a boat and proceeded to teach from there. He told another story:

"A farmer went out to plant his fields. As he scattered the seeds, some fell on the path and the birds had a feast. Some fell on areas where there wasn't much topsoil. The seed sprouted but didn't keep growing because it had no roots and the sun dried it out. A few seeds fell in areas where weed seeds had also fallen; and when they all sprouted, the thorns choked the good plants. Thankfully, some ended up on the good soil, sprouted, and produced a crop that was thirty, sixty, and even a hundred times what was planted."

Later, when He was alone with His disciples, they asked what point He was trying to make with the story about the farmer and why He taught using stories.

Jesus responded, "God has given you the tremendous privilege of learning the mysteries of His Kingdom. Not everyone shares that blessing. You have responded well to what you've heard so far and more will be revealed. The rest, who have listened but not really heard, watched but not really seen, will lose out. It's exactly what Isaiah predicted, 'Hearing, you will hear and not understand; and seeing, you will see and not perceive; for the heart of this people has grown dull. Their ears are hard of hearing, and their eyes they have closed; lest they should see with their eyes and hear with their ears, lest they should understand with their heart and turn so that I would heal them.'

"But as I said, you are getting in on a blessing which for centuries prophets and godly men longed to see and hear. Now, do I really need to explain this parable of the seeds to you? It really is so basic. You need to understand this one before you can possibly interpret any others.

"The seed is God's Word, His message. The hard-packed path is a picture of those who fall under the sound of the truth but won't receive it at all. Immediately the devil, like a hungry bird, comes and removes the very idea from their heart, eliminating all possibility of future life.

"Those represented by the stony ground seem truly glad to hear the Good News, and they respond positively at first. But as soon as they encounter opposition or ridicule, they give it up and the possibility of good fruit is lost.

"Then there are those who, likewise, are happy to attend the meetings and be around the message; but once they get home and life gets busy, they fall back into the multitudinous distractions and temptations of this world. Their so-called 'belief' ends up being unfruitful.

"And then there are those like you: the good soil. Your hearts are hungry for truth and you receive it into your lives, let it change you from the inside out, and in the end, watch it reproduce in countless benefits to yourselves and others.

"My message is like a lamp to help people find their way. But light, to be useful, has to be out in the open. It is so important that you let it expose the secrets of your heart rather than hiding your true self in darkness. Ultimately, every secret will be out in the open, so why not take advantage of this opportunity to be changed? If you do, you will see and hear more and more. If you shut out the light, you'll end up in utter darkness.

"And don't ask Me how this process of transformation works. No farmer would have a harvest if he went out and kept digging up the seed to see what was happening to it. He leaves it alone and the miracle happens; the dirt and sun and rain do the work. Before long a green shoot appears, then the head forms, and finally the ripe grain is ready for harvest. That's when the farmer goes to work!

"Since we're talking about seeds and harvest, here's another story:

"Once a farmer planted his crops and returned home to await the harvest. What he didn't know was that an enemy sneaked in at night and threw seeds of worthless weeds all over the field. Once the plants were up and growing, the farmhands noticed the different kinds of leaves and asked the farmer how it happened that there were so many weeds mixed in. He recognized the dirty work of an enemy but warned them not to attempt to pull the weeds, saying, 'If you did that now, you'd pull up the good plants, too. We'll have to separate the wheat from the weeds at harvest time.'

"The mustard seed is another example of how the Kingdom works. It's incredibly tiny and doesn't seem like much when you plant it; but once it starts growing, it gets so large and strong that birds can build their nests among its branches.

"Ladies, here's one for you:

"The Kingdom message is like yeast. It doesn't take very much to affect a large batch of dough, does it?"

Even this story-telling aspect of Jesus' ministry had been pre-dicted in the Old Testament. There's a verse that says, "I will open My mouth in parables; I will utter things which have been kept secret from the foundation of the world."

Later, Jesus' disciples asked Him to explain the story about the farmer. He said, "In this story, I am the farmer planting the good seed. The field is the world, the good seeds are all who belong to the Kingdom, and the weeds are Satan's 'children.' The enemy, of course, is Satan. The harvest is the final judgment when time comes to an end, and My angels are the ones who bring in the harvest.

"In the same way that farmers around here separate out the worth-less stalks and burn them, I will send out My angels to gather up those who persist in rebellion and wickedness. I will see that they are thrown into the furnace where there will be unbearable regret as they reap what they have sown. Meanwhile, the ones who have learned Kingdom ways will shine like the sun in their Father's Kingdom.

"Are you getting the message? Do you see the importance of the Kingdom?

"It's like a treasure that was buried in a field. When a man discovered it, he perceived the extravagant value. Then he went and sold everything he owned so he could buy the field and have that treasure. Or maybe it's more like an unusual pearl in a merchant's bucket. Someone who knew about pearls saw it and sold everything he had in order to buy it.

"Spreading the Kingdom message is like fishing with a big net. The net is put in the water and dragged back to shore. Once there, they get to work saving the good fish and throw-ing out the useless ones. Judgment Day will be like that when My angels separate the good from the bad. Again, it won't be a good time for the wicked. They'll realize after it's too late that they didn't get away with their sinful lives.

"Does this make sense to you?" Jesus asked.
"Yes, Lord," they replied.

"And so it is," Jesus went on, "that everyone who studies the Kingdom of Heaven is like a homeowner who skillfully utilizes fresh new things as well as familiar old ones."

Having concluded the stories for the present, they departed. It had been a long day dealing with the crowds, so Jesus told His disciples they were going to take a boat across to the other side of Galilee. While the men worked the sails, Jesus slept. It wasn't long before a windstorm kicked up and began churning the waves so violently that the small vessel began to fill with water. The disciples, recognizing the danger, were frantic, but Jesus slept soundly at the back of the boat.

Finally, one of them, yelling over the sound of the storm, woke Jesus, saying, "Lord, help us! We're about to go under! How can You sleep at a time like this?"

Jesus, unflustered, replied, "Why are you so worked up? Do you not believe who I am?"

He stood up and told the wind and waves to settle down. Everything became completely still. "Like I said, fellows, did you forget who was with you in the storm? If you believe, you won't fear."

The men, who had weathered their share of storms in the past, couldn't believe what they had just seen. After Jesus went back to lie down, they kept asking one another, "Who is this man? How did He do that? How did He get the weather to obey Him instantly?"

No sooner had they landed on the other side in the Gadarene district than they saw two wild, demon-possessed men coming toward them. One of them was naked and covered in scars. Townsfolk had tried to subdue him with chains and shackles, but he always broke them to pieces. He spent his life, day and night, wandering through the hills and cemeteries, screaming and cutting himself with stones.

When he saw Jesus, he ran up to Him and fell on his knees before Him. The demon-spirit cried out from inside the man, "Why have You come here, Jesus, Son of the Most High God? Are You here to torment us before our time?"

Jesus asked the demon its name, to which it replied, "Legion, because there's a swarm — thousands of us — in here. Please don't destroy us! If You have to throw us out of this man, let us go into those pigs over there. Please don't send us to our doom yet."

Jesus commanded them to go then to the pigs, a herd of about 2,000. The pigs went crazy and ended up running en masse right down into the lake where they drowned. The disciples gave the man some clothes and he sat with them, having become perfectly sane.

You'd think the whole countryside would have been relieved; but instead, they came out to where Jesus was and pleaded with Him to leave, afraid of what else He might do. So Jesus and His disciples returned to the boat. The man who had been delivered from the demons begged to go along. "No," Jesus told him, "you go back home now and tell your friends how the Lord God has demonstrated His love for you. Explain everything." And he did, sharing his testimony throughout the entire district.

They got back in the boat and headed across to another town. As you might imagine, a crowd gathered quickly, among them one of the leading men of the synagogue whose name was Jairus. He was desperate to see Jesus and fell down before Him, saying, "It's my daughter. She's on the verge of death. If You would come and touch her, I know she would be well again." (The girl was twelve years old.)

Jesus went with him as did the disciples and the throngs of people. In the crowd was a woman who for twelve years had suffered from hemorrhaging, a condition the doctors couldn't remedy. She had spent her life savings and was only getting worse. *If only I could touch that Man's robe,* she thought, *I'm sure I'd be healed.* So she pushed her way through the multitude and came up behind Him, getting just close enough to touch His garment. Immediately she could feel that her body had changed, had been restored to health.

At the same time Jesus perceived that power had gone out of Him; so He turned around and asked, "Who just touched Me?" No one said anything.

Then the disciples said, rather incredulously, "Who touched You? With the crowd pressing on us like this, you ask who touched You?"

But Jesus persisted, "Someone touched Me; I know it. I felt the energy flowing out of Me."

Then He saw her. And she knew that He knew. Shaking with fear, she fell down in front of Him and poured out her story. He pulled her to her feet and said, "It's all right. You believed and now you're well. Go. Enjoy. Your troubles are over." And she went her way, a happy woman.

In the time it took for this interruption, Jairus' daughter had died. Someone came to notify him of his daughter's death and to let him know there was no point in troubling Jesus. It was too late now. Jesus, however, having heard the report, encouraged Jairus not to give up, saying, "Trust Me, she will be healed."

As they arrived at the home, the mourners had already begun their clamorous lament with flutes and wailing moans. Jesus stopped them, saying, "What's all this commotion? The girl isn't dead; she's just sleeping." Instantly the crowd laughed at Him as though He were crazy. They knew she was dead.

Jesus took three of His disciples, Peter, James, and John, and the girl's parents into the room where she was lying. He made everyone else leave the room. Going over to the girl, He took her hand. With two words, "Talitha cumi!" (which means, "Little girl, arise!"), He changed everything. She sat up and looked around, got up and started walking, and asked for something to eat. Her parents were beside themselves with relief and joy. Jesus gave them strict orders not to tell anyone about what had happened. But how could a miracle like this be kept secret? Before long everyone knew about it.

Leaving there, he heard two blind men in the crowd who kept shouting, "Son of David, have mercy on us!" After they had entered a house, Jesus asked if they really believed He could help them. "Yes, Lord," they replied.

He touched their eyes and said, "Receive what you have believed!" And their eyes were opened. Again, Jesus warned them not to talk about this, but they spread this good news everywhere they went.

A little later they brought to Jesus a man who could not speak; a demon had entered him, causing this condition. Jesus cast out the demon. The man spoke. And the people marveled, saying, "We've never seen anything like this!" But the Pharisees kept spreading the idea that Jesus got His supernatural powers from the devil.

When Jesus and the disciples went to His hometown of Nazareth, it was a different story. The people heard Him teach in the synagogue and were impressed, but then they reasoned that He couldn't be anything special because they all knew His parents and siblings. Rather than taking Him seriously, they were offended at His audacity. Jesus reminded them of the old saying, "Prophets get respect from everyone except the home folk."

Because of this, very few miracles were done in Nazareth. He did lay hands on one or two, but He was amazed at the general unbelief.

Such was not the case throughout the rest of the region, however. Crowds gathered, the Good News was proclaimed, the sick were healed, and He taught freely in their synagogues. Jesus looked with compassion on the masses; they were like flocks of sheep lost and wandering without a shepherd. He told His disciples, "There's so much to be done, so many needs, and so few to do the work. Pray that the Lord of the harvest will call in more workers!"

It was at this point that Jesus began to send out the disciples in pairs to proclaim the Good News, heal the sick, and cast out demons. This was His commissioning speech:

"Your message is simply, 'The Kingdom you've been longing for, the Kingdom of God, has come.' Take this message exclusively to the lost sheep of Israel. They must be the first to hear it and have opportunity to respond. Heal the sick, cleanse the lepers, raise the dead, and cast out the demons. As generously as you have received, give.

"And don't worry about provisions. Don't bother taking extra food or clothing because as people hear your message, they'll provide what you need. When you enter a town, look for someone sympathetic to what we're doing. If they are hospitable, bless them and don't feel bad about staying in their homes.

"Whenever folks reject you and refuse to hear the message, then as you leave town, shake the dust off your sandals as a sign of judgment. I tell you, they will suffer worse things than Sodom and Gomorrah in the Day of Judgment!

"I realize that I'm sending you out like sheep into an environment filled with wolves. You'll need to be sharp and discerning, like serpents, while remaining as gentle and harmless as doves. The time will come when they will take you before tribunals, whip you, and mistreat you because of Me. When that happens, don't be worried about how to respond: the Spirit of your Father will speak through you in those situations.

"It won't be easy. Families will be divided with brother turning against brother, fathers turning against their own children, and children turning in their parents to be executed. Even if everyone hates you because of Me, don't turn back, don't give up! If they harass you in one city, go on to the next. Before long, I will come and rescue you.

"You know, don't you, that students grow up to be like their teachers? If they think I, your Teacher, am Beelzebub, you can be sure they'll treat you the same way or worse!

"Don't be afraid of them. They won't get away with it forever. Be bold; expose their wicked schemes. The worst they can do is kill your body; they can't touch your soul. Your Father, who happens to know every time a little sparrow gets hurt, cares so much more for you than for those birds. Trust Him.

"Don't be ashamed of Me or of the stigma that may be associated with being My follower, and I will honor you openly before My Father in heaven. It's those who turn on Me, denying what they've seen and heard, whom I must deny before My Father.

"I think you're beginning to realize that following Me and living in the Kingdom of God will mean realigning your priorities. Earthly relationships, even close family ties, may have to be severed; but unless having Kingdom life means everything to you, it means nothing. Ironically, to have My life, you will have to lose yours.

"So as you go, be encouraged. All who open their hearts to you are opening their hearts to Me, and all who accept Me accept My Father. Those who treat you as God's messenger will be rewarded as though they themselves were carrying the message. All those who assist you will be rewarded as partners in your work. Nothing you do for Me will go unnoticed or unrewarded — even as simple a thing as giving someone a cup of cold water."

With that, Jesus sent them on their way; and they took the message everywhere, anointing and healing the sick, casting out demons, and issuing an urgent call for all to repent. Jesus also went about teaching and preaching throughout the region.

When reports of Jesus' activities reached Herod's palace, Herod was unnerved. Rumors were flying that John the Baptist, whom he had just had beheaded, was resurrected and had supernatural powers. Herod looked for an excuse to meet Jesus for himself.

Herod, you may recall, had imprisoned John for meddling after John publicly rebuked him for living with his sister-in-law Herodias. She was furious with John and insisted that he be taken out, which Herod would have done in a heartbeat except that the populace revered him as a prophet of God. She got her way, however, during Herod's next birthday celebration. Herodias' daughter entertained the guests with a provocative dance, which led Herod to offer her "up to half the kingdom." She deferred to her mother, who told her to ask for John's head on a silver platter at once.

Herod was suddenly sobered and regretted his impulsive offer. Nevertheless, to avoid embarrassment before his guests, he complied and had the executioner carry out the act. The head was delivered to Herodias; the party was over. John's disciples were notified, and they came to get his remains so they could give him a proper burial. Messengers were sent to tell Jesus what had happened.

When Jesus heard what Herod had done to John, He took a boat and went off to a deserted place by Himself.

Shortly after that, the disciples returned from their mission trip with many stories to tell. They had been kept so busy that they were exhausted and hungry, so Jesus had them get in a boat with Him to get away for a time of rest. They escaped the crowds and found a quiet place near Bethsaida.

The crowds took note of where they were headed and proceeded to run that direction on foot. The boat had barely reached their destination when they saw the multitude approaching.

Jesus said to Philip, "What are we going to do? These people will need to eat. Is there somewhere close by where we could get some bread?" It was a trick question because Jesus knew what He had in mind.

Philip had no idea and retorted, "It would take nearly a year's wages to buy enough just to give that crowd a snack!"

Jesus, touched by the hurts and hopelessness of the people, who were like sheep having no shepherd, spent the rest of the day explaining the Kingdom message and healing their sicknesses. By late afternoon some of the disciples urged Jesus to send the crowd away so they could find food and lodging. Jesus, testing them because He knew what He was going to do, said, "No need for them to go away, you feed them."

They repeated Philip's line that between all of them they didn't have nearly enough money to afford that. Jesus asked them to find out what food might be available among the people. Andrew found a boy who had a couple of small fish and a handful of rolls. Jesus asked if He could have them. He then told His disciples to organize the thousands of people into groups of fifty and to prepare for a picnic supper.

Jesus held out the boy's lunch, looked up to heaven, and gave thanks for the abundance. Then He began to hand the food to the disciples who, in turn, passed it out to the people. The people ate their fill and the food kept coming. When everyone was finished, Jesus told His disciples to collect any extra food so nothing would be wasted. They gathered twelve baskets full of leftovers. They had just served a meal for five thousand men plus women and children.

Needless to say, the people were ecstatic and wanted to make Jesus king right then and there. They said, "Undoubtedly, this is the promised Prophet who will set things straight!"

Jesus could see what they intended to do, so He quickly had the disciples get in the boat and head across the lake. Meanwhile, He sent the crowd on its way and once again went up a nearby mountain to pray by Himself. He prayed late into the night.

As the boat was making its way toward Capernaum, another storm whipped up the sea, making it hard for the disciples to make headway. They had traveled quite a few miles from shore, and Jesus, seeing their dilemma, walked on the water to where they were. When the disciples saw Him, they thought they were seeing a ghost. He looked like He was going to walk on by; but when He got close enough where they could hear, He said, "It's just Me, nothing to be afraid of."

Peter replied, "Lord, if it's really You, let me walk over to You."

Jesus said, "Come."

Peter climbed over the side of the boat and began walking on the water toward Jesus — that is, until he looked around at the waves and became afraid. The moment he did that, he began to sink. So he cried out, "Lord, save me!"

Jesus took his hand and pulled him up, saying, "Why did you start to doubt?"

They walked back to the boat and as soon as they had gotten in, the wind stopped. The disciples were speechless. When they finally spoke up, they said to Jesus, "You really are the Son of God, aren't You?" The next thing they knew, they were at the shore.

The next day the crowd went down to the lake looking for Jesus. They knew the disciples had taken their boat and that there hadn't been another boat available, so they couldn't figure out where Jesus had gone. They finally took boats themselves to Capernaum and found Him and His disciples there. Their first question was, "Teacher, how did You get here?"

Interestingly, Jesus didn't answer their question. Instead, He challenged the motives of their hearts by saying, "I see you are very diligent in looking for Me but only because I fed you. It would be far better for you to spend your efforts looking for truth that will produce God's kind of life. God has given Me the authority to pass that life on to you."

"So what exactly should we be doing?" the people asked.

Jesus answered them, "The most important thing God wants you to do is to trust in Him and believe that He sent Me to you."

"Okay," they replied, "but aren't You supposed to give us some miraculous sign that You are sent by God? You know, kinda like back in Moses' day. He gave them bread from heaven to eat." From their response, it was apparent that they were still trying to get another free lunch.

Jesus tried to help them see the difference between bread made of wheat and bread made of truth. "You know, don't you, that it wasn't Moses who sent that manna from heaven? My Father did that, and He is doing it again by sending Me down from heaven. This real bread will give life to the whole world."

"Well," they replied, "by all means give us some of that bread!"

"I am that 'Bread of Life.' Whoever comes to Me in faith will find his deepest hunger and thirst more than satisfied. Here you are hearing every word I say but not taking hold of it. So be it. Everyone My Father gives Me will come to Me, and I will hold on to them right to the end. I'm not here to do what I want to do but only what pleases the Father. It is His delight to give Our kind of life to anyone who entrusts themselves to Me. On that Final Day there they will be, still with Me forever."

Some of the Jews got really upset after He said that. "How can He claim to have 'come down from heaven?' Why, we know His parents, Joseph and Mary. We know where He came from."

"Stop the whispering," Jesus said. "I don't expect you to believe. No one can come to Me unless My Father first inclines their heart to Me. Do you remember the verse that says, 'and they shall all be taught by God?' That's what I'm talking about. All who come to Me for life do so because they've experienced My Father at work in their souls. Not that you can see Him, for only I have ever seen the Father; but I guarantee that if you entrust yourself to Me, you will have Our kind of life in you forever.

"As I said, I am that 'Bread of Life.' Your forefathers ate the manna in the wilderness but they eventually died. I'm telling you that if you eat of Me, you will never die."

The Jews retorted, "How can this Man give us His flesh to eat?"

Jesus said, "Unless you feed on Me — on my flesh and blood — you cannot have life. Only those who get their sustenance from Me have Me living in them. My Father is fully alive and He fills Me with life. In the same way, I will fill with life anyone who feeds on Me. Again, let Me remind you that this is a very different kind of bread and a different kind of life than what your fathers experienced in the desert."

Jesus brought this teaching in the synagogue at Capernaum. Later, some of His disciples were complaining, "What on earth was He talking about? I wish He wouldn't make it so hard to understand."

Jesus, perceiving their agitation, said to them, "Does My teaching frustrate you? If you can't figure it out now, how will you understand it once I'm gone? But it's not about figuring it out. Only the Spirit can produce life, not your human intellect. The words I'm speaking give life when the Spirit reveals them. Some of you just won't believe." (Jesus had known right from the first who would betray Him.) "As I said, no one can come to Me unless My Father has given them the ability to come."

It was at this point that many who had accompanied Him turned away and stopped walking with Him. He asked the Twelve, "Do you want to leave as well?"

Simon Peter was quick to answer, "Lord, where would we go? You are the only One whose words produce real life. We're convinced that You are the Messiah, the Son of God."

Jesus responded somewhat pensively, "Yes, I chose all twelve of you, didn't I? And yet one of you is a devil." (He was, of course, referring to Judas who would later betray Him.)

Jesus went from there back to the land of Gennesaret. The people recognized Him right away. They ran throughout the region gathering all who were sick so that wherever He went many awaited His touch or begged to touch the hem of His garment. All who did so were made perfectly well.

He continued ministering in the northern region. He stayed away from Judea because He knew that the Jews there were looking for an opportunity to kill Him. So the Pharisees and scribes from Jerusalem came to where He was teaching.

Looking for proofs that He couldn't be who He claimed to be, they challenged Jesus about the disciples' disregard for orthodox rituals of cleansing. The Jewish religious leaders had complicated rules about washing just about everything — even how they were to run the water over their hands. "Why don't Your disciples follow the long-standing Jewish traditions?" they asked.

Jesus had one word for them, "Hypocrites!" He went on, "Isaiah nailed it when he described you with these words, 'These people draw near to Me with their words, honor Me with their lips, but their hearts are far from Me. What they call worship is meaningless. They've turned their man-made rules into divine oracles.' Yes, you Pharisees aren't nearly as concerned about what God says as you are about what your traditions tell you. In fact," Jesus added, "your traditions actually cause you to break God's laws. You know the clear command to 'honor your father and mother,' but you overrule that with this gimmick called 'Corban' (meaning devoted to God) so that people will give to you what ought to be used for supporting their elderly parents. You've basically rewritten God's commands to suit yourselves, which you do with a lot of other things as well."

Jesus turned to the listening crowd and said, "Listen up! You've been given a long list of things to avoid eating or touching, but I'm telling you that none of that matters! The problem isn't what you put into your mouths but what is in your hearts and comes out of your mouths. If you have ears, I hope you're hearing this!"

Later when He was alone with His disciples, they said, "Did You realize that the Pharisees were offended by what You said?"

Jesus replied, "Don't mind them. Any plant which My Father hasn't planted will be uprooted soon enough. They are blind leading the blind; the whole bunch will end up in the ditch together."

Then Peter asked, "What did you mean about things we eat or things we say?"

Jesus answered, "You still don't get it, do you? My message is all about what's inside, not the externals that religion tends to focus on. The food you eat doesn't go into your heart but through the stomach, digestive system, and eventually out of the body. In that sense, no food is clean or unclean when it comes to your spiritual well-being. How thoroughly you wash your hands before eating isn't of great significance to God either. What He does care about is the filth that exists deep in the core of your beings: the evil thoughts, murders, adulteries and sexual fantasies, stealing, coveting, lying, deceiving, conniving, blasphemies, and pride."

Some days later Jesus went to the region of Tyre and Sidon where He wouldn't be recognized. Even there a local Gentile woman came to the house where He was staying. "Won't You have mercy on me, Lord, Son of David?" she begged. Over and over she cried out, "My daughter is severely oppressed by demons. I know You can help her!"

The disciples were irritated and urged Him to send her away. So Jesus rebuffed her by saying, "I've been sent to help the lost sheep of Israel, not the Gentiles."

She didn't let that stop her but came and threw herself at His feet, begging Him to help her. Appearing to be unmoved, Jesus responded, "As the saying goes, don't give to the dogs what is meant for the children to eat."

To which she replied, "Yes, Master, but even the little dogs under the table get to eat the crumbs that fall from the children's plates."

Jesus was touched by her determination and said, "Woman, you are persistent and I'm blessed by your faith. Your wish is granted; your daughter is healed." The woman returned home and found it just as Jesus had said; the demon was gone and her daughter rested comfortably on her bed.

From there Jesus went around the Sea of Galilee into the region of Decapolis. The people of the region brought to Him a man who was deaf and had difficulty speaking. Jesus took him away from the crowd to heal him. He spit on His finger, touched the man's tongue, and then put His fingers in his ears. With a deep sigh Jesus looked up to heaven and said "Ephphatha," which means "be opened."

Immediately the man could hear and speak plainly. Jesus told the crowd not to tell what had happened, but that didn't stop them from spreading the word. More and more came to Him and He healed them all. When the multitude saw all these miracles, they gave the credit to God and said about Jesus, "Everything He does is amazing!"

Once again they found themselves with a crowd on hand and nothing to eat. In fact, they had been with Him for three days solid. "I can't send them away like this or they may faint," Jesus told His disciples.

"And where in this wilderness do You expect us to come up with bread?" the disciples questioned.

"Well, what do we have to work with?" He asked them.

"Seven pieces of bread and a handful of small fish is all we've come up with," they replied.

"Good," Jesus answered, "have the crowd get seated for dinner."

Jesus took the bread, gave thanks, and broke the pieces. Handing them to the disciples, they then distributed the bread among the people. He did the same with the fish. Everyone ate till they were full. When they gathered up the leftovers, there were seven large baskets full. This time He had fed over four thousand people. After sending the crowd on its way, Jesus and the disciples got into a boat and headed across the Sea of Galilee toward Dalmanutha (also called Magdala).

Again, the Pharisees and Sadducees were there to hound Him. They kept telling Him they just wanted one more supernatural sign to prove His credentials. Jesus sighed deeply in His spirit and rebuked them, saying, "In the evening, if the sky is red, you predict a nice day ahead; but if the sky is red in the morning, you predict bad weather. What hypocrites you are! You can read the signs in the sky but can't figure out the signs of the times we're in. This adulterous generation, wanting anything but God, keeps looking for signs. The only sign I can leave with you is the sign of the prophet Jonah." With that, Jesus left them.

He and His disciples headed back across the lake; but when they got there the disciples remembered that they didn't have food with them.

Jesus wanted to warn them about the influence of their leaders so He said, "Beware of the leaven of the Pharisees and Sadducees and the leaven of Herod."

Well, the disciples immediately thought He was upset that they forgot to bring along enough bread. Jesus, of course, knew what they were thinking and said, "Hold on, guys, no matter how many times I say this, you aren't catching on. You think I'm talking about food and that I'm upset that we don't have some. Have you forgotten that we fed more than five thousand? How many leftovers did we have?"

"Twelve baskets," they answered.

"Then just the other day we did it again, feeding more than four thousand," He said. "Do you recall how many baskets we had after that meal?"

"Seven," they replied.

Jesus went on to say, "So you surely can't believe I'm worried about whether we have enough to eat today, can you? That is not at all what I was referring to when I said to watch out for the leaven of the Pharisees."

Then the disciples realized that He was warning them to not allow the Pharisees' beliefs to get mixed in with His teaching.

Later they arrived at Bethsaida where a blind man was presented to Him. The people begged Jesus to heal him. He took the man by the hand, and they walked away from the town. Jesus spit on His hands, laid them on the man's eyes, and asked him to open them. "What do you see?" asked Jesus.

"I see men, I think. They're kinda fuzzy, more like walking trees."

Jesus laid His hands on his eyes once more and then had him look up.

"Now I see everything!" he exclaimed. "And it's all so clear!"

Jesus sent him home, specifically asking him not to tell anyone what had happened.

Then they went up to Caesarea Philippi in northern Israel where Jesus could get away to pray. When His disciples joined Him, He asked them, "What are you hearing from the crowds? Who do they say I am?"

"Some are convinced that you're John the Baptist," they answered. "Others say Elijah, Jeremiah, or another of the ancient prophets come back to life."

"And what about you?" Jesus asked. "Who do you say that I am?"

Simon Peter, always quick to speak, spoke for the rest by saying, "You are the Messiah, the Son of the Living God."

"You are blessed, Simon, the son of Jonah," said Jesus. "This was revealed to you by My Father in heaven, and it is this rock-like conviction that will build My church so that even the gates of hell can't stop it. As you go, you will be given the wisdom and ability to bring about on earth what God is doing in heaven." But He gave strict orders that they not yet say anything publicly about His being the promised Messiah.

Jesus' Final Year: Preparing to Suffer

From this point in His ministry, Jesus began to openly state that He would suffer at the hands of the Jewish leaders, that they would have Him killed, and that He would rise up on the third day.

One time after hearing this, Peter took Him aside and began to rebuke Him, saying, "There's no way this could happen to You, Lord!"

Jesus looked at Peter and said, "You don't know what you're saying. Satan is using you to trap Me. Be gone, Satan! And you, Peter, are relying on your own understanding and don't have a clue what God is doing."

Jesus gathered the people and His disciples around Him and began to explain what it meant to truly be His disciple. "Following Me means giving up your right to run your life the way you want to. If you're willing to 'lose' your agenda by embracing Mine, you will find the real meaning of life — even if it costs you everything you now think is so important. However, if you pursue earthly success, it could cost you your very soul.

"At the end of history I will come, shining with My Father's glory and accompanied by holy angels, to reward each of you according to what you've done. If the record shows that you've been too embarrassed or ashamed to identify with Me in front of your friends and this godless world, I'll be ashamed of you.

"There are some in this crowd who will actually get to see a glimpse of what that Kingdom glory is like before they die!"

About a week after He said this, Jesus took three of His disciples, Peter, James, and John, to the top of a high mountain to pray.

While they were praying, Jesus' body began to glow brighter than anything the disciples had ever seen. His face radiated light like the sun and His robe glistened with indescribable brilliance.

The disciples had been dozing when all this began. Suddenly two men, also glowing, appeared and began discussing Jesus' impending death. Somehow the disciples recognized them as Elijah and Moses. By the time they were fully awake, the two men were getting ready to leave.

Peter, not sure what to say and overwhelmed by what they were seeing, blurted out, "Master, Teacher, this is incredible! Would You like us to build three shelters, one each for You, Moses, and Elijah?" We're not sure what Peter was thinking when he suggested this, but then he didn't know what he was saying either.

Immediately they were enveloped by a massive brilliant cloud which frightened them. Then a voice spoke out of the cloud, saying, "This is My precious Son who is a delight to Me. Listen to Him." At this the disciples fell on their faces to the ground in utter terror.

Jesus came right over to them and touched them gently, saying, "It's all right, don't be afraid. Get up now." They looked around and everything was normal. Just the four of them were left standing at the top of the mountain.

As they made their way down the mountain, Jesus told them they must not say a word about this experience until after He had risen from the dead. They couldn't figure out what He meant about rising from the dead, but they did keep quiet about the amazing scene they had witnessed.

The scribes had been saying that Jesus couldn't be the Messiah because Elijah hadn't come yet to set things straight. The disciples asked Jesus what He thought about that. He answered by saying, "It's true. Elijah does come first to set things in order for the Messiah. Also the Messiah will suffer rejection, but the scribes miss that point. I'm telling you that Elijah has come and they didn't realize who he was, so they ignored him. And they're about to mishandle Me before long."

When Jesus explained it this way, the disciples realized that He was talking about John the Baptist fulfilling the Elijah role.

The day after their mountaintop experience, Jesus found a crowd gathered around His disciples. They were arguing with the Jewish scribes. Of course, when the people noticed Jesus, they all ran to Him. Jesus asked the scribes what they had been discussing; but before they could answer, a man burst from the crowd and cried out, "Lord, have mercy on my son. He has seizures and the devil throws him into convulsions. Sometimes he foams at the mouth, gritting his teeth; and sometimes he falls into a fire or into the water. I took him to Your disciples for healing, but they couldn't cure him."

"Oh, you poor, lost people," Jesus said. "How much longer can this go on? Go, get your son and bring him to Me."

The instant the boy saw Jesus, the demon-spirit threw the child to the ground in convulsions and he began foaming at the mouth. Jesus asked the boy's father how long he had been having this trouble.

"Ever since he was a young child, Sir," he replied. "If there's anything You can do for him, please do!"

Jesus said, "If you trust Me, anything is possible."

To which the man answered, "Oh, I believe in You; help me overcome any unbelief!"

Jesus went to the boy and addressed the evil spirit, saying, "Deaf and mute spirit, I command you to leave him and never return." With a shriek and a final convulsion the demon came out of him, and the boy lay limp on the ground. The people thought he had died; but Jesus took him by the hand and lifted him up, handing him to his father. Everyone was amazed at how powerfully God had worked.

Later, when they were alone, the disciples asked Jesus why they had been unable to heal the boy. "Some cases require that you have a stronger faith. This is something you develop over time through prayer and fasting. Eventually, if the situation called for it, you would be able to tell that hill to move over to the other side of the valley. Nothing would be impossible."

They continued ministering around Galilee, but Jesus tried to avoid the crowds. When He was alone with His disciples, He reminded them that He was going to be betrayed, turned over to men who would kill Him, but that He would then be raised up on the third day.

Naturally, they were very upset by this and couldn't comprehend it, but they were too afraid to ask Jesus to explain further.

One day in Capernaum a temple tax collector found Peter and asked him whether Jesus paid the temple tax. "Of course," Peter told him.

But later, when they were in the house discussing the situation, Jesus said, "Simon, when a king decides to collect taxes for some project, do his own subjects have to pay taxes or does he collect it from foreigners?"

Peter quickly said, "Only from the foreigners."

Jesus went on, "So the local citizens don't have to pay, right? Technically, we shouldn't have to pay the temple tax; but to avoid causing a scene, we will pay it anyway. I'll tell you what, take your fishing rod down to the lake and catch something. The first one you catch will have a coin in its mouth that will be enough to cover the taxes for both of us."

One day on their way back home to Capernaum, the disciples began arguing with each other over who deserved the top positions in Jesus' Kingdom. When they got to the house, Jesus asked them what the lively discussion was along the road. Of course, no one wanted to admit what the topic was.

Jesus sat down and invited the others to gather around Him. "I'd like to talk about true greatness," He said. "Whoever wants to be most important must serve others, making their concerns more important than his own."

The disciples were confused. "How does that work when it comes to deciding who sits on which throne in the Kingdom of Heaven?" they asked.

So Jesus called over a small child and had him stand where all could see him. "First of all," Jesus said, "you can't get into the Kingdom of Heaven unless you change and become humble like a child. In My Kingdom, the least is the greatest. Whenever you extend yourself even to one little child, you are giving yourself to Me and to the One who sent Me. That's how you become the greatest in the Kingdom of Heaven."

John, wanting to draw a clear line between those who were working for the Kingdom and those who were not, said, "Teacher, we saw someone who isn't one of us casting out demons using Your name. We stopped him because he wasn't with us."

But Jesus said to him, "Oh, no, don't stop someone from using My name to do miracles. Folks doing that are less likely to turn around and say something nasty about Me. In situations like this, if they are not against Me, we will consider them on our side. Yes, even so simple a gift as a cup of water given in My name will carry with it a reward."

With the child still in their midst, Jesus went on to warn His disciples, "Whoever causes one of these little ones to stumble into sin will wish he'd been thrown into the middle of the ocean with a stone tied to his neck when he sees what torment is coming to him.

"Offenses will happen in this world but woe to those who instigate them. Just how serious is this matter? If it's your hand causing you to sin (violence, stealing, etc.), it would be better for you to cut it off and to go through life one-handed than to end up with two hands in the eternal fire that never ends.

"If it's your foot that makes you sin (taking you down forbidden paths), cut it off and throw it from you as far as you can. Limp through life if you have to, but don't end up with both feet, burning in the relentless fires of hell.

"If it's your eye that leads you into sin (covetousness, lust, etc.), it would be better to pluck it out and throw it away. Would you rather get into God's Kingdom with one eye or keep both to see the fire of hell from which you can never escape?

"Fire, like salt, either destroys or purifies. Everyone goes through the fire in one way or the other. Purify your lives so that you don't end up destroyed by fire! Let this affect how you treat one another.

"And be especially careful how you treat these little ones. You may not see much in them, but I tell you they have an angel holding them before the face of My Father in heaven. He sent Me to save little lost ones like this.

"Take a shepherd, for instance, who has a hundred sheep to care for. If even one gets lost, does he not go far and wide to rescue that one? And isn't he completely joyous when he finds it? That's how My Father feels about every one of these poor, lost children.

"In your relationships, when someone wrongs you, don't harbor resentment. This is where you can help each other like a purifying fire or like salt that still works to preserve and enhance. Go privately to them and explain what they did wrong. If they see it and respond humbly, you've won them back. If they don't, take along a couple of witnesses who can hear both sides. If they won't listen to them, only then do you take public action and seek the intervention of the group. If they stubbornly refuse to heed the counsel of these many 'grains of salt,' cut them loose; don't go any further.

"As you agree together in these difficult situations, all of heaven will work with you in bringing about restoration. Even when it's just two or three of you, I'm there as an unseen Witness."

Peter was starting to comprehend God's desire for reconciliation and asked, "Lord, how far does this go? Should I be expected to forgive my brother up to seven times over?"

Jesus told him, "No, Peter, not seven times. How about seventy times seven? Let Me illustrate:

"Once upon a time there was a king who decided it was time to settle up with his workers. Among them was a man who owed him millions of dollars. There was no way the man could pay back such a huge amount; so the king instructed that he, his wife, and his children be sold so that he could recover at least something of the enormous debt.

"The worker, stunned by the harsh reality of this judgment, fell down in front of the king, saying, 'Master, if you'll just bear with me a little longer, I'll pay it all back.' The king, in an unthinkable act of compassion, forgave the entire debt and set the man free from all obligation to repay.

"On his way home the worker encountered an associate who owed him about half a year's wages. He grabbed the man by the throat and said, 'Pay up what you owe me, and I mean right now!'

"The other was distraught and cried out for patience, saying, 'Give me a little more time and I'll pay it all back.' But the one who was demanding payment showed him no mercy, throwing him into debtor's prison until the debt was repaid.

"The other workers, knowing all that had happened, were so upset they went right to the king to tell him what the man forgiven of his debt had just done to a co-worker.

"The king called the man back to his palace to set him straight. 'You are a wicked servant! Here I forgave you that huge debt just because you begged me for mercy. How could you come down on this other man for such a comparatively trifling amount? You showed no pity, therefore I have no pity on you.' With that the king had the man sent to the torturers until he found a way to pay back the millions he owed.

"My point is this: unless from the core of your being you truly forgive those who wrong you, My Father in heaven will have to deal with you in this same way. He is serious about grace ruling your relationships!"

Sometime later when the Feast of Tabernacles was approaching, Jesus' brothers found Him and mockingly suggested that, if He were going to become king, He should go where the crowds are, to Jerusalem. (None of His siblings believed who He was at this point.) Jesus told them to go on without Him because it wasn't time for Him to go. "You go have a good time," He told them. "You won't face any trouble, but I will when I go because I am publicly pointing out what's wrong with their lives." They went on ahead, but He remained in Galilee a few more days. Then Jesus and His disciples made their way south through Samaria, hoping to attend the feast secretly.

He sent a couple of disciples ahead to prepare a place for them to eat and rest, but the residents of that village refused to welcome them. James and John were furious and asked Jesus if they should, like Elijah of old, command fire to come down from heaven and consume them.

Jesus, however, rebuked them, saying, "Certainly not. I have not come to destroy but to save men's lives." So they proceeded on to another place.

Along the road they encountered a scribe who boldly proclaimed that he would follow Jesus to the ends of the earth. Jesus warned him that it was no easy life he'd be signing up for. "I can't even find a room for the night," He said. "Even the wild animals have it better off than Me right now."

Jesus invited another in the crowd to follow Him. The man showed some interest but said he would have to wait until his obligations at home were taken care of. "There are plenty of others," Jesus answered, "who can take care of those earthly matters. You should be out proclaiming what really matters: the Kingdom of God."

Another claimed he would follow Jesus but gave the excuse that he needed just a little more time with his family and friends back home. Jesus warned him that if he left the fields now, having already begun "plowing" with Him, he was simply not the kind who could enter the Kingdom of God.

Before arriving in Jerusalem, Jesus was the main topic of conversation. Everyone was on the lookout for Him. The people had mixed opinions about Him, some saying He was good while others felt that He was deceiving the people. None of this talk went on openly because they knew the Jewish leaders were out to get Him.

Halfway through the feast (it lasted eight days), Jesus went to the temple and began teaching. Again, they marveled at His ability to explain things so well, especially since He had never had formal training.

Jesus made a point of explaining that His "great teaching" wasn't something He came up with but that He was only passing on to them what the One who sent Him wanted Him to teach. He went on to tell them that those who truly want to do God's will would know that what He taught came from God and wasn't just something He had made up Himself. He wasn't saying these things to become famous or to make people think He was someone important. Rather, He was seeking to honor God, who had sent Him to teach these things. "Anyone," He told them, "who seeks to honor the person in authority over him would be telling the truth and could be trusted. You claim to hold Moses up in such high esteem. Don't you believe that he gave you the Law from God? Yet none of you obeys what he taught either. If I speak for God as Moses did, why do you want to kill Me?"

The crowd reacted with, "You're crazy! Who's trying to kill You?"

Jesus said, "I healed a man on the Sabbath and this astonished you. But you break the Sabbath all the time when, to fulfill the circumcision command, you have to perform the task on a Sabbath. If you do this for a routine practice, why do you get so upset when, on the Sabbath, I make a man completely well? If you just think this through sensibly, you'll have to agree that I'm right."

Now some in the crowd spoke up, saying, "Isn't this the One the Jews are trying to kill? Here He is teaching in public, and they're not doing anything about it. Have the rulers come to the conclusion that He is the Messiah after all? But that couldn't be because we know where He came from. They say that the true Messiah will appear mysteriously, no one knowing where He comes from."

"Yes, you know Me and My upbringing, but you don't really know who sent Me because you don't know Him. I do know Him and am here because He sent Me to you," was Jesus' response.

"Really," the crowd began to wonder, "what more could the Messiah do than this Man has done so far?" And some believed. But when the Pharisees saw what was going on, they sent some officers to apprehend Him.

Jesus told the crowd, "I won't be around much longer. I'm going back where I came from and you can't get there from here."

This really had them bewildered. "Where could He possibly go that we wouldn't find Him?" they asked. "Is He going to other countries, looking for Jews scattered among the nations? And what does He mean that we can't follow Him where He's going?"

On the final day of the feast, Jesus stood up and shouted, "If anyone is thirsty, he should come to Me and drink. Believe in Me, and as the Scriptures promise, out of your innermost soul will flow rivers of living water." (We now know that He was describing what would happen when His followers received the Spirit. This hadn't happened yet because Jesus' work on earth wasn't finished.)

The crowd was divided in their opinion about Him. Some were solidly convinced that He was the Messiah or the great Prophet they had been hoping for. Others couldn't reconcile the fact that they understood Jesus to be from Galilee when they knew that the Messiah would have to come from Bethlehem in Judah, David's hometown.

While some were trying to silence Him, no one could actually get their hands on Him. In fact, the officers returned to the Pharisees empty-handed. The religious leaders demanded why they hadn't brought Jesus; their reply was, "We never heard anyone speak quite like He does."

The Pharisees fumed, "What? Surely you're not falling for Him, too? Look around you; none of us Pharisees are taken in by His teaching. This accursed crowd doesn't know the first thing about the Law."

Nicodemus, one of the Pharisees who, unbeknownst to them, had privately visited with Jesus, spoke up, "Well, our law doesn't condemn a man before it hears his side of the story, does it?"

The Pharisees glared at him, "You? Are you on this Galilean's side? C'mon, you know that no prophet comes out of Galilee!"

After this, everyone went to their homes, but Jesus went to the Mount of Olives. Early the next morning He was back teaching in the public court of the temple near where the offering chests stood. A crowd quickly gathered around Him. The scribes and Pharisees, trying to trick Him into doing or saying something they could turn against Him, brought a woman to Him, saying, "Sir, this woman was caught in the very act of adultery. The Law of Moses requires that we stone her to death. What do You say?"

Jesus didn't answer them directly. He bent down and started doodling in the dirt as if He hadn't heard them. They kept prodding Him with the question until finally He stood up and said, "All right then, let's begin. Whoever among you has never sinned can be the first to throw a stone at her." He stooped down again and started writing something in the dirt. Whatever he wrote apparently brought conviction on the accusers; and one by one, beginning with the oldest, they walked away, leaving the woman alone with Jesus.

When Jesus finally stood up and saw that they were gone, He asked the woman where her accusers were. "Has everyone left? Does no one condemn you?"

She quietly answered, "No one, Sir."

Jesus comforted her and said, "Then neither do I. Go on now and be done with sinning!"

Turning to the crowd, Jesus said, "I am the light of the world. If you come with Me, you won't stumble in darkness but will enjoy living in the light."

The Pharisees in the crowd interrupted Him, charging, "You make all these claims for Yourself, but all we have is Your word on it. We need more than that."

So Jesus answered them, saying, "They may be My words but that doesn't mean they are unreliable. I know I speak the truth because I know where I am from and where I am going. You see things from your limited perspective, but I have the Father as My witness."

"And where is this Father You speak of?" they asked.

Jesus answered them, saying, "It's obvious that you don't really know Me, otherwise you would automatically know who My Father is. One of these days I'll be gone; you'll look for Me in vain and die in your sins. You can't join Me where I'm going."

Some said, "Is this guy going to kill Himself? Is that why He says we can't follow Him or won't be able to find Him?"

Jesus went on, saying, "You are from down here; I am from up above. You are part of this world system; I am not. That's why I said that you will die in your sins: you refuse to believe in Me."

So they asked, "Who are You, anyway?"

He answered them, saying, "I am what I've been saying from the beginning. I could say a lot more, but I only say what the One who sent Me tells Me to say." They still didn't realize that He was talking about God, His Father. "Once you've nailed Me to a cross, you'll find out who I am. Then you will finally realize that I've been speaking for My Father and always do what He wants Me to do."

There were some who believed in Him at this point. To them He said, "Just keep holding on to what I have said; live by it and you will know that you've found truth, for you will be truly free on the inside."

Some others overheard Him and retorted, "What do You mean 'truly free'? We're Abraham's descendants and we've never been enslaved to anyone."

Jesus replied, "There are all kinds of slavery. Everyone who sins becomes a slave to sinning. A slave doesn't have a permanent place in the family but the son does. So if the Son makes you free, you are truly free. I hear you claiming to be Abraham's descendants, yet you want to kill Me. You won't listen to what I'm saying. I listen to My Father and you're listening to your father."

"Abraham is our father!" they shot back at Him.

"Come now," Jesus said, "if you were really children of Abraham, you'd be more like him. Here I come telling you the truth about yourselves which I heard from God, and you're ready to kill Me. Abraham wouldn't do anything like that. You're behaving just like your father."

"At least we weren't born out of fornication," they snapped, implying that He had been, since there were rumors about His mother's unplanned pregnancy and all. "We have one Father — God."

"Well, that's strange," Jesus said. "If God were your father, you would love Me since I came directly from Him. But as it is, you can't hear a word I'm saying because you are just like your father the devil; and you do everything he tells you to do. He was a murderer from the start and can't stand truth. He is the father of lies and that's his native tongue. Now, when I speak truth, you won't listen and believe because these are God's words; and you're not of God at all."

The Jews came back at Him again, saying, "We were right when we said You were a Samaritan and had a demon, weren't we?" (For the rumor suggested that Mary got pregnant on her way through Samaria to visit her aunt Elizabeth in Judea.)

Jesus didn't mince words. "I do not have a demon. I say that I am honoring My Father; you say I am not. There is One who knows, and we'll let Him be the judge. I can promise you this, that anyone who takes Me at My word and lives by it will live and never die."

"Well," they responded, "there's the proof that You're out of Your mind. Abraham and the prophets are all dead, yet You're promising that if people follow You they won't die? That would make You greater than them. You're not trying to tell us You're greater than Abraham, are You? Or greater than the prophets?"

Jesus answered them, "It wouldn't matter to you what I say about Myself. The only thing that does matter is what My Father says, the One you call your God. Well, I'm telling you that you don't know God, but I know Him personally. I am committed to doing whatever He says. And speaking of Abraham, he was delighted when he saw Me coming."

"Right," they said sarcastically. "You're not even fifty years old and You want us to believe You've seen Abraham?"

Jesus answered, "The fact is, before Abraham was, I AM."

Hearing that phrase from Jesus' mouth threw them into a frenzy. They looked for stones to kill Him on the spot. Jesus was able to walk right past them and out of the temple area.

Passing by, they saw a blind man sitting beside the road. He had been there many times, having been born blind. The disciples, assuming that all handicaps were the direct result of some sin, asked Jesus, "Teacher, was it this man's sins or his parents' that caused him to be born blind?"

Jesus surprised them with His answer, "His blindness has nothing to do with sin, neither his own nor his parents. This is an opportunity for Me to demonstrate how God works. The time is coming when it will be too late for miracles. While I am here, I bring light to this darkened world."

Upon saying that, Jesus spat on the ground and made a clay compress with the saliva and dirt. After putting the mixture on the man's eyes, Jesus sent him to wash it off in the pool of Siloam (a play on words since Siloam means "sent"). So the man went, washed, and came away seeing everything for the first time.

Everyone in town knew the man and couldn't believe their eyes. "Is this really the same guy who's been begging all these years?" they asked. Some decided it must be someone who just looked like the man.

"No," the once-blind man said, "I am the very one!"

"No way!" the people replied. "How did your eyes get healed?"

"Quite simply," the happy man explained. "A man named Jesus made some clay and put it over my eyes. Then He sent me to Siloam to wash it off. I did and here I am — seeing you!"

"Where is He?" the people inquired.

"I couldn't tell you," he answered.

It wasn't long before the man was taken to the Pharisees because this happened to be the Sabbath . . . again. They also asked the man for details, "How exactly did you get your sight?"

So the man told his story again, "He put clay on my eyes, I washed it off, and now I can see."

Some of the Pharisees were adamant, "Obviously this Man can't be from God because He keeps on doing work on the Sabbath, which is against God's Law."

Others, though, queried, "How could a mere man who is a sinner do miracles like this?" They couldn't agree on what to do so they asked the blind man his opinion. "What do you think about this Man who opened your eyes?"

"Seems to me He must be a prophet of some kind," answered the man who had been blind.

The "blinded" Pharisees decided this must be a hoax and that this fellow hadn't really been blind and then healed. They asked someone to bring his parents to them for questioning. "Tell us," they demanded, "is this your son and was he born blind? And if so, how do you account for the fact that his eyes are working just fine?"

The parents didn't hesitate but said, "Yes, he is our son and he definitely has been blind since birth. As far as the healing goes, you'll have to ask him. We weren't there and he's old enough to speak for himself." You see, they knew that the Jewish leaders had threatened to excommunicate from the synagogue anyone who publicly aligned themselves with Jesus. That's why they deferred to their son when it came to commenting on his healing.

Back to the son they went, saying, "Listen, fellow, give the credit to God, not this sinner whom you claimed healed you."

The formerly blind man, the object of everyone's attention, said, "I couldn't tell you whether or not He's a sinner. All I can say is once I was blind and now I can see!"

Trying to get him to change his story, they asked again how the healing had occurred. The man, a little put out at their interrogation, said, "I've been through this once and you wouldn't listen. Why are you asking again? Are you thinking that maybe you will become His disciples now?"

"Humph," they stormed, "you're the one who is obviously His disciple. We're Moses' disciples because we know he heard directly from God. As for this man, we don't know anything about Him."

"Isn't this amazing?" the man replied. "You don't know where He is from but He has opened my eyes. Everyone knows that God doesn't listen to sinners; but if someone serves God and wants to do His will, then God uses him. Never in the history of mankind have we heard of someone who was born blind being healed — until me. What I'm saying is that if this man weren't from God there would be no way He could have done this miracle."

The Pharisees had had enough. "You good-for-nothing low-life. What do you mean trying to teach us? We're the teachers around here!" they barked. "Now, get out of here!" And they threw him out.

Jesus heard about this and went to find the man. "Do you believe in the Son of God?" Jesus asked.

"Who is He, Lord? I'd love to believe in Him."

Jesus said, "You're looking at Him. It's Me." The man believed and worshiped then and there.

Jesus said to those who were standing around, "Yes, I came to shake things up. I'm doing these things in order to help the blind see and to declare as blind those who think they see."

Some Pharisees heard this comment and asked, "Are you calling us blind?"

To this Jesus replied, "If you realized how blind you are, I wouldn't condemn you; but since you think you're fine, I leave you in your sin."

Jesus ended the day talking about sheep and shepherds since He saw the masses of people as helpless, wandering sheep. "At night the sheep are safely contained inside the walls of their fold, and the night watchman protects the doorway. Some will try to get to the sheep by climbing over the wall. They are up to no good.

"The shepherd, known to the night watchman and to the sheep, comes to the door and leads out the sheep, calling them each by name. The sheep don't mind following him because they know and trust the shepherd, but they shy away from strangers or anyone whose voice they don't recognize.

"I am the door. Those who come through Me will have real life, safety, and all they need. Anyone else who claims to be the way to life is actually a thief. The sheep won't listen to him.

"I am also the good shepherd. You can tell the difference between a good shepherd and a hireling by how they respond to trouble. If a wolf comes, the good shepherd will lay down his life if he has to in order to protect the vulnerable sheep. The hireling only cares about his own safety and runs for his life. I am that good shepherd. My sheep know Me, and My Father knows Me as well as I know Him. I will lay down My life for My sheep.

"The reason the Father loves Me is because I'm willing to lay down My life so that I can take it up again. No one can take My life from Me; I choose when and where I will lay it down. I have the authority and the ability not only to do this but also to raise it up again just as My Father told Me.

"I'll be gathering in other sheep, too. All of you will become one big happy flock under one Shepherd."

Hearing this, the crowd was again divided. Some decided Jesus was deranged and possessed, wondering why anyone in their right mind would listen to Him. Others exclaimed, "Since when does a demon or someone possessed by a demon go around opening blind eyes?"

Sometime later, Jesus commissioned seventy of His followers to go two-by-two throughout the region of Judea as preparation teams for His ministry. He instructed them in much the same way as He had His twelve disciples when they went out previously in Galilee.

"There's a great harvest out there and not enough workers. Pray that the One in charge of the harvest will call out more workers. You're going into difficult places, like lambs going to the wolves. Go with confidence and determination, and don't let anyone distract you. Don't make a big production of it either; just go from city to city telling the people that the Kingdom of God is here. If a city opens its gates to you, great! Don't feel bad about taking up their offer of hospitality: a laborer deserves his wages.

"If a city rejects you, then tell them that the Kingdom of God is upon them, but not for blessing. They will be in for the same harsh rebuke I gave in Galilee to the cities of Chorazin, Bethsaida, and Capernaum. Anyone who rejects your message is rejecting Me. Sodom and Gomorrah will get off easier on Judgment Day than these cities will."

They went out and did everything Jesus had said. When they returned, they were ecstatic, saying, "Lord, even the demons had to obey us when we rebuked them using Your name."

Jesus' response to their enthusiasm was, "You haven't seen anything yet! I saw Satan fall like lightning from heaven. You'll have My authority to trample scorpions and serpents and anything else the enemy throws at you, without being hurt. But that's not the thing that should excite you most. The best thing of all should be knowing that your names are among those written in heaven."

Jesus, overcome with joy in His spirit, lifted His eyes to heaven and said, "Father, I love the way You work! I love how You hide these things from the know-it-alls and reveal them to those who are childlike. I love knowing that You know Me and that I know You. And I love revealing what You're like to these I have chosen."

Then He looked at the disciples and said, "I hope you realize what a privilege you have. A whole lot of prophets and kings longed to see the things you're seeing and to hear what you're hearing!"

One day a lawyer came up to Jesus and tested Him with a question, "Teacher, what do I need to do to inherit this eternal life You speak of?"

Jesus, as He often did, responded to the question with a question, "What is your understanding about how the Law answers that question?"

The lawyer answered, "You shall love the Lord your God with all your heart, with all your soul, with all your strength, and with all your mind; and your neighbor as yourself!"

Jesus commended the man, saying, "That's it! Do that much and you will have the life you're asking about."

The man, wanting to justify himself, asked Jesus whom he should think of as a neighbor.

So Jesus proceeded to tell this story:

"There was a man making the trek from Jerusalem down to Jericho when some thieves overpowered him, beat him, and left him half naked beside the road. Shortly a priest came along and noticed the man but went out of his way to avoid getting too close. Then a Levite passed the same spot and quickly crossed to the other side of the road and went on his way as though he hadn't noticed the man lying there.

"A while later a despised Samaritan was making the same journey and happened upon the scene. Filled with compassion, he cleaned the wounds, put a blend of oil and wine on them, and bandaged him carefully. He put the man on his packhorse and led him to the nearest inn, providing food and shelter for him. In the morning he left extra funds with the innkeeper and told him to take care of the fellow, adding, if it cost more he'd pay up when he came through again.

"Which of these three," Jesus asked the lawyer, "was the true neighbor of the man who had been viciously attacked?"

The lawyer responded, saying, "Obviously it was the one who extended himself to care for the man."

Jesus answered, "That's right! Now you follow suit."

Once, when Jesus was near Jerusalem, He spent some time at the home of Martha and Mary. While Martha busied herself with all the meal preparations, Mary just sat at Jesus' feet drinking in every word He spoke. After a while Martha was pretty frustrated about having to do all the work while her sister sat and enjoyed their guest. She said to Jesus, "Lord, don't You care about me? Couldn't You at least send Mary in to help me?"

Jesus said to her, "Martha, Martha, you're going to too much trouble. We don't need much really, just one thing. Mary is getting in on what's most important, and I don't want her to miss out on it."

One day, after Jesus had been praying, His disciples asked if He would teach them how to pray. He was more than willing and reiterated what He had taught at the beginning of His public ministry before many of them had joined Him.

"Here is how you should pray:

"Our Heavenly Father,
may Your name be honored in our lives,
may You be in charge of our lives
and may Your heart's desire be accomplished
here on earth the way it is in heaven.
We recognize You as our Source
and ask only for what we need for this day.
We know we need Your forgiveness
and we extend that forgiveness
to all who wrong us.
Finally, protect us from the evil one
and his temptations."

Jesus went on to describe His Father's heart and how they should ask Him for what they need:

"Suppose you are in a situation where someone drops in on you unexpectedly when you have no food in the house and the stores are closed. Even though it is quite late, you have a neighbor who you know would help you. So you go to his house and arouse him. At first he calls down to explain that everyone is in bed and he can't help you. You stand there and keep appealing to his kindness. Eventually, if not because you're a friend, he'll get you what you need just so he can get back to bed.

"When you pray, ask and keep asking until you receive. Seek for what you need and don't stop until you find it. Knock and keep knocking until doors are opened.

"Even though you're sinful humans, you don't ignore the requests of your friends or children, nor do you give them things they don't need. If you know how to give good gifts to your children, how much more willingly do you think your heavenly Father will give His Holy Spirit to all who ask Him?"

In Judea He encountered many of the same situations He had seen in Galilee. Once for instance, He cast a demon out of a man who had been made mute by the evil spirit. Immediately the man was able to speak. The crowd was in awe. But as usual, there were skeptics in the group who claimed that Jesus was possessed by Beelzebub, prince of demons, who enabled Him to cast them out.

Jesus anticipated their criticism, "I know what you're thinking; but really, think about this: If a kingdom is divided against itself, how can it keep going? What good would it do for Satan to cast out those doing his dirty work?

"And another thing, if the only way I'm able to cast out these spirits is by the power of Beelzebub, how is it that your own sons perform exorcisms? What would they say about this accusation?

"If, however, I'm empowered by God's hand to cast out demons, then the Kingdom of God has come upon you here and now.

"If a well-armed man guards his estate, everything is safe until an even stronger man overpowers him. In that case the stronger man can strip him of his weapons and take everything he owns.

"Whoever is not actively on My side is working against Me; and if you're not helping, you're making things worse.

"And one more thing, it's not enough just to get rid of a demon; because if nothing better replaces it and the person's soul remains empty, the demon will to return with even more wicked spirits to take possession. In that case, the man's condition is far worse than it was originally with just one demon."

About this time a woman in the crowd, overcome with all that Jesus was doing and saying, shouted out, "How blessed and proud Your mother must be!"

Jesus heard her and said, "An even greater blessing rests upon all who hear what God is saying and live by it!"

Crowds of people pressed around Jesus, demanding that He give them more miraculous proofs of His identity.

"Evil is reigning over your lives; you keep looking for yet another sign. Do you remember Jonah? He was sent to Nineveh to rebuke them for their wicked lives. I am to this generation what Jonah was to that city.

"Do you know about the Queen of Sheba? She went to great lengths just to hear Solomon's wisdom. I am greater than Solomon yet you won't listen to Me. The Queen will be a witness against you on Judgment Day, as will the people of Nineveh. At least they repented when they heard what Jonah had to say.

"I'm talking about the difference between living in darkness and living in the light. I'm speaking about how you view life. If you have good vision, seeing things as they really are, life is good. If your vision is blurred or blocked, everything gets complicated. Stumbling around affects you and those around you. That's why you must stay in the light!"

As if to give Jesus a chance to elaborate on these things, a Pharisee invited Him to dinner. The first thing the man observed (and was critical of) was Jesus' failure to go through the thorough cleansing ritual before sitting down. Jesus knew He had raised some eyebrows so He explained:

"Talk about the wrong way of looking at life! You Pharisees are obsessed with how things appear on the outside, oblivious to what's wrong on the inside. It would be like taking this cup and washing the outside but leaving the inside full of scum and filth. Surely you don't think the One who made you only focuses on external rituals and performance, do you?

"You're meticulous about measuring out one-tenth of every tiny spice and herb to show how serious you are about tithing when all the while you completely miss the justice and love of God. I'm not saying you should be careless about your giving, but put first things first.

"The problem with you Pharisees is that you're addicted to the recognition you get everywhere you go.

"Do you want to know what you are, you scribes and Pharisees? You're just like unmarked graves covered with grass so that those who walk over the area have no idea what's dead and rotting underneath."

One of the religious experts said, "You're being pretty hard on those guys and getting close to incriminating us as well."

Jesus continued His diatribe:

"Woe to you, too, you lawyers! You make up so many rules, which you yourselves don't follow; you cause the people to live under unbearable burdens.

"Sure, you're all about building fancy tombs for the prophets of old, but your own fathers were the ones who murdered them in the first place. That makes you accomplices in their wickedness. Do you want to know what God says? 'I will send them prophets and apostles and some of them they will kill and persecute. Therefore I am going to hold this present generation accountable for all the innocent blood shed from Abel to Zecharaiah who was slain between the altar and the temple.'

"Yes, it's you experts in the Law who have the key to truth, and you not only don't use it for your own benefit but hide it so that no one else can enter in."

As you might imagine, these comments ignited a firestorm of reactions among the scribes and Pharisees. They lit into Jesus with all kinds of questions and accusations, looking for some way to catch Him incriminating Himself.

Then Jesus went out to speak to the crowds of people who had gathered. Directing His comments to the disciples, He said:

"Be careful that the teachings of the scribes and Pharisees don't contaminate your minds. They think they can hide their private lives, but I'm telling you that everything will one day be out in the open — excruciatingly public!

"Don't be manipulated by their threats. Even if they kill your body, they can't destroy your soul. Live your life before God who has power over body and soul! Know that He cares deeply about you, keeping track of the littlest details like the number of hairs on your head. Why, He's aware of every sparrow, and you're worth far more to Him than they are.

"Don't be ashamed to identify with Me here on earth, and I'll be proud to introduce you to the angels of God in heaven. But if you turn your back on Me, I'll have to do the same.

"Know, too, that if someone misjudges or speaks against Me, they can be forgiven. But if they assign the work of the Spirit to Beelzebub, they cannot be forgiven.

"You shouldn't concern yourselves about how to respond when the authorities interrogate you. The Holy Spirit will put the words in your mouth at just the right moment."

While Jesus was giving these profound warnings and instructions, someone in the crowd thought they might get Him to help arbitrate a family feud they were having over inheritance monies. "Teacher, would you tell my brother to divide the inheritance with me?" the man asked.

Jesus answered him by saying, "Excuse Me, but since when have I been assigned to handle your case?"

That ended the conversation, but Jesus used the opportunity to talk about the dangers inherent in possessions. "Guard yourselves against the tyranny of covetousness," He said, "because you know that a good life isn't defined by the number of things you own.

"Have you heard the story about the wealthy businessman who prided himself in how successful his investments had become? 'Why, I think I'll just tear down these little warehouses and build some huge ones that can handle all that I'm accruing!' he boasted. Then he said to himself, 'Buddy, you're in great shape! Take it easy now; you're set for life! Let's party!'

"What he failed to consider in all this was what God might have in mind. 'You're a fool,' God said. 'Tonight you will die and then what good will all this do you? Who will benefit from all your stuff?'

"This is the situation for everyone who bases their entire life on what they can get here and now but doesn't value what God considers riches," Jesus explained.

"So that's why I urge you not to stress out about the everyday things of food and clothing. Life is much more than food, and there's more to the body than what you put on it. Besides, just look at the ravens. They don't spend their lives stockpiling food; God provides for them what they need every day. You're a lot more precious to Him than those birds.

"Who has ever been able to extend his life one minute by worrying over it? If you can't do something as simple as that, how do you expect to control the bigger issues?

"Discouraged about your limited wardrobe? Why? Look at the lilies in that field. They are so stunning that not even Solomon in all his finery was as beautiful as they are, but those plants are going to be dead and gone in a few days. How much more do you think your Heavenly Father is concerned about addressing your needs than He is about those flowers?

"No, you don't need to fret over all those details. The pagan world doesn't know any better, but you do. You have a Father who knows just what you need. So concern yourself with the things that matter to Him and He'll take care of the rest.

"Do you realize what I'm saying, little flock? Your wonderful Father is excited about giving you His Kingdom! Don't sell yourselves short. Sell your surplus, give away as much as you can to the poor, and start depositing real assets in your heavenly account where it is safe and sound. Once you put your treasure in what has eternal value, you'll find that your heart's desires will be more and more centered around things that really matter.

"But don't let this Kingdom-of-Heaven-centered living make you complacent about life on earth. You have a job to do here. Serve faithfully in the little things, always aware that your Master will be returning. You never know when it will be; let Him catch you doing the right thing, always ready for Him to show up."

Peter, wondering whether Jesus meant this instruction exclusively for His faithful disciples or for the crowd, asked, "Lord, this story You're telling, is it for us or for everyone?"

Jesus explained how the Day of Reckoning will work:

"Suppose a master appoints one of his stewards to oversee the day-to-day affairs of the household. If, upon returning to his estate, that master finds that his steward has faithfully fulfilled his duties, he will be rewarded with even greater responsibilities and privileges. But if the servant, instead of caring for the workers as the master would have, mistreats them and spends his days in drunken parties, what do you think will happen when the master suddenly shows up? It won't be a pretty sight.

"Now, as to your question about the crowds. If this servant didn't know what his master expected from him, then his punishment would be less severe than if he knew the master and was well aware of what his job assignment was. In other words, if you've been given much, you'll be accountable for much.

"Mind you, I am going to light a fire someday that will purify this earth. But first I must go through a fiery trial Myself, which I wish was over with. I'm not here to smooth things over but to expose and distinguish right from wrong even though it may break up families and cause division."

Turning to the crowd, Jesus said, "You're so good at predicting tomorrow's weather by reading the signs, but you're blind to the signs of the times in which you're living. If you realized what was coming, you'd get busy making things right. Instead you're carelessly going on with life like a wrongdoer who, instead of confessing and working things out quickly with his adversary, waits to show up in court and ends up 'getting the book thrown at him.'"

Jesus used a couple of recent tragedies to emphasize His point:

"You've heard about the Galileans who were murdered by Pilate while bringing their offerings to the temple the other day. Do you suppose this happened to them instead of someone else because they were worse sinners? Of course not. That's why I'm telling you to repent and make things right while you still have a chance. Tomorrow something like this could happen to you, and it would be too late to change.

"The same goes for the eighteen unfortunate souls lost when the tower in Siloam collapsed recently. They had no idea their lives would be cut short. Things like that happen suddenly and randomly whether or not we expect them. Likewise, you have no control over when it could happen to you. Repent, get serious about what matters most!"

Then He warned the people with this story:

"A certain man had a fig tree planted. Year after year came and went as the man waited, hoping for a harvest. Finally, he instructed the workers to cut it down, saying, 'Look, for the last three years I've been expecting some fruit to show up on this tree and it produces nothing. It's a waste of valuable space. Cut it down so we can plant something in its place.'

"The worker asked if he might not give it one more year, saying, 'Sir, let me work the soil and fertilize it just one more year. If there's still nothing, then we'll cut it down.'"

It just so happened while Jesus was teaching in one of the synagogues on the Sabbath, a woman showed up who had suffered a crippling illness for eighteen years. Jesus noticed her and called her to come to Him. When she came, He laid His hands on her and said, "Ma'am, I remove this infirmity from your body." Immediately, she stood up straight and praised God for the miracle.

The man in charge of the services in the synagogue, however, was upset and addressed the crowd, "Now, listen to me. There are six days in the week for doing work. If you need to be healed, come on those days, not on the Sabbath!"

Jesus didn't miss a beat. He answered the man with these words, "Why, you hypocrite! Every one of you, whether it's the Sabbath or not, unties his donkey from the stall and leads it over to the water tank for a drink. So why shouldn't I release this woman, who is a daughter of Abraham, from the sickness in which Satan has held her bound these eighteen years?"

The crowd was thrilled by Jesus' miracles and forthright exposure of the religious leaders. His adversaries, on the other hand, were embarrassed and agitated.

"I've said it before and will say it again," Jesus declared, "God's Kingdom may not look like much in seed form; but once it takes root and begins to grow, it will be like the mustard tree, large enough for birds to nest in.

"Or you could liken it to yeast: just a pinch will affect a large loaf."

One day, during the winter Feast of Dedication (Hanukkah), Jesus was in Jerusalem walking in the section of the temple known as Solomon's Portico. A crowd surrounded Him. Some prodded Him with this question, "Why are You keeping us in suspense? If You are the Messiah we've been waiting for, just say so."

"I have made it quite clear," Jesus answered, "but you won't believe Me. I've done plenty of miracles as My Father instructed Me. That should be sufficient evidence for you, but you can't believe Me because you aren't My sheep. As I said before, My sheep hear My voice; I know them and they willingly follow Me. I give them God's life, and they are forever secure under My care. Besides, My Father, who has given them to Me, is greater than all; and He too holds them securely in His hand! The Father and I are one."

At this statement, the Jews picked up stones to stone Him.

"My Father has blessed you with many good works through Me. For which of those works are you now ready to stone Me?" Jesus inquired.

The Jews answered curtly, "We're not stoning You for what You've done but for what You've claimed. You, being just a man, are claiming to be God. That is blasphemy!"

Jesus responded, "Concerning some of your ancestors, your own Law quotes God as saying, 'I said, "You are gods."' So if He spoke of them in that way, why do you call it blasphemy when I, whom the Father sent into the world, say that I am the Son of God?

"If I'm not living up to the claim by doing works which are obviously of God, then don't believe Me. If, however, you will accept My works as being from God, then you'll be able to know and believe that the Father is in Me and I am in Him."

Again, this was too much for the Jews. They tried to grab Him, but He slipped away.

After this, Jesus went across the Jordan to where John the Baptist's ministry had started. The people remarked that even though John hadn't done miracles, everything he had said about Jesus proved true. And many believed in Him.

As Jesus went from town to town, He continued teaching as He made His way back toward Jerusalem for the last time. Once, someone approached Him and asked whether everyone would eventually be saved or just a few.

Jesus answered him, "You must be serious now about entering the narrow gate to life. There will come a time when many will try to get in but will discover that they missed their chance. It will be like the situation where many get invited to a party but show up late after the doors are bolted shut. They may knock as hard as they want, but the master will tell them he doesn't know them. They'll try to explain that they knew him and were part of the crowd when he was in their town, but he will counter with the final word declaring that he, in fact, did not know them and that they were not qualified to enter. The host will tell them, 'Go away, all of you who persisted in doing evil.'

"I tell you," Jesus went on to explain, "that they will be filled with regrets and unbearable grief when they see Abraham, Isaac, Jacob, and all the prophets sitting down in God's Kingdom while they themselves are on the outside looking in. To make it even worse, they'll watch as folks come from every corner of the earth to enter in while they are excluded.

"Indeed, many who think they're at the head of the line will be at the end, and many who barely expect to get in will be welcomed first."

While Jesus was explaining these things, some Pharisees came to warn Him that Herod was out to kill Him.

Jesus said, "You can tell that fox that I've got a few more days' work here — casting out demons and healing the sick, but then I'm on my way to Jerusalem because it wouldn't do for a prophet to die anywhere but there.

"O Jerusalem, Jerusalem," He lamented, "you who kill the prophets and stone to death everyone sent to help you! You won't believe how often I've wanted to gather you safely under My wings like a hen gathering her brood, but you wouldn't come to Me. Now your grand 'house' will stand desolate and empty; and you won't see Me again until the day you declare, 'Blessed is He who comes in the name of the Lord.'"

One Sabbath day Jesus was invited to break bread in the home of a Pharisee. While they were dining, in came a man who had a disease that made his arms and legs extremely swollen. Everyone watched Jesus closely to see what He would do.

Jesus posed a question to the lawyers and Pharisees who were there. "Is it against the Law for a person to heal on the Sabbath?" He asked.

They wouldn't answer Him. So Jesus healed the man and sent him on his way. Then Jesus said to His host and to the religious experts, "Which one of you, if your donkey or ox falls into a hole on the Sabbath, wouldn't rush right out to help it?"

Again, they were silent.

Meanwhile, Jesus had noticed how the guests had all come in jockeying for the best seats, so He gave them something else to think about. "Next time you're invited to a wedding feast, don't rush to the best seat in the house because someone may come in who deserves the honor more than you do. Then you will be humiliated while everyone watches as you get moved down to the end. Instead, pick a back row so that when the host sees you, he says, 'My good friend, please, come sit by me.' Folks will be impressed with that. My point is that everyone who is motivated by pride will be humbled, and everyone who is genuinely humble will be honored."

Turning to the host, Jesus said, "Next time you put on a special event, don't invite your peers who can reciprocate by inviting you to their homes. Instead, invite those who truly need special care: those who are poor, handicapped, and sick. Then you'll be in for real blessing — not because any of them could possibly do something for you, but because of the reward waiting for you at the resurrection of the upright."

Someone sitting nearby picked up on this and remarked what a blessing it would be to eat bread in the Kingdom of God.

So Jesus responded with this story:

> "Once upon a time a man planned a great feast and sent out dozens of invitations. On the day of the affair, he sent out his staff to notify everyone that the meal was prepared.
>
> "Well, much to the chagrin of the host, they all came up with excuses for missing the meal. One had to go check out some property he'd purchased, another had to try out his new yoke of oxen, and still another said he'd just gotten married and couldn't make it.
>
> "When the staff returned with this report, the man was furious. 'Fine, then,' he said, 'go out in the streets and invite everyone you can find, even if they're poor and handicapped!'
>
> "After they realized there was still room for more guests, he told them to go further and find the homeless to fill up the empty seats. There was no way he was going to welcome those he had first invited if they changed their minds."

By this time Jesus was used to the crowds of people who accompanied Him everywhere. He decided to explain what it took to be a true disciple. "Do you want to be My disciples?" He asked. "Are you prepared to pay the price? Will you follow Me even if it costs you everything you now hold dear — family, friends, yes, even your own life? If you aren't willing to take up your cross, you can't go on with Me.

"I'm saying this to save you the embarrassment of starting something you can't finish. That would be like starting to build a house but not having enough money to ever finish it, or like a king recklessly going to war with another king before evaluating the odds of his success.

"In other words, following Me can't be done without forsaking everything and everyone else. Those who hold on to their agenda while claiming to endorse Mine are like salt that has no flavor, good for nothing but to be thrown out. I hope you are hearing and understanding all this."

The Pharisees and scribes noticed that there were a lot of tax collectors and sinners in Jesus' crowds. Jesus heard about their murmuring and decided to tell some stories to help them understand what was happening.

"A number of you own sheep, don't you?" Jesus asked.

"Suppose you have one hundred sheep and one wanders off on its own and gets lost. You think nothing of leaving the ninety-nine and searching high and low until you find it, right? Once you've rescued the wayward sheep, you call together all your friends to celebrate the good news. Don't you know that there's more celebrating in heaven over one sinner who repents than over ninety-nine others who don't need to repent?

"Ladies," He went on to say, "when was the last time you lost a valuable coin? I'm sure you turned on all the lights and swept out every last corner until you found it. You too couldn't wait to tell your friends your good news. I'm telling you that every time a sinner repents that's how the angels in heaven rejoice!

"Or think about it this way:

"A certain man had two sons. The younger one decided he didn't want to wait for his dad to die before benefitting from the inheritance, so he asked for his portion ahead of time. The father complied and divided his estate.

"With all this money in hand, the young man left the confines of the ranch and headed for the big city. There he found plenty of ways to squander the wealth on wanton pleasure. But the money was soon gone, and the region where he was living went through a severe famine. The son ended up being so hungry he was willing to take a job feeding pigs out in the country just so he could eat something, even if it was pig food. No one gave him anything.

"One day as he thought over his life, he came to his senses and said to himself, 'What am I doing here? I'm so much worse off than any of my dad's hired hands; I should just go home and see if he'd hire me on as a servant.' He made up his mind to go home, and he prepared just what he would say to his father.

"As the young man was nearing the home place but still quite a ways off, his father saw him. Overwhelmed with love, the father ran to meet his son and hugged and kissed him, then hugged him some more.

"The son began his prepared speech, 'Father, I have sinned against heaven and against you with what I've done. I'm no longer worthy to be treated as a son . . .' But before he could explain about wanting simply to be a hired worker, the father called out to the servants, 'Run, get my best robe to put on him, my signet ring for his hand, and new sandals for his feet. Go prepare a prime veal feast and call the neighbors! We've got reason to celebrate now that my son who was lost has been found. It's like he was dead and has been raised to life again!'

"Did I mention that there were two sons? Well, the older brother was out in the fields when all this happened. When he came in that evening and saw the festivities, he asked what all the noise was about. A servant let him know that his brother had finally returned home and that his dad had killed the fatted calf in celebration.

"This made the older brother so jealous and angry that he refused to join the party. His father came out and pleaded with him to join them. Fuming, the older son replied, 'I can't believe you're doing this for him! Here I've been slaving away while he's been wasting your money on prostitutes. I've kept all your rules religiously all this time, and you've never so much as given me a goat to eat with my friends. But for him you've killed our best calf.'

"The father tried to reason with him, saying, 'Son, yes, you've been faithful. Everything I have is yours, but don't you see that we must celebrate this miracle? He was dead and is now alive. Your brother was lost, but now he's found.'"

Later, when He was with His disciples, He told another story to warn them against being careless or passive in their responsibilities.

"Once there was a wealthy banker who hired a manager to handle all his accounts. Someone had accused the manager of being irresponsible, so the banker called him in to get a full accounting of his activities.

"It ended up that the banker fired the manager. This put the manager in a tough dilemma. He knew he didn't have skills to get another kind of job, and he was too proud to beg for a living. So he came up with a scheme to get all his clients indebted to him.

"He called each of the clients who owed money to the banker and one by one authorized a significant reduction in the amount owed. The debt of one, who owed a hundred measures of oil, was lowered to fifty; the debt of another, owing a hundred bushels of wheat, he reduced to eighty; and so on.

"The banker had to admit the fellow had been creative in providing for his future, and he commended his ingenuity."

Jesus concluded that story by observing that the pagans, in many cases, were more shrewd about these things than were the "sons of light."

Jesus went on to explain the proper use of material goods. "Be shrewd in your use of money. Use it in ways that will benefit you and others for eternity and don't be careless. Only when you are faithful in the little things, can you be entrusted with great ones. If you're careless with money, how can you be trusted with true eternal riches? Be faithful with what others entrust to you and you will truly prosper.

"Having said that, I am not suggesting that you set your hearts on financial prosperity. If you do, you will end up becoming disloyal to God. You can't serve both God and money; these are two different masters."

There were Pharisees in the audience; and since in their hearts they loved money, they scoffed at Jesus' warnings. Jesus put them in their place by stating, "You're all about image and getting honor from men, but God knows what's going on in your hearts. You can be sure that whatever men value is probably an abomination to God."

Jesus continued, "The Law and the Prophets were your guides until John came preaching the Kingdom of God; now crowds are rushing to get in. That doesn't mean the Law is null and void. For instance, 'whoever divorces his wife and marries another is committing adultery and whoever marries a divorced woman likewise is committing adultery' is a law that hasn't changed and won't until heaven and earth disappear.

"Once there was a very wealthy man who lived a life of luxury. Outside his gates sat a poor beggar named Lazarus whose body was covered in sores which the dogs came and licked. He survived off of scraps gleaned under the rich man's table.

"Eventually, both Lazarus and the rich man died. Lazarus was carried by angels to Abraham's bosom, but the rich man found himself in the torments of Hades. Across the bottomless chasm he could see Lazarus being held in Abraham's arms; so he called out, 'Father Abraham, have mercy on me. Could you send Lazarus here with a drip of water to cool my tongue? I'm burning up in these flames!'

"Abraham answered, saying, 'Son, do you recall the luxury and abundance you enjoyed back on earth while Lazarus had nothing? Well, the tables are turned and he's getting the blessing now. Besides, as you can see, there's an impassable gulf between us; no one can get from one side to the other.'

"The rich man then begged Abraham to send someone to warn his five brothers who were still living so that they could avoid ending up in the torment he was suffering.

"Abraham again answered, saying, 'They have the Scriptures which are adequate for their instruction if they will just listen to them.'

"The rich man countered with, 'No, Father Abraham, it would be far more effective if someone would come back from the dead and speak with them.'

"But Abraham said, 'If they're not willing to listen to Moses and the prophets, they won't be persuaded even though one were to rise from the dead.'"

Speaking to His disciples (although the Pharisees may have been within earshot), Jesus said, "Everyone is bound to encounter temptations and stumbling blocks along the way, but woe to those who cause them! They'll wish someone had thrown them overboard at sea with a millstone tied around their neck to keep them from stumbling others. Let this be a warning to you."

Then Jesus reiterated His instructions about forgiveness. "If someone wrongs you in some way, confront them about it. If he responds humbly, forgive him. Do this even if seven times in a single day he repents and asks you to forgive him. Forgive liberally!"

The disciples were flabbergasted. "Lord, You're going to have to increase our faith if we have to treat others like that."

Jesus said, "It's not a matter of greater faith. Why, the tiniest amount of faith, rightly directed, could tell this mulberry tree to 'go jump in the lake' and it would do so."

To help His disciples see that it isn't a matter of flexing some random faith muscle but that true faith is a matter of acting on what you've been told to do (just as Jesus trusted His Father's wisdom and always did what He instructed), Jesus illustrated His point with this word picture:

> "When a wealthy landowner sees his servant coming in from a long day in the fields, he doesn't say, 'You must be ready for a good meal. Come, relax, eat with me.' No, because he's a servant, he's expected to get right into the kitchen, fix the meal, and serve it. Only when everything is cleaned up can he sit down to eat. And is the boss expected to come find the servant to thank him for all his work? Of course not. The servant has just done what was expected of him. You are servants. At the end of the day, however long it has been, your attitude should be, 'I'm blessed to be a servant, just doing my job.'"

During this time Jesus got word that His friend Lazarus was seriously ill. Do you remember the story of Mary and Martha? Jesus had a very special love for them and often stayed at their home in Bethany. Mary was the one who would later anoint the Lord's feet with fragrant oil and wipe them with her hair.

So when the sisters sent word to Him, saying, "Lord, Your dear friend is very sick," Jesus told His disciples, "It's all right, this sickness won't result in death; rather it will provide a good opportunity for God to express His power through Me." That's why, in spite of how dearly He loved them, He chose to wait two more days before heading to Bethany.

"We've got to go back to Judea again," Jesus said.

His disciples were very troubled and asked, "Rabbi, is that a good idea? Aren't the Jews looking for You to stone You? Are You sure You should go back now?"

Jesus explained to them that His work was not finished and that Something (the "light of the world") inside Him was compelling Him to go in spite of any dangers. If He let Himself be controlled by what might happen, He would just be stumbling around going nowhere.

He told His disciples, "Our friend Lazarus has fallen asleep and I need to go wake him up." That made no sense to the disciples who understood that a good sleep was necessary for someone to get better. Jesus, of course, was referring to Lazarus' death, but the disciples didn't know that. Jesus explained, "Lazarus is dead. For your sakes, I'm glad I didn't go there sooner. Come now, let's get going."

Thomas, not too pleased with the risk they were taking, said to his companions, "Let's go; we might as well all die together."

Upon arriving in Bethany, they discovered that Lazarus had been in the tomb for four days. Martha and Mary had many friends, some from Jerusalem (about two miles west), who were there comforting them in their loss. When they got word that Jesus was near, Martha left the house and ran to where He was. "Lord," she burst out, "if only You had come sooner, my brother wouldn't have died. But I trust You; I know that God listens to You and gives You whatever You ask for."

Jesus comforted her, saying, "Your brother will rise again."

"Yes," Martha agreed, "in the great day of resurrection, I know."

But Jesus responded, saying, "Martha, I am the resurrection and the life. Whoever believes in Me, though he dies, will surely live. In fact, whoever lives and believes in Me won't ever die. Do you believe this?"

Martha, choking back tears, said, "Yes, Lord, I believe that You are the Messiah, the Son of God, who came into the world." After saying this, she hurried back to where Mary was and said, "The Teacher is here and He's asking for you." So Mary hurried out to where Jesus had met Martha. When the crowd saw her leave, they followed her, assuming that she was going to the grave to mourn there.

Mary fell at Jesus' feet and repeated what her sister had expressed earlier, "Lord, if You had been here, my brother wouldn't have died."

When Jesus saw them all overwhelmed with sorrow, He groaned deep in His spirit and was troubled. "Where have you laid him?" Jesus asked, weeping. They offered to take Him to Lazarus' tomb.

Along the way the mourners noted Jesus' tears and said to one another, "He must have really loved Lazarus!" Others remarked, "Yes, but if He could open blind eyes, shouldn't He have been able to prevent this death?"

Jesus' spirit was still groaning deep within Himself as they arrived at the tomb. He ordered them to take the large stone away from the entrance to the cave. Martha recoiled at this, saying, "But, Master, he's been dead for four days. The smell will be terrible."

Jesus simply said, "Didn't I tell you that if you trust Me you would see God's power at work in a glorious display?"

At His command they took the stone away. Jesus lifted up His eyes toward heaven and said, "Father, thank You for hearing My request. You always listen to Me, but I long for these standing here to know and believe that You sent Me to them."

Then Jesus looked toward the tomb and in a loud voice shouted, "Lazarus, come out of there!" Moments later Lazarus shuffled out of the cave with the grave-wrappings wound around him from head to foot. "You'd better untie him," Jesus said.

Needless to say, this was enough to convince many of the Jews to acknowledge Jesus' claim to be the Messiah. But there were some who rushed off to Jerusalem to alert the Pharisees about Jesus' latest exploit.

The Pharisees were beside themselves. They called a council to discuss their dilemma. "What can we do?" they pondered. "If we let Him keep working these miraculous signs, everyone will believe in Him. Then the Romans will surely come and wipe out everything we've got left."

One of them, Caiaphas, who had the honor of being high priest that year, said, "Can't you all see now that it's either Him or us? Getting rid of Him is the only way to save all the people." (What Caiaphas didn't realize is that, as high priest, God had caused him to prophesy that Jesus would die for the nation and, in fact, for all people.)

Because of this statement, they determined to find a way to kill Jesus. Having to avoid public places, Jesus took His disciples out to the remote areas of Ephraim, north of the city.

As they passed through one of the villages, a group of ten lepers, keeping their distance from the rest, called out, "Jesus, Master, won't You have mercy on us?"

Jesus looked in their direction and simply told them to go show themselves to the priests. This was the requirement in the Law of Moses for any who claimed to be cleansed of leprosy. Trusting Jesus' word, they began to make their way toward the temple. All ten of them got healed.

A while later one of them, the only Samaritan in the group, came back, found Jesus, and fell at His feet overwhelmed with thankfulness. Jesus asked, "Where are the others? Weren't there ten that got healed? How is it that you, a foreigner, were the only one who came back to thank God for the miracle? My blessings on you, friend," Jesus said. "Your obedient trust has made you well."

Now the Pharisees, who were forever saying that one day the Kingdom of God would come and deliver them from all their troubles, asked Jesus when He thought that might happen. He answered them by explaining many things about the Kingdom.

"You are looking for a physical event, but you need to know that the Kingdom of God is not external but internal. It is something that takes place inside you."

He directed further insights to His disciples:

"There's a time coming when you will wish I was with you like I am right now. And you will hear rumors that I've returned to this place or that place, but don't believe it. You'll know it when I return; it will be as obvious as lightning that lights up the sky from one end to the other. However, before any of that, I must endure excruciating pain and be rejected by this generation.

"When I return, it will be as sudden and unexpected as the flood in Noah's day. The people were going about their lives as if this life were all there was, right up to the day Noah entered the ark. And just like that, the flood destroyed them all.

"Or like the residents of Sodom: everyone was going about their routines. Who would have believed that, in a matter of moments after Lot left the city, fire and burning sulfur would fall from heaven and consume them all?

"That's how it will be when the Son of Man is revealed. Everyone will be going about business as usual. But I'm warning you not to be part of that crowd, not to so love this life that you lose everything. Be ready to run and don't look back. Remember what happened to Lot's wife.

"This will happen so suddenly. Two will be working side by side or sleeping in the same bed; one will be lost while the other, rescued."

The disciples, intrigued by these predictions, asked Jesus where this was going to take place. Jesus answered with a cryptic analogy, saying, "You know where the carcass is because you can see the vultures circling."

As grim as this scenario was, Jesus, not wanting His disciples to lose heart or give up praying, shared this story:

"In a certain city lived a judge who was not particularly respectable. Once, a widow approached his court with a desperate appeal, saying, 'Please protect me from this predator who is harassing me.'

"The judge couldn't care less about the woman's plight, so for the longest time he did nothing. She kept coming back until finally he said to himself, 'I wish she'd leave me alone. The only way I'm going to be relieved of her nagging is if I take care of the problem,' which he did."

Jesus said, "Do you see what it took to get that judge to take action? If he, being selfish and ungodly, was finally willing, how much more do you think God is ready to avenge His dear children who are crying out to Him day and night for deliverance? Yes, it may seem to be taking a while, but He will avenge and it will be sudden. But," Jesus went on to say, "when I return, will I find that kind of persistent faith?"

Knowing that some who were listening to Him felt superior in their status before God and looked down on the rest, Jesus told this story:

> "One day two men went up to the temple to pray. One was a tax collector; the other, a Pharisee. The Pharisee stood in a prominent place and lifted his voice, saying, 'God, I thank Thee that I am not like these wicked people around me — thieves, adulterers, and that tax collector over there. I hasten to remind Thee that I fast twice a week and give a tithe of all my possessions.'

> "Meanwhile, the tax collector, off in a corner and ashamed to lift his face toward heaven, kept beating his chest in remorse, saying, 'God, have mercy on me. I am such a sinner.'

"I want you to know," Jesus explained, "that it was this tax collector who went home at peace with God and not the Pharisee. God lifts up those who are humble, but He humbles all who exalt themselves in His presence."

Jesus continued teaching and healing the multitudes as He journeyed in Galilee and in the region across the Jordan River.

Some Pharisees came again with another test question to see if Jesus upheld their Law. "Teacher," they inquired, "is it lawful for a man to divorce his wife for any reason at all?"

Jesus, in turn, asked them a question, "What did Moses say about this?"

They said, "He permitted a man to write a certificate of divorce and let her go."

Jesus, knowing that once again they were twisting the clear intent of God's Law to make it fit their lifestyle, said, "Yes, that provision was made, but only because of your hard hearts. You do know, don't you, that divorce was not God's desire from the beginning when He 'made them male and female'? He made it quite clear right from the start that 'for this reason a man shall leave his father and mother and be joined to his wife, and the two shall become one flesh.' What has once been joined into oneness by God, man should never attempt to tear apart."

"If that's the case," the Pharisees replied, "then why did Moses give this instruction about a certificate of divorce?"

Jesus answered, "As I said, Moses did this because of the hardness of your hearts even though it was not as God originally intended. I can assure you that anyone who does divorce his wife for any reason other than her unfaithfulness and then marries another is guilty of adultery. Likewise, anyone who marries the divorced woman is committing adultery."

Later, when they were away from the crowds, Jesus' disciples asked Him about this issue. So He reiterated, saying, "Whoever divorces his wife and marries another commits adultery against her; and if a woman divorces her husband and marries another, she commits adultery."

His disciples were amazed at these stringent demands and said, "In that case it would be better not to marry at all."

Jesus responded to them, saying, "Not marrying isn't necessarily the answer. The celibate life is an exception to the rule. Yes, there are a few born with the capacity to remain single, others have celibacy imposed on them, while some may be called to give up marriage in their service to the Kingdom. If you're among that select group, then, yes, it is better not to marry."

Once, when they were out and about, the people were bringing their little ones to Jesus and asking Him to lay hands on them and bless them. Jesus' disciples saw what was happening and were upset with this seeming waste of Jesus' time.

Jesus, on the other hand, was displeased with the disciples for their attitude and said, "Let the little children come to Me. Don't prevent them because the Kingdom of God is open to them. In fact, no one can receive the Kingdom unless they come into it with childlike trust." He loved holding the youngsters and blessing them.

They continued on their way and a local official came running up to Jesus. Kneeling in front of Him, he asked, "Good Teacher, what exactly do I need to do to get this special God-kind of life You're describing?"

"What do you mean by calling Me good?" Jesus asked. "God alone is good. Are you approaching Me on those terms? You know the commandments, all you have to do is keep them."

"Which ones in particular?" the man asked.

Jesus said, "You shall not commit adultery, you must not murder, steal, lie, or cheat. Honor your father and your mother and love your neighbor as yourself."

The young man, feeling relieved, said, "Teacher, I have kept all of those since I was a child. Is that all I need to do?"

Jesus looked at the man with compassion and said, "Just one more thing. Go sell all your possessions and give the money to the poor. Then your treasure will be in heaven. Once you've done that and are willing to stop living for yourself, come, follow Me."

The man's countenance fell. He was heartsick at this last instruction because he was very wealthy and couldn't bring himself to let go of his possessions.

As Jesus saw the man walk away, He too became heavy-hearted. With sadness in His voice, He said to His disciples, "It is so hard for wealthy people to enter the Kingdom of God."

The disciples were stunned, having assumed that prosperity was a sure sign of God's approval.

Jesus addressed them, saying, "Do you want to know how hard it is for the rich to enter the Kingdom? It would be easier to put a camel through the eye of a needle than for a rich man to enter the Kingdom of God."

This blew the disciples away. They looked at each other in astonishment and wondered aloud, "Then how can anyone ever be saved?"

Jesus heard them and replied, "With men this is impossible, but not with God. With God all things are possible."

Peter, trying to grasp this concept, asked, "So if that's the way it works and we've left everything to follow You, what will be our reward?"

Smiling, Jesus told him, "I promise you that in the new creation when I am on the throne in glory, you who have followed Me will sit on twelve thrones, ruling over the twelve tribes of Israel. In fact," Jesus went on to explain, "anyone who has sacrificed the comforts and conveniences of this life in order to serve Me and advance the

Kingdom of God can be confident that they will be rewarded a hundredfold in this life and enjoy God's life with Him forever! Things are not always as they appear. Those who seem to be missing out, always in last place, will one day have it all and find themselves in first place, while those who are enjoying 'the good life' now may find themselves in a world of hurt in the long run.

"Let me explain rewards in the Kingdom of Heaven:

"A landowner needed to hire some laborers to work his vineyard. First thing in the morning he went to the labor pool and employed a handful of men. A few hours later he decided that he needed additional workers and went back to hire some more. This happened twice more during the day with the last group getting hired with just an hour's worth of work left in the day.

"At closing time the men came through the line to receive their pay, the last hired being paid first. To their surprise, they received a full-day's wage even though they had only worked for an hour. By the time the first crew came through, they were certain that they would get a bonus for having worked all day; but to their chagrin, they too received a day's wage.

"These workers complained to the landowner that he'd been unfair since they weren't given more than the latecomers. He dismissed them with the comment, 'Friends, I have not wronged you. Didn't you agree to work for the amount you were paid? Take it and be satisfied. If I, with my own money, choose to be generous with these others, have I broken some law? Perhaps my kindness exposes some evil in your hearts.'"

Jesus concluded by reminding His disciples again that in the Kingdom, the last will be first and the first last. Then He added, "For many are called but few are chosen."

After this, Jesus led His disciples toward Jerusalem, but they were growing anxious about the trouble that might be awaiting them. Along the way He took them aside and told them plainly, "Yes, we are on our way up to Jerusalem, and everything the prophets wrote about the Messiah will be fulfilled. I am going to be betrayed to the chief priests and scribes; they will condemn Me and hand Me over to the Gentile magistrates who will, in turn, mock Me, insult and whip Me, and finally, crucify Me. But on the third day I will rise again."

This was such a foreign idea for the disciples that they couldn't process it, and they dismissed it from their minds.

Further along, James and John, along with their mother, came to Jesus and knelt down with a request, "Teacher, will You promise to do what we ask?"

Not ready to make any promises, Jesus asked them, "What is it that you want Me to do for you?"

Their mother answered for them, "I'd like my boys to have positions of honor on either side of You when You reign over Your Kingdom." Apparently her sons had put her up to this.

Turning to James and John, Jesus said, "I don't think you realize what you're asking. Are you prepared to go through the kind of trouble I'm facing?"

In blissful ignorance, they replied, "Oh, yes, we can do that!"

Jesus said, "Yes, you will experience much the same abuse and difficulty; but when it comes to awarding thrones, that is My Father's business. We'll have to leave that with Him."

As you might imagine, once the other disciples caught wind of this, they were really upset with James and John. But Jesus used the situation to further explain the nature of His Kingdom. "You are used to thinking of authority and leadership the way this world exercises it, where the one in charge makes everyone serve him. That is not My idea of authority nor will it be yours. As I see it, if you want to be considered great in My Kingdom, you must be the lowest servant. I am your example of how this is done. I did not come to be served but to serve and to let My life pay the price so others can go free."

Their journey toward Jerusalem took them through the old city of Jericho. Two blind men were sitting along the road and heard the crowd approaching. One of them, named Bartimaeus, asked what all the commotion was about. Someone told him that Jesus of Nazareth was passing through town. Immediately, the men began to shout

out, "Jesus, Son of David, have mercy on us!" Over and over they repeated this until some tried to silence them. This only made the blind men more desperate and they cried out even louder, "Have mercy on us, O Lord, Son of David! Have mercy on us!"

Jesus heard them and instructed that they be brought to Him. So some in the crowd hurried to the two men and said, "C'mon, hurry, the Master is asking for you!" They threw off their blankets and made their way through the crowd to where Jesus was.

He asked them, "What would you like Me to do for you?"

"Teacher, I want to see!" said one of them. "Lord, open our eyes!" replied the other.

Filled with compassion for them, Jesus reached out and touched their eyes, saying, "Receive your sight! Go on your way now. Your faith has made you well."

They couldn't believe their eyes! They were seeing! They praised God — as did the whole crowd — and began following Jesus.

Just a little further down the road, Jesus came to a place where a large sycamore tree stood. Looking up, He saw a grown man sitting on one of the branches. A local tax collector, in fact the head of tax collecting in Jericho, had heard that Jesus was coming; and he was anxious to see for himself the Man everyone was talking about.

This man had a disadvantage; he was rather short in stature and couldn't see much when crowds were around. That's why he had climbed up the tree, to get a better view. To his surprise, as Jesus approached the tree, He stopped and, seeing the man up in the tree, spoke to him by name, "Zaccheus, come down here. I'd like to get to know you!" Zaccheus dropped down out of the tree and invited Jesus to his home.

Now tax collectors were despised by everyone because it was common practice for them to overcharge citizens, keeping the surplus to enjoy a life of luxury themselves. Needless to say, they didn't have a lot of friends. When the crowd saw Jesus heading home with Zaccheus, they were appalled that He would keep company with sinners like this.

Zaccheus, however, was deeply touched by Jesus' genuine interest in him. Suddenly, as if he had been blind, he saw what was of real value. "Lord, I'm going to see to it that half of my estate gets sold and the proceeds distributed to the needy in this town," Zaccheus declared. "And besides that, if I've overcharged anyone, I commit to repay them four times the amount I took."

Blessed by this change of heart, Jesus said, "Today salvation has come to this house. Zaccheus has shown himself to be a true son of Abraham by this decision. The whole reason I came was to seek out lost ones like him and rescue them."

Because His followers were assuming that He was getting ready to set up His Kingdom on earth, Jesus told this story as they continued toward Jerusalem.

"A certain prince was called away to conduct kingdom business, so he commissioned ten of his servants to oversee some of his investments. He gave each of them a pound of silver to manage.

"It so happened, while the prince was away, that the citizens, who hated him, sent a delegation to let him know that they didn't want him ruling over them any longer.

"In time, the prince returned and called in the ten servants to account for their business dealings. The first to show up had multiplied the value ten times what he'd been given. 'Great job,' the prince remarked, 'you've proven yourself faithful; I'm putting you in charge of ten whole cities!'

"The second servant had been able to increase the investment by five pounds of silver, and the prince rewarded him with control over five cities.

"The next servant appeared carrying a small handkerchief and explained, 'Sir, here is the pound of silver you left with me. I was too afraid of what you would do if I lost it, and I didn't want to take any risks.'

"'Why, you worthless fool!' the prince exclaimed. 'If you knew I a shrewd investor, you could have at least put it in the bank to get a little interest!' Then, turning to the others, he said, 'Take this man's silver and give it to the first man, the one who earned ten pounds with his.' They wondered why he would give it to the one who had so much already.

"'Let me assure you,' the prince concluded, 'that everyone who has used what I have given them will be given more, and any who have nothing to show for their lives will lose everything. And as for those citizens who sent word that they didn't want me ruling over them, bring them here and kill every one of them.'"

When He had finished the story, Jesus continued up to Jerusalem.

Passover was approaching. Days in advance many Jews from outlying areas converged on Jerusalem to complete the purification rituals. Everyone was talking about Jesus, wondering whether He would have the nerve to make a public appearance. The chief priests and Pharisees had issued an edict requiring anyone who knew of Jesus' whereabouts to report to them they could arrest Him.

Six days before the Passover, Jesus came to Bethany. Many Jews also came from far and wide. Although they came partly to see Jesus, they were even more curious to see with their own eyes this man Lazarus who had been raised from the dead not too many weeks earlier. Realizing that this recent miracle had caused even more Jews to believe in Jesus, the chief priests conspired to kill Lazarus as well.

Jesus attended a supper at the home of Simon the leper. Lazarus was there with them, and Martha helped serve the meal.

Mary came in with a flask of fragrant oil of nard. She broke open the container, poured some on Jesus' head and feet, and then wiped His feet with her hair in an act of humble devotion. The whole house was filled with the fragrance of the oil.

When His disciples saw this, some of them were indignant and rebuked her. Judas Iscariot, son of Simon, said, "What a waste! We could have sold that for thousands of dollars and given it to the poor!" At that point no one knew that Judas' motives weren't out of concern for the poor; but as treasurer for the group, he had been siphoning funds for his own use.

Hearing the commotion, Jesus rebuked them, saying, "Leave her alone! She's done the right thing. There will always be poor to take care of, but you won't always have Me around. She unknowingly has pre-anointed my body for burial, and this sacrificial act of devotion will be included in the telling of the message as it goes around the world."

JESUS' FINAL WEEK

Sunday

The next day Jesus sent two of His disciples ahead to the village with these instructions, "Just as you enter the town, you'll notice a donkey tied up with her colt beside her. Untie them and bring them to Me. If anyone asks what you're doing, just tell them, 'The Lord needs them,' and they will approve."

So the disciples went and found everything just as Jesus had said. They untied the beasts, explained to the owners what they were doing, and led the donkeys back to Jesus. They laid their outer robes on the colt and Jesus mounted.

A crowd began to form as Jesus made His way toward Jerusalem on the donkey. It wasn't until weeks later that Jesus' disciples realized this was a fulfillment of an Old Testament prophecy which said, "Tell the daughter of Zion not to fear. Behold, your King is coming to you, humble, sitting on a donkey, yes, a colt, the foal of a donkey."

As more and more people joined the procession, they began to cheer exuberantly and to spread a royal carpet of palm branches ahead of Him, celebrating with loud shouts of praise all the miracles they had witnessed.

Their chants and cheers climaxed in a veritable coronation hymn: "Hosanna to the Son of David! Blessed is the One who comes in the name of the Lord! Hosanna! Lord, save us! Blessings on the King of Israel!"

In the crowd were some who had seen Jesus raise Lazarus, as well as many who had just heard about it. The Pharisees were beside themselves. "We're getting nowhere! The whole world has gone crazy for this Man." One of them called to Jesus and urged Him to silence the throng.

Jesus shouted back over the commotion, "Right now, if I silence the people, the stones would take up the shouting!"

At one point, as Jesus looked at the walled city, tears filled His eyes and He lamented, "If only you knew what this day could mean in bringing real peace for you. But you are unable to see it. You will see, in the days to come, your enemies surround you, invade and destroy everything — the buildings and you and your children — all because you missed the opportunity God provided."

The city was all abuzz as the parade made its way through the gates. Some visitors asked, "Who is that Man?"

"Jesus, the prophet from Nazareth of Galilee," they answered.

Jesus went straight to the temple, and many who were blind or lame were brought to Him to be healed. The chief priests saw all this, even children dancing around, waving palm branches, and singing, "Hosanna to the Son of David!" They were outraged and asked Jesus if He were hearing them.

"Yes. I think you may have read the passage that says, 'Out of the mouths of little children God has brought forth praise.'"

After taking time to thoroughly look over the temple courts, Jesus and the Twelve headed back out to Bethany for the night since it was late in the day.

Monday

On their way back to Jerusalem the next morning, Jesus and his disciples saw a fig tree beside the road. Feeling hungry, Jesus went to see if there were any ripe fruit on it. Finding none, He cursed the tree, saying, "You will never bear fruit again!"

Upon their arrival at the temple, Jesus went directly to where money-changers were sitting and upended their tables, scattering coins everywhere. He drove out the people selling doves and various other religious goods. He prevented anyone from conducting business in the temple courts. To those who were observing, He declared, "Doesn't Scripture say, 'My house shall be called a house of prayer for all the nations'? Look, you have turned it into a den of thieves!"

Among the thousands who made the pilgrimage to Jerusalem for Passover were some Greeks. They approached Philip, one of Jesus' disciples from Bethsaida in Galilee, and asked if they might be able to meet Jesus. Philip found Andrew and together they went to Jesus.

Jesus indicated that the time for meeting and ministering to the crowds had passed; it was now time to focus on one thing, His impending suffering. He said, "It is time for Me to complete My purpose. You know that a grain of wheat must fall to the ground and die or it remains forever a single grain. Only when it dies can it produce much grain. So it is that whoever loves and tries to hang onto his life ends up losing everything, but whoever dies to himself gains life that goes on forever as God designed it. If someone really wants to serve Me, they have to stay at My side all the way; and they can be confident that My Father will reward them."

Jesus seemed to live in two worlds simultaneously. Often, in the midst of talking with the people around Him, He would speak directly to His Father as though He were part of the same audience. This was one of those occasions. "My soul is in turmoil right now and I want to cut and run. But how can I ask My Father to change Our plans? This is the main reason I came. Father, carry on with the plan and reveal how awesome and wonderful You are!"

Right then a voice came from the heavens, saying, "I have been demonstrating that and will continue doing so!" Only Jesus discerned the words.

The crowd looked around in awe, thinking it had thundered. Some said, "An angel has spoken to Him."

Jesus explained, "This voice wasn't for My sake but for yours. Time is up for this world and for the one who has been running it into the ground. As I am 'lifted up from the earth,' people everywhere will turn toward Me."

Since the phrase 'lifted up from the earth' was commonly used to describe death by crucifixion, this really confused the hearers. They said, "The Old Testament said our Messiah would reign forever. If you are the Promised One, how can you talk of dying like this?"

Jesus didn't answer their question directly but exhorted them, saying, "You have seen the light and have begun walking in it. Soon that light will be gone; but if you continue walking in the light you have seen and entrust yourself to it, you will become children of light who do not stumble around in darkness. Those who walk in darkness don't know where they are going."

After saying this, Jesus left the temple area and hid Himself from the crowds.

For several years the people had heard His words and had seen the miracles, but they still wouldn't entrust themselves to Him. Isaiah had foreseen this hundreds of years before when he wrote, "Lord, who has believed our report? Does anyone recognize God stretching out His mighty arm to save?" Isaiah was given a vision of all these events and described it in God's words: "Their eyes have been blinded and their hearts hardened so they cannot see and will not believe. They cannot turn to Me and let Me heal them."

There were, however, a handful of Jewish leaders who did privately embrace Jesus' teaching; but, more concerned about getting man's approval than God's, they didn't admit publicly to believing. They feared the disgrace of being put out of the synagogue.

Later that day, Jesus spoke out again to the people, saying, "Everyone who believes in Me is actually believing in the One who sent Me, and whoever sees Me is seeing the One who sent Me. I came into the world as light so that no one who believes in Me has to stay in the dark. Anyone who has heard My words and rejects them will be judged, not by Me, but by the truths they have heard from My mouth.

That's because I always, only spoke what My Father wanted Me to say. His words produce eternal life in all who accept them."

While Jesus was teaching, the crowds were listening in astonishment. However, the scribes, chief priests, and leaders were discussing just how to get rid of Him; but their hands were tied because of the people and because they were afraid of Jesus.

That evening, Jesus once again left the city.

Tuesday

The next morning as they passed the fruitless fig tree, the disciples noticed that it had withered from the roots up and was completely dead. "Teacher," Peter exclaimed, "look at that! The fig tree You cursed yesterday is already dead!"

Jesus replied, "When you know and trust God and He prompts you to tell that mountain over there to throw itself into the sea, it will happen. That is, if you believe and don't doubt Him. When you pray, expect Him to 'move mountains' and He will. Moving mountains and withering fig trees is not as important, though, as forgiveness. You must forgive any who have wronged you so that you can enjoy unhindered forgiveness from your Father in heaven."

While in the temple explaining His message to all who would listen, Jesus was approached by a group of official interrogators made up of the chief priests, scribes, and elders. These men demanded that He explain His credentials, saying, "Who, exactly, gave You the authority to do and say all that You do?"

Jesus came back at them with a question and said, "First, you tell Me whether John's baptism was something God initiated or just a man-made fad. Then I'll tell you where I get My authority."

This put them between a rock and a hard place. They knew they couldn't admit it was God-given because then Jesus would ask them why they hadn't embraced it. But they also knew that if they openly claimed it was just a fad, the multitudes who revered John as a prophet would have stoned them. So they gave a non-answer by saying, "We do not know where it was from."

Jesus, in turn, said, "Then I won't be telling you where My authority comes from either."

Jesus then began telling a story to them:

"Once upon a time a man had two sons. He said to the one, 'Son, go work in my vineyard today.' The boy retorted with 'No, I don't feel like it!' But then later he felt bad about it and went to work after all. Meanwhile, the father had gone to the second son with the same instruction and the boy quickly agreed to obey. But as it turns out, he ended up not going to work even though he had said he would.

"Now," Jesus asked, addressing those who had questioned His authority, "which of the two actually obeyed the father?"

They answered, "The first son."

Jesus said, "That's right! And I tell you that tax collectors and prostitutes will be getting into God's Kingdom ahead of you. John came explaining how to get right with God, but you didn't want anything to do with it. These sinners believed, yet you still wouldn't rethink your position.

"Here's another story for you:

"A wealthy landowner planted a vineyard and built all that was needed for producing wine. He then hired a crew of workers to manage the enterprise while he went to a far country. At harvest time the man sent a servant to visit the operation and bring back a sample of the fruit. Astonishingly, the hired crew beat the servant and sent him off with nothing.

"So the owner sent a second messenger to his vineyard. This one they also beat; threw stones, hitting him in the head; and sent him away empty-handed.

"One after another, the servants sent to inspect the vineyard were beaten and some were killed. Finally, the landowner had had enough. This time he would send his only son to examine the work. 'Maybe they will respect him,' the man reasoned, 'knowing how much I love him.'

"But when the workers at the vineyard saw the son coming, they conspired, saying, 'Look, here comes the heir of this place. All we have to do is kill him and it will all be ours!' So they took hold of him, dragged him outside the vineyard, and killed him."

Jesus turned to the crowd and asked, "Now, when the owner comes back to deal with these workers, what do you suppose he will do?"

"He'll kill them all," the people shouted, "and put other people in charge of the place!"

Then Jesus turned to the religious leaders and prodded them, asking, "Is that what he'll do? Give the vineyard to others to tend?"

"Certainly not!" they replied, for they knew that Jesus' story was pointed at them.

He looked at them and said, "It's just what Scripture said would happen, 'The stone rejected by the builders has become the chief cornerstone. This was the Lord's doing and it was marvelous in our eyes.'

"So I say to you, the Kingdom of God will be taken away from you and given to others who will produce good fruit. Stumble on that cornerstone and you will be broken to pieces. Let that stone fall on you and you will be crushed!"

Now the Pharisees were desperate to find some way to silence Him. They knew He was calling them the hired workers. But they couldn't risk offending the massive crowd who believed Jesus was a prophet sent from God. So they went off to make plans.

Jesus didn't back down but kept telling more stories:

"There once was a great king who prepared a marvelous wedding feast for his son. Once everything was ready, he sent servants out to call the guests. At first, no one would come; so he sent out more messengers, extending the invitation. This time some totally ignored the invitation and went about their business; others beat the servants and even killed some of them.

"This made the king furious. He sent his army to destroy them and burn their cities. Then he said to his servants, 'The feast is ready and no one on my original guest list was worthy of the honor. Go out and find anyone willing to come, good or bad, rich or poor.'

"So the servants gathered a hall-full of people who were thrilled and astonished at the privilege of being invited. However, someone came in trying to be part of the festivities without receiving the proper robe. When the king saw the man, he asked him, 'Friend, where is your robe?' But the man had no answer. The king ordered his servants to throw him out, out into the darkness, out where there is nothing but grief and regrets. Many are invited," Jesus concluded, "but few actually participate in the king's feast."

Meanwhile, the Pharisees cooked up a plan where they would get some of their interns along with a few political activists to ask Jesus a question that would get Him in trouble with the Roman officials, prompting them to take action against Him. These interrogators found Him in the temple and asked, "Teacher, we really respect You and Your teaching and appreciate that You're not beholden to anyone. We were just wondering, should we who are Jews be paying taxes to Caesar, or not?"

Jesus, of course, saw through their hypocrisy and called them on it, saying, "You hypocrites are just testing Me. Show Me one of the coins used for paying taxes."

So they brought Him a denarius. He looked it over and asked, "And whose image is this on here?"

Together they replied, "Caesar's!"

Then Jesus answered, saying, "Give to Caesar what is his and give to God what is His."

Frustrated by Jesus' amazing ability to answer them so plainly, they left without further questions.

In their place some Sadducees, who don't believe in an afterlife, came up with another trick question. "Teacher," they said, "Moses commanded that if a married man dies without any children, then his brother has to take the widow to produce offspring to carry on the family line, right? So there was this fellow who died, having six brothers. One after another, the guys died after taking the first brother's widow, before any had a chance to produce children.

Eventually, after the seventh brother had died, the woman also died. So our question is, in the resurrection, which of the brothers will have her for a wife since all of them had married her?"

Jesus confronted their arrogant ignorance by responding, "Ah, you're revealing how little you know of the Scriptures or how God works. Yes, marriage is the normal pattern in this life, but in the resurrection it won't be that way. God's children will relate on a much higher level, more like the angels. And since we're on the subject of resurrection, haven't you read the story of Moses at the burning bush when God spoke to him, saying, 'I am the God of Abraham, the God of Isaac, and the God of Jacob'? He referred to them as still alive and living in His presence. By denying the possibility of resurrection, you make a serious mistake!"

The crowd was most enthusiastic with Jesus' answer. Some of the scribes even commended Him, saying, "Good answer, Teacher!" And they were hard-pressed to come up with another question.

Hearing how Jesus had silenced the Sadducees, the Pharisees tried to think of other questions. A lawyer had heard Jesus' pithy answers, so he asked Him, which of the commandments in the Law was the most important.

Jesus said, "The first commandment is 'Listen, O Israel, the Lord our God is the only God. You must love the Lord your God with all your heart, with all your soul, with all your mind, and with all your strength.' That is the most important command; and the second-most is like it, 'You must love your neighbor as yourself.' Every other rule and truth in the Old Testament is built on the foundation of those two commands."

The attorney said, "I like that! It makes sense that, since God is over all, we should love Him completely and wholeheartedly. I can see where loving Him and loving my neighbor is far more important than all the burnt offerings and sacrifices I could present."

When Jesus heard that sincere response, He said, "You are very close to understanding and entering the Kingdom of God."

Jesus went over to where the Pharisees had gathered and posed a question to them. "This Messiah you are looking for, whose Son is He?"

Without hesitation they answered, "The Son of David, of course."

"If that's the case," Jesus went on, "how is it that David, in the Psalms, calls the Messiah his 'Lord'? You know the place where the Holy Spirit inspired him to pen these words: 'The Lord said to my Lord, "Sit at My right hand until I make Your enemies Your footstool."' How can David refer to his son as 'Lord'?"

This really stumped them. No one dared attempt an answer. Again, the common people thoroughly enjoyed Jesus' ability to out-smart the authorities.

Jesus was fed up with the way the religious leaders had misled the people. He lit into them:

"These scribes and Pharisees know the Law of Moses; and to the extent that they teach his commands, you should obey. However, I'm not saying you should follow their example and live the way they do. They are experts at saying the right thing and not doing it. Yet they make up tons of rules which they pile on you, never intending to follow them themselves. Beware of them!

"You can see through them. They are all about public image and getting honor from you. They make sure you address them as 'Rabbi' to distinguish themselves from the rabble.

"No one deserves the exalted role as 'Teacher' except for the Messiah. Everyone else is on equal standing with each other. No mere human should take on the title of 'Father' as though he deserved absolute obeisance; that privilege is reserved for your Father in heaven. True greatness is defined by being a devoted servant, looking out for the welfare of others more than for your own. Self-seeking, proud individuals will all be humbled eventually; but those who humbly give themselves away to others will be greatly honored.

"But you scribes and Pharisees, you frauds! I don't envy what you've got coming to you! You are not only missing the Kingdom, but you're also doing your best to make sure no one else can get in! You hypocrites! Every one of you is ravaging the meager possessions of widows, all the while making a show of your long, flowery prayers. You should know better! You will be in for a stiffer judgment.

"Woe to you, the whole lot of you — specialists in the Law, scribes, deceivers! You're going around the world to win converts; but once you do, they are twice as much a son of hell as you are. You're just a bunch of blind guides! Promises and vows are a joke with you. You let people off who 'swear by the temple,' saying it doesn't count unless they 'swear by the gold of the temple.' Someone else swears by the altar and you nullify it unless they swear by the gift on the altar. Fools! Which is greater, the altar or the gift that gets consumed on it? Can't you see that if someone swears by the altar, they're including everything offered on it as well? And if anyone swears by the temple, they're testifying to Him who dwells in it! The one who swears by heaven is making himself accountable to the throne of God and the One who sits on it.

"And another silly show you put on is with your tithes. You're sure to drop in the tiny portion of mint, anise, or cumin seed while you neglect the really weighty matters like justice, mercy, and faith. There's nothing wrong with being careful to give God His due, but you'd better make sure you're being faithful with all of His commands. As it is, you make sure to strain out a gnat from your cups all the while you're swallowing a camel.

"You are in for a rude awakening, hypocrites! You've spent all your time washing the outside of the cup while on the inside you're full of greed and gluttony. You're nothing more than whitewashed tombs: you look good on the outside but you're rotting away on the inside. Outwardly you appear holy but your hearts are caldrons of wicked thoughts and deceitful schemes.

"Scribes, Pharisees, frauds, you make monuments to dress up the tombs of the prophets and boast that if you'd been living in the days of your fathers, you wouldn't have persecuted God's messengers. Hah! You are sons of your fathers, that's for sure! And you're about to finish the job they started.

"Serpents, a brood of vipers — that's what you are! How on earth do you think you can avoid eternal judgment? Every messenger I've sent to you, whether prophets, wise men, or scribes, you've either killed, crucified, scourged in the synagogue, or persecuted from city to city. I tell you that your generation will see the culmination of blood-guilt from innocent Abel to Zechariah, son of Berechiah, whom you murdered between the temple and the altar.

"O Jerusalem, Jerusalem, the one who kills the prophets and stones all who are sent to her! How often I wanted to gather your children together as a hen gathers her chicks under her wings, but you were not willing. From this day forward you will be barren and desolate until the day you cry out, 'Blessed is He who comes in the name of the Lord!'"

All this Jesus said while sitting in the public courts of the temple. Across from Him were the large offering chests where worshipers could be seen making their contributions. The rich, of course, had significant donations. About that time a widow passed by, throwing two pennies into the coffer. Jesus pointed her out to His disciples, saying, "You know what? That poor widow has just put in more than all the rich. They gave a portion off the top of their wealth, but she just contributed every last penny she owned."

As they made their way out of the temple that afternoon, His disciples called attention to the massive stones that made up the magnificent temple square. Jesus used their comments to prophesy of things to come. "Yes," He told them, "look around at all these great structures. There's a day coming when not one stone will be left in place, but all will be dismantled and scattered."

The disciples were amazed. "Teacher, tell us more! When is this going to happen? How will we know when all this will occur?"

Passing through the city gates, they climbed up the Mount of Olives across from the temple, overlooking the great city. Jesus answered them, saying:

"You must be very cautious because in that season many will claim to be speaking for Me or even say 'I am He,' or 'The time has come!' You'll hear reports of conflicts and wars, but that won't necessarily mean it's imminent. In those days nations will war violently against each other; natural disasters like earthquakes, plagues, and famines will multiply; and even the skies will be filled with frightening phenomenon. All this is just the beginning of the end.

"But even before that, you will face tremendous persecution and suffering. You will stand trial before kings and authorities for My sake, but don't spend time worrying about your defense or what you should say. At the right time I will put the words in your mouth which will silence the prosecution. All this will simply provide more opportunities for you to testify about Me.

"Don't be surprised if you are opposed by some of your closest friends and relatives. Some of you will be killed. All of you will be hated because you represent Me. But I will be working behind the scenes and will see that even the hairs of your head will be preserved. Only persevere and never give in, never give up!

"When you see Jerusalem surrounded by armies, then it's time to run. And I mean run! Don't go back into the house for valuables; just get to the mountains! Oh, what a trial this will be for those who are pregnant or nursing their young. The devastation this city will experience will be so sudden and violent and thorough that no one in the city will avoid either the sword or being dragged away as captives.

"Jerusalem will be trampled by Gentiles and left desolate until the era of Gentile domination is complete. In the days leading up to this, there will be false teachers everywhere. People will display unbridled selfishness; any semblance of love will go cold. But those who keep the faith through it all will be saved, and the message of salvation will be proclaimed worldwide before the end comes.

"The prophet Daniel wrote of a time when some blasphemous idol would be set up in the Holy of Holies. By all means, if you hear that this has happened, flee to the hills! Pray that this doesn't happen in winter or on the Sabbath! The kinds of suffering experienced during this time will be worse than any in history; and if the Lord doesn't intervene and cut it short, not a single person could survive. But, for the sake of His own, He will put a sudden end to the devastation.

"At some point the sun will go dark, as will the moon; the oceans will erupt in violent uproar; and stars will fall from the heavens. Because of the terror, men's hearts will fail.

"Then a sign in the heavens will indicate My return. I will appear in clouds with majestic glory. I will blow the trumpet, and My angels will gather My people from every corner of the earth. When that happens, look up, lift up your heads; for your day of ultimate deliverance has come!

"The trees serve as a great illustration of this. After a long winter, when you see little buds and then fresh green leaves on their branches, you know that summer is right around the corner. In the same way, as all these signs converge, you can be sure the Kingdom of God is close.

"You can count on these things happening not just in some future generation, but you yourselves will experience some of it. Heaven and earth will pass away but My words will not.

"As to the precise timing of all this, no one, not even the angels of heaven, could tell you. Only My Father knows that plan.

"I only urge you not to lose heart nor to get caught up in the pleasures and priorities of this world. Those are nothing but traps to distract you from what is best. Pray that you might escape all this destruction and be found worthy to stand before Me. Remember, you won't know for sure when it will all come about.

"Think of it like this:

"A man goes off on a long trip and leaves servants in charge of his house. Each one has specific tasks. The butler should keep alert and watchful at the door because there's no telling when the master might return. It could be any time of day or night. Woe to the ones he finds asleep! That's why I urge you to keep your eyes open for Me.

"Remember the story of Noah? Everyone was just doing their own thing, partying, and living as though this life were all there was. No one, even though they had been warned, was ready for the flood when it took them away. That's how sudden and shocking My return will be. People will be working side by side and suddenly one of them will be gone. Watch! Be ready!

"If a master had forewarning of a thief breaking in, he would be prepared to prevent him from doing so. That's what I'm talking about. You must be alert and ready for My return!

"You know that a faithful servant will be rewarded when his master returns and finds him doing his job. But the servant who decides the master may never return and spends his time partying and abusing the other workers will face dreadful consequences when the master does return. That unfaithful servant will end up where all hypocrites do — in the torment of eternal regrets and suffering.

"Or picture this:

"Ten virgins were invited to be part of a bridal procession. Five were wise and they made sure they had extra oil for their lamps. The other five were careless and didn't take time to prepare. The festivities ended up being delayed by several hours and the ladies fell asleep. Around midnight they were suddenly awakened by the joyful announcement of the bridegroom's arrival. Quickly, they gathered their things to join the procession. However, the five foolish girls couldn't get their lamps going. They asked the others for some of their fuel, but they couldn't spare any. 'Sorry,' they said, 'you'd better go find a shop to buy some yourselves.' They hurried off in pursuit of oil. Meanwhile, the celebration began. When the five foolish virgins finally got there, they knocked and begged to be admitted; but the bridegroom looked out and said, 'Sorry, I don't recognize you!'

"So I say, be ready! Watch! I am coming but can't tell you when.

"Do you remember the story I told you before about the merchant who left his servants with money to invest? Some were diligent and prospered while others simply buried the coins to keep them safe. Do you recall how the man rewarded those who had been responsible with what had been entrusted to them and how he welcomed them as partners? But the one who was irresponsible and lazy, who miscalculated the character of the merchant, lost everything.

"When the great Day comes and I am seated on the throne, surrounded by holy angels, all peoples will be brought to Me to be judged. Just as a shepherd separates the sheep from the goats, so I will divide all mankind into two groups.

"To those on the right I will say, 'Come into the Kingdom prepared for you since the beginning of creation. Receive My Father's blessing because when I was hungry, you fed Me; when I was thirsty, you gave Me a drink; even though I was a stranger, you welcomed

Me; when I was naked, you clothed Me; when I was sick, you visited Me; and when I was in prison, you came to encourage Me.'

"Stunned, the righteous will ask when they had seen Him in these desperate conditions. I will tell them that every time they did it for a needy fellowman, it was as though they were doing it for Me.

"Then, to the 'goats' on My left I will declare, 'Depart from Me, you wicked, self-centered ones! The eternal fire prepared for the devil and his angels will be your destiny because when I was hungry, thirsty, and naked, you did nothing. Because I was a stranger, sick, and in prison, you avoided Me and despised Me.'

"This group will likewise be perplexed, wondering when they had had occasion to do something for Me. I will explain to them that every time they had opportunity to serve the needs of others and refused, they were rejecting Me. These will be sent into eternal punishment while the righteous will enjoy life with God forever."

At the conclusion of this, Jesus reminded His disciples that the Passover was just two days away and that He was going to be crucified.

The chief priests and Pharisees had issued an edict requiring anyone who knew of Jesus' whereabouts to report to them so they could arrest Him.

The chief priests, scribes, and elders of the people were assembled in Caiaphas' palace, plotting just how they would apprehend Jesus and have Him killed. They had decided to wait until after the feast to avoid a riot by the masses of people; but just then Judas, one of Jesus' disciples, came to them, offering his assistance. "What will you pay me to help deliver Jesus over to you?" he asked. Pleasantly surprised with this new inside contact, they gave him thirty pieces of silver. Judas assured them that he would alert them to the next opportunity when they could capture Jesus without crowds of people being involved.

Because it was evening, Jesus and the disciples camped out on Mount Olivet.

Wednesday

In the morning Jesus sent Peter and John into the city to make preparations for their Passover meal.

"Did You have any place in mind?" they inquired.

"Yes," Jesus answered, "as you enter the city, you'll come upon a man carrying a pitcher of water. Just follow him. When he reaches his destination, explain to the master of the house that I have sent you. Tell him My time has come and we plan to keep the Passover at his place. Ask to see his guest room, and he will take you to a large upper room already furnished. You'll just need to arrange the final details."

His disciples went and found everything just as He had described. There they prepared the Passover.

Jesus knew that His time on earth was drawing to a close and that He would be returning to His Father. He loved His followers deeply and was preparing to demonstrate it in the greatest way possible.

That evening as they reclined around the large table, Jesus began by saying, "You can't imagine how much I have looked forward to tonight's meal together! I am about to face tremendous suffering, and this will be our last Passover together. We won't be together like this again until it is fulfilled in the Kingdom of God."

Then He took the cup of sanctification, gave the blessing, and passed it around, saying, "Take some, all of you. The next time I partake will be when the Kingdom of God comes."

There had been no little rivalry among the disciples about who got to sit in the places of honor. Jesus, being satisfied with the honor given Him by His Father, didn't need to prove His greatness to anyone. He knew where He had come from and where He was going; so since no one else had performed the lowly task of washing the guests' feet, He got up to do it. He removed His outer robe, took up a basin and towel, and began wiping the feet of each disciple.

When He got to Simon Peter, Peter said, "You shouldn't be washing my feet!"

Jesus explained to Peter that he would understand later why He was doing this. Peter recoiled, "I'll never let You do this, Lord!"

Jesus said, "If I don't wash you, you don't belong to Me."

To which Peter replied, "In that case, Lord, wash me from head to toe!"

Jesus smiled and said, "You've already bathed; this is just to get today's dust off your feet. You are already clean. Well, most of you are!" He knew who was about to betray Him; that's why He said that they weren't all clean.

When He had finished, He put His robe back on and returned to His place at the table. "Do you know why I have done this?" He asked. "You call Me 'Rabbi' and 'Lord' and you are right. Your job is to learn from Me. I have just set an example by washing your feet. This is the way you must serve each other. The servant is not greater than his master, so you must not think yourselves above such lowly service. Now that you know this, you can only enjoy deep happiness if you live this way.

"As I've said before, do not follow the example of this world's leaders. They dominate and control the lives of those under them. Your authority, like Mine, does not work that way! Humble, genuine service defines great leaders. Again, I say, you are used to a system in which the younger serves the elder, yet here I have ministered to you.

"Because you have stuck with Me through the ups and downs of the past three years, I will give you places of dominion just as My Father has given Me a Kingdom. Someday you will sit at My table in My Kingdom and rule over the twelve tribes of Israel.

"I don't speak of all of you, however, for the Scripture must be fulfilled which says, 'He who eats bread with Me has lifted up his heel against Me.' I am forewarning you so that when it happens, you will be convinced that I Am Who I Am.

"Rest assured that whenever someone responds to you as My messengers, they are accepting Me, just as you, by responding to Me, have accepted the One who sent Me."

After saying this, Jesus was visibly troubled and said, "Yes, one of you sitting here tonight will betray Me."

The disciples were hurt by this; and some nervously asked, "Lord, is it I?"

Jesus said, "It will be the one to whom I pass the matzah after dipping it. Yes, Scripture must be fulfilled; but as for the one who betrays Me, it would have been better for him if he'd never been born."

The disciples were more perplexed than ever and began questioning each other, trying to figure out who among them might be the guilty one.

With brazen mock innocence, Judas himself asked, "Rabbi, am I the one?"

To which Jesus replied, "You know who you are."

Simon Peter nudged John, who was beside Jesus, to get him to ask once more. Jesus told him to watch closely to whom He handed the dipped matzah. Jesus then took some bread, dipped it, and handed it to Judas.

Immediately, Satan entered Judas. As Judas rose from the table, Jesus said, "Carry out your plans quickly." Judas went out; darkness had fallen.

In spite of all the clues, the disciples thought nothing of Judas' exit, assuming that since he held the money, Jesus had sent him out either to buy something else for their meal or to help the poor.

Once Judas was gone, Jesus said, "God's glorious plan is unfolding before your eyes. The genius and perfection of how He works everything out through Me will be indescribably brilliant.

"My dear children, before long I must be gone from here. You will look for Me, but as I told the Jewish crowds, 'Where I am going, you cannot come.' But once I'm gone, you must love one another the same way I have loved you. The one thing that will set you apart as being My disciples will be your love for each other."

Peter picked up on the fact that Jesus was going away and asked, "Lord, tell us where You're going."

All Jesus said was, "You can't follow Me there right away, but someday you will."

Peter replied, "Lord, why can't I follow You right now? I mean, I'm ready to follow You to prison or even to death!"

Jesus told Peter, "You think so, don't you? The fact is that before the rooster crows tomorrow morning, you will deny Me at least three times. Dear Simon, what you don't know is that Satan has asked for you, to sift you like wheat. But I have prayed for you, that you won't utterly abandon Me. Once you have been restored, you will be a real source of strength for your brothers.

"Do you remember," Jesus asked the men, "when I sent you from city to city and told you not to bother with taking along provisions? Did you ever run out of what you needed?"

"Not once!" they replied.

"Well, this time it's different," Jesus said. "Prepare for trouble. Get your money out of the bank and sell whatever you have to in order to buy a sword. Everything written about Me in the Scriptures is about to be fulfilled, even the phrase, 'He was condemned as a criminal.'"

"Lord, we've got two daggers here!" someone said.

"All right," Jesus remarked, "that's enough about swords."

As they were eating, Jesus took bread, blessed it, and broke it. As He passed it around to the disciples, He said, "Take, eat: This is My body which is given for you. Whenever you eat this, think of Me."

Afterward He lifted up the cup of redemption, gave thanks, and passed it around, saying, "Drink from it, all of you. This is My blood poured out for many, ushering in a whole new covenant which takes away all your sins. The next time we share this cup will be when we are together in My Father's Kingdom."

For the next hour or so Jesus shared His heart with the disciples, saying, "I have not told you all this to trouble you. You believe in God, so I urge you to trust Me when I tell you that in My Father's house there are magnificent mansions. I'm going ahead of you to get your rooms ready. Once they are, I will come back to get you so that we can spend eternity together. You know all this already, and I've explained the way to God's Kingdom to you."

But Thomas spoke up, saying, "Lord, we don't know where You are going, so how could we possibly know the way?"

Jesus answered, "I am the Way, the Truth, and the Life; no one can come to the Father except through Me. Truly knowing Me is how you know the Father. Since you know Me, you know Him and have seen Him."

Philip didn't understand this and asked, "Please, Lord, if You will introduce us to the Father, then we'll be able to say that we've seen Him and know Him."

"Philip," Jesus replied, "are you saying that you don't know Me? We've been together for so long. How many times have I told you that I am in the Father and He is in Me? That's why I say that if you have seen Me, you've seen the Father. How can you ask to see Him as though it's a new concept?

"Let me say it again, I am not just saying words that I've come up with. No, the Father who lives in Me is the One at work. If you can't take My word for it, then believe because of the works you've seen Me doing. Everyone who trusts in Me will do the same amazing works and even greater things because I've gone to My Father. In that day you can ask the Father, using My name, to do great works. I will do those works through you, and all the glory the Father has endowed upon Me will be enhanced as a result. If you love Me, listen and live by My instructions.

"I am going to ask My Father to give you another companion, One who will be with you forever. The Spirit to whom I am referring is a mystery to the rest of the world, but you are acquainted with Him because He has been alongside you. Though the world cannot receive Him, He will be in you. So you see, I am not abandoning you like orphans.

"I am going to come to you, and you will 'see' Me in a way the world cannot. I will be alive inside you; and you'll get to experience what it means that I am in My Father, you are in Me, and I am in you.

"Whoever loves Me listens to and follows My instructions. And if someone loves Me, My Father and I will love them and I will reveal Myself to them."

Judas (not Iscariot) said to Him, "Lord, how are You going to show Yourself to us without the world being able to see You?"

Jesus said, "Listen to Me. If you love Me, you will be carrying on My work. My Father is delighted when that happens, and together We will make Our home inside you. This does not apply to those who show that they don't, in fact, love Me because they aren't faithful to do what I've instructed. I tell you this on My Father's authority; it was entirely His idea and plan.

"I'm telling you all this, giving you a 'heads-up,' before I'm gone; but the Spirit will help you understand it. As I said, My Father will send Him at My request; and He will bring to mind the many lessons you've learned from Me.

"I trust that this settles your anxious hearts. I want to leave with you a kind of peace the world couldn't possibly offer. I'm not telling you these things to trouble you, but rather to enable you to trust Me and to be overjoyed with Me that I get to return to My Father who is everything to Me.

"It's time now. The ruler of this world is about to attack; but don't worry, he has no claim on Me. I must go through with this to show the world how much I love My Father and that I am willing to do whatever He asks of Me. Come now, let's be on our way."

When they had sung a hymn, they went out, crossed the Kidron Valley, and headed up the Mount of Olives.

Passing through a small vineyard, Jesus turned to His disciples and said, "Think of Me as the True Vine and My Father as the Gardener. He lifts up and secures the branches that aren't bearing fruit and trims the ones that are so that they will be more productive.

"My words have had a pruning affect in your lives. See that you stay closely bonded to Me, letting Me live in and through you. Don't think for a moment that I'm asking you to go do things on your own: No branch can produce fruit unless it's attached to the vine. Are you seeing the picture? I am the Vine and you are the branches. As long as you are getting your life from Me, you'll produce a lot of fruit. Apart from Me you can't hope to do anything. Anyone who won't get their life from Me is like a branch all withered and dry, good for nothing but to be burned in the fire.

"Do you want to be known as My disciples? Get your life from Me. Let My words be like the life-giving sap flowing from the vine into the branches. Then you will find new desires taking shape deep within. As you ask Me for those things, I will answer; you'll be very productive and My Father will be thrilled. That's what makes a real disciple.

"Remember, love is what this is all about. You've experienced My love, and I've explained that it flows from My Father's love for Me. Now you can live inside that love by doing what I tell you, just like I live inside My Father's love by hearing His heart and doing whatever He asks Me to do.

"I'm so eager for you to enjoy the kind of life that I have. Your whole being will be filled with inexpressible pleasure. More than anything else, I want you to demonstrate the same kind of love you've experienced from Me. Loving like this means, ultimately, being willing to lay down your life for your friends.

"You have become My friends by doing what I've asked of you. Ours is not a servant-master relationship since servants aren't privy to their master's thoughts and long-term plans. Because you are friends, I have openly shared with you everything My Father has told Me.

"It is so important that you love one another because the world isn't going to love you. If you were part of the world system, they would; but I have chosen you to come out of the world, so they will hate you just like they have hated Me.

"Those who have accepted My word will accept your message, but you can be sure that anyone who has persecuted Me will harass you as well. They do that because they don't know the One who sent Me. They have heard My words and seen My works, so they are accountable for their response. Those who haven't seen and heard may have an excuse for not believing. That's not the case with these agitators. They actively oppose both Me and My Father. Their own Scriptures predicted it, saying, 'They hated Me without a cause.'

"But remember, I just explained that the Father will be putting the Spirit of Truth in you to help you as you spread the word about Me. The Spirit will testify to you about Me. You have been with Me since the beginning of My ministry and will be effective witnesses.

"It's not going to be easy, but I'm telling you ahead of time so you don't stumble when they kick you out of the synagogues. In fact, some of them will even believe they are doing God's will by killing you.

"I didn't say anything about this until now because I've been here with you, taking the brunt of the rejection. Now that I've told you, you're so focused on what might happen when I leave that you aren't interested in where it is that I'm going or that I get to reunite with Him who sent Me.

"Someday, after the Spirit has entered you, you'll realize why it is to your advantage that I go away. Believe Me, as soon as I leave, I'll send Him to you. Then, as you spread My message, the Spirit will help people see how wrong it is NOT to believe in Me. He will use the fact that I have returned to My Father to convince them that I was right about how to be accepted by God. He will also cause them to realize they will either face judgment along with the ruler of this world or experience liberation from his domination because his authority has been broken.

"There's so much more to say, more than you could digest right now; but that is another reason why I will send the Spirit. Do you recall that whenever I taught, I was being told by My Father what to say? Similarly, after I'm gone, the Spirit will take what is Mine and explain it to you.

"First, though, I must leave you. In a day or so you won't see Me, then shortly after that you will see Me again: I have to go to My Father."

The disciples looked at one another and asked, "What does He mean — 'not seeing,' 'seeing,' 'going to the Father'?" They couldn't figure it out.

Jesus could tell they were confused, so He said, "Very soon, when you cannot see Me, you will be distraught. The world will rejoice while you weep. Then, soon afterward, your sadness will turn to joy. It's kind of like a woman in labor. The process is painful; but as soon as the child is born, she feels tremendous joy at bringing another person into the world. Be encouraged. I promise you that the season of sadness will turn into joy the moment you see Me again. Finally all your questions will be answered; you won't need to ask Me to explain.

"I have shared My heart with you; and because you have begun to desire the same things I do, you can pour out your hearts to the Father. Ask Him your questions and tell Him what you need. Because you have devoted yourself to Me, the Father loves you and longs to meet your needs. Fellowship with Him will fill you with intense joy!

"He sent Me into this world and soon I will return to Him. I can hardly wait!"

The disciples were feeling a bit less troubled and said things like, "Now we understand what You're saying," and, "You have answered all our questions," and, "We have no doubt now that You came to us from God."

"Do you believe? Really?" Jesus asked. "What you don't realize is that you're about to scatter and leave Me all alone — except for the Father who is always with Me.

"Just know that no matter what the world throws at you, in Me you will have peace. Yes, take heart, I have overcome the world."

After saying this, Jesus looked up toward heaven and said, "Father, it's time. Complete the glorious plan You have for Me so that I can display Your supreme authority and goodness. Finally We can give them Our kind of life: an indestructible aliveness that is energized by their intimate companionship with You, the only true God, and with Me, the One whom You have sent to make it all possible.

"I have been faithful to do everything You asked Me to do. I have shown them just how incredibly wonderful You are. I can hardly wait to return to You and to the glorious life We had together long before this world existed!

"These here with Me, Father, have heard every word You told Me to share with them. I have shown them exactly what You are like. Now they are convinced that You sent Me, that You have been speaking through Me, and that I get My very life from You. They have responded to Your word and have entrusted themselves to You.

"My heart goes out to them as I prepare to leave this world while they must remain in it. I want them to know that they belong to You and that You have given them to Me. I want them to see how their lives are intertwined with Mine in a glorious bond. Oh, Holy Father, watch over them and protect each of these whom You have given to Me. Recreate Our oneness in them. While I was with them, I kept them safe on Your behalf. I didn't lose any of them except, of course, the son of destruction, as the Scripture had predicted.

"Yes, I am coming Home! But I am talking with You about this while I am still with them. I so long to see them filled with the joy and pleasure I experience.

"Now that they have received Your Word, they are no longer part of the world any more than I am. And the world hates them for it. I'm not asking that You zap them out of the world but that You protect them from the evil one. Their relationship to the world is now what Mine has been; our life, our identity is not defined by the world.

"Continue to set them apart from this world by the truths of Your Word. I have dedicated Myself to them and to their becoming utterly distinguished by the truth. Just as You sent Me into this world, I am sending them into the world.

"As they proclaim the message, many more will believe; and I lift them up to You as well, Father. Recreate Our unique oneness in all of them. They have realized that You are in Me and I am in You. Now show them that together, all of them are in Us. When the world sees their unity and love, then they will be persuaded that You sent Me.

"You treat Me with such dignity and delight, Father; and I have passed that on to them so that they can enjoy Our kind of relationship with each other. What a picture: I in them and You in Me, the ultimate definition of oneness. Yes! When the world sees their amazing oneness with Us and each other, they will know for sure that You sent Me and that You love them every bit as much as You love Me.

"O Father, all this makes Me more eager than ever to have all of them living with Me there. I want them to see for themselves how glorious it is to be at Home with You, to experience Your love in person. Yes, You loved Me long before We laid the foundations of this world.

"O righteous Father! This world doesn't have a clue what You are really like! But I know You, and these with Me believe You sent Me to them. I keep telling them more and more about You because I want the love You have for Me to be in them and I want to be in them."

As the group approached the grove of olive trees known as the Garden of Gethsemane, Jesus turned to the disciples and said, "It is written, 'I will strike the Shepherd and all the sheep will scatter.' Tonight this will be fulfilled as every one of you gives in to fear and runs away."

Peter rebuffed Him, saying, "Lord, what are You talking about? Even if all the others abandon You, I could never do that!"

Jesus looked at him and said, "Oh, Peter, by the time the rooster crows a second time tomorrow morning, you will have denied Me three more times!"

This really bothered Peter and he protested, saying, "Even if it means dying with You, Lord, I'd never deny You!" And all the disciples conveyed similar sentiments.

Jesus encouraged them to wait while He went on a little farther to pray. "Pray that you won't give in to temptation," He told them. He invited Peter, James, and John to go on with Him. They could see that He was very troubled.

"The burden is crushing Me," He told them. "I need you to stay with Me."

Then Jesus went a little farther on and, kneeling down, said, "Father, oh, Father, how can I drink this awful cup? Is there any way out? Yet whatever You decide is best, for I do want what You want." Right then an angel appeared to Him from Heaven to strengthen Him.

Weighed down with the burden, Jesus fell on His face and cried out, "Abba, dear Father, all things are possible with You. Could You possibly take this cup away from Me? O Father, I surrender My desires to Your perfect plan." The intense pressure He felt even caused small blood vessels under His skin to burst so that He was sweating blood.

Eventually He got up and returned to where He had left Peter, James, and John. They too had been emotionally drained and had fallen asleep. "Peter," Jesus said, shaking him, "how can you sleep? Can't you stay alert even for an hour?

"Wake up!" He said to them. "Watch! Pray that you don't give in to temptation! The spirit is willing and ready, but the flesh is extremely weak!"

He left them again and spent more time crying out to His Father. Finally He said, "My Father, if there is no other way to deal with this, I will drink it. I do want Your desires to be accomplished."

When He returned to the disciples, they were once again asleep; He could hardly rouse them. So He left them and went off alone to pray.

He came to His disciples a third time and woke them. "All right, men! That's enough sleep! The betrayer is approaching; get up! Let's go!"

Now Judas, who betrayed Him, knew where to find them because Jesus often met there with His disciples. No sooner were the disciples on their feet than Judas showed up leading a crowd of soldiers and officers from the chief priests and Pharisees, all carrying lanterns, torches, swords, clubs, or other weapons.

Judas had given them a signal to watch for: he would single out Jesus by greeting Him with a kiss. Judas was in the lead and, seeing Jesus, immediately went up to Him and kissed Him, saying, "Rabbi! It's You!"

Jesus looked at him and replied, "Friend, what are you doing here? Would you betray Me with a kiss?"

Jesus knew what was going on so He asked the crowd, "Who are you looking for?"

They answered Him, "Jesus of Nazareth."

Without hesitation, Jesus replied, "I AM." Instantly, the whole lot of them, including Judas, fell backwards to the ground.

When they had gotten back on their feet, Jesus asked them again whom they were looking for. "Jesus of Nazareth," they said.

"I am the One you are looking for," Jesus answered. "There's no reason to detain these others." With that He fulfilled the Scripture that said, "Of those whom You gave Me, I have lost none."

As the soldiers were taking hold of Jesus, one of the disciples asked, "Lord, is this why we needed swords?" And Peter, not waiting for a reply, took a swing at the nearest assailant, cutting off his right ear. It happened to be a fellow named Malchus, one of Caiaphas' servants.

Then Jesus said to Peter, "No, this is not the time or place for swords. Using swords to defend yourself only means you're likely to die by the sword.

"Surely you know Me well enough to know that if I wanted to, I could ask My Father and He would send more than seventy thousand angels to protect Me. But if He did that, the Scriptures would not be fulfilled. No, I must drink the cup which My Father has given Me."

Then Jesus said to His captors, "Hold on just a moment." He reached out and touched Malchus' ear. Immediately it was healed.

Turning to the crowd, Jesus said, "Really now, you come out under cover of night with weapons to arrest Me? I sat with you daily in the temple. Wouldn't it have been a lot simpler to seize Me then? But no, it had to be this way. You prefer darkness to light. And this way, every detail written by the prophets gets fulfilled."

About this time all the disciples left Him and ran for their lives. The troops tied Jesus with ropes and led Him out of the Garden. A boy had come out to watch the drama unfold; but when someone tried to grab him, he bolted and ran off naked, leaving them holding the sheet he had wrapped around himself.

Thursday

The late-night procession led first to the estate of Annas, the High Priest emeritus. His son-in-law, Caiaphas, was the official High Priest. It was Caiaphas, you may recall, who had previously counseled the tribunal that they would all be better off if one man were sacrificed for the people, thus avoiding a riot and increased tension with Rome.

Simon Peter and John followed from a distance. As they neared Annas' residence, John was ushered in because he was acquainted with Annas; but Peter was left at the gate. John asked one of the maids to go get Peter and let him in, which she did. When she saw him, she said, "You're one of that Man's disciples, aren't you?"

Peter denied it flatly, saying, "No, I'm not!"

It was the middle of the night and quite chilly, so some of the servants and officers had built a small fire in the courtyard. Peter joined them and they sat together warming themselves.

Meanwhile, inside the house, the High Priest grilled Jesus about what He taught and who His disciples were.

"You don't have to ask Me," Jesus said. "I've been teaching in your synagogues and in the temple all along. I have no secret agenda. Ask anyone here; they can tell you what I've said."

One of the officers standing near Jesus slapped Him across the face, saying, "Is that how You talk to the High Priest?"

Jesus said, "Did I say something that wasn't true? If not, why do you hit Me?"

Outside, where Peter was warming himself, another servant girl came up to him. After looking him over closely, she said, "This man was with Jesus of Nazareth." The others who were sitting there turned to him and said, "You aren't one of His disciples, now, are you?"

Peter answered them all tersely, "I don't know what you're talking about. Woman, I don't know that Man."

Peter decided to move a safe distance away from this group, so he found his way to a porch area. It wasn't long before yet another servant came to where he was. He was a relative of Malchus, whose ear Peter had cut off. He took one look at Peter and said, "Hey, I saw you with Jesus there in the Garden! You are one of them!"

Peter said, "Man, I am not!" As he turned to leave, a rooster crowed in the distance.

Annas, getting nowhere with his investigation, decided to send Jesus over to Caiaphas' palace. So once again Jesus was bound and led through the dark streets of Jerusalem. There, a great number of priests, elders, and scribes had come together.

Peter again followed as far as the courtyard and watched the mock trial from a distance.

The officials were scrambling to find someone who would testify against Jesus so that He could be condemned to die. Many came forward, but their testimonies conflicted. It looked like nothing could be found against Him. Finally, two of them said they had heard Jesus talk about destroying the temple. One said, "I heard Him say, 'I will destroy this man-made temple and within three days I will build one that is not man-made.'" The other man's charge was similar but not exactly in line with it.

Caiaphas stood up and asked Jesus, "Aren't You going to defend Yourself against these claims?"

But Jesus remained silent. He would not answer.

"I'll make You talk," the High Priest said, spitting out his words. "I adjure You by the Living God to tell us whether You are the Messiah, the Son of God."

Jesus answered and said, "I AM. And you will one day see the Son of Man sitting at the right hand of the Almighty and coming on the clouds of heaven."

Shouts of "Blasphemy!" rose from all around the room. The High Priest tore his robe in mock horror at the claim. "Who needs witnesses? Every one of us has heard His blasphemy! What do you say?"

First one and then another of the elders and leaders spoke up in a chorus of, "He deserves the death penalty! He must die!"

Those nearest Jesus took up the verdict and began beating Him and spitting in His face. Someone blindfolded Him, and several slapped Him on the face and then mocked Him, saying, "Prophesy, Messiah! Who just hit You? You should know!" This abuse went on until sunrise when He was taken to stand trial before the whole Sanhedrin.

Peter, meanwhile, was facing his own interrogation in the courtyard where he had been sitting. A servant girl walked up to him and said, "You were with Jesus of Galilee."

Peter glanced around nervously and said to all who were nearby, "I don't have a clue what you are talking about."

A few minutes later when he was standing near the gate, one of the servants who had confronted him earlier began telling everyone, "This fellow was with Jesus of Nazareth." But again he denied it with a curse.

Another hour passed and someone who had been standing there said, "This guy has to be one of His followers. His Galilean accent gives him away!"

Then Peter began to curse and swear. "I'm telling you," Peter retorted, "I don't know whoever it is you're talking about!" Before he finished the sentence, the sound of a rooster crowed for the second time that morning.

Peter could see Jesus from where he was standing, and at just that moment Jesus turned and looked at Peter. All of a sudden Peter remembered what Jesus had said to him a few hours earlier concerning these denials. Immediately Peter went out and wept bitterly.

As dawn was breaking, the whole council came together and made Jesus, already disheveled by the earlier abuse, stand and testify. "If You are the Messiah, tell us," they demanded.

"If I said yes, you would not believe Me," Jesus answered. "And if I were to question you, I'm sure you would not answer and you certainly would not let Me go free. Let Me just say that someday you will see the Son of Man enthroned with honor at the right hand of the Almighty."

"So then You are claiming to be the Son of God?" they asked.

"You have obviously come to that conclusion," Jesus replied.

"That's all the evidence we need," the council declared. "We have heard it straight from His own mouth."

When Judas, the betrayer, realized that Jesus wasn't going to escape this time, he was overcome with remorse. He returned to the chief priests and elders and confessed, "I have sinned by betraying innocent blood."

"We can't do anything about that!" the religious leaders retorted. "The deed is done."

At that, Judas threw the thirty pieces of silver on the floor of the temple at their feet and hurried out. He attempted to hang himself but ended up falling to his death.

This turn of events caused no small dilemma for the chief priests. "What are we going to do with this money?" they asked. "Because it's blood-money, we can't just put it back in the treasury. That just wouldn't be right."

After a brief discussion, it was decided that they would use it to buy an outlying field where potters discarded their scraps. Their plan was to turn it into a cemetery for strangers. Over time, the field became known as the Akeldama, the "Field of Blood." This fulfilled Jeremiah's prophecy which said, "And they took the thirty pieces of silver, the value set on Him by the children of Israel, and gave them for the potter's field, as the Lord directed me."

Once the Sanhedrin had condemned Jesus, they simply needed the Roman governor's consent. Because Israel was occupied territory, the Jewish leaders could not carry out capital punishment. Even though it was still quite early, they dragged Jesus to the Praetorium, Pontius Pilate's courtroom, and called for the governor. The Jewish leaders sent in emissaries rather than defile themselves by entering a Gentile facility since it was Passover.

Pilate, irritated at having to conduct business at this early hour, came into the square and asked, "What are the charges against this Man?"

The spokesman said, "If He hadn't done something wrong, do you think we'd be bringing Him to you?"

To which Pilate replied, "You have your own courts for petty crimes. Go try Him according to your Law."

The Jews said to him, "But you won't let us put anyone to death!" The policy to which they were referring would lead to the fulfillment of Jesus' words when He said that He would be lifted up, indicating death by Roman crucifixion as opposed to the Jewish method of stoning.

Someone in the crowd shouted, "This Man has been disturbing the peace and telling the people they shouldn't pay taxes to Caesar. He claims to be the Messiah, the true King of Israel. He's nothing but trouble."

Pilate called for Jesus to be brought to him for questioning and asked Him outright, "So, are You the King of the Jews?"

Jesus responded by asking him, "Why are you asking — for your own sake or just because of what the others are saying?"

Pilate was affronted by this and retorted, "I'm no Jew! Your people, Your chief priests are the ones who brought it up. What have You done to cause all this trouble?"

Jesus said, "My Kingdom isn't in this world. If it were, I'd call the subjects of My Kingdom to defend Me against these Jews. But My Kingdom isn't from around here."

"So," Pilate exclaimed, "You are a King then!"

Jesus answered him, "Yes, in the truest sense of the title. I came into this world for one reason: to tell people the truth. Everyone who desires truth receives My testimony."

This conversation wasn't going where Pilate had expected and he asked sarcastically, "Truth? What is truth?" He turned to the crowd and announced that he could find no crime worthy of prosecution.

That caused pandemonium as the chief priests and elders standing just outside the doorway began shouting, the crowd taking up all manner of accusations against Jesus. Jesus just stood there not saying a word.

Pilate turned to Jesus and said, "You hear their accusations! They've got some pretty serious charges. Aren't You going to say something?"

But Jesus remained silent. Pilate marveled at His composure.

Once again Pilate called to the crowd, "I find no fault in this Man."

"No! No!" they shouted, "He has stirred up this nation from here all the way to Galilee!"

"Galilee?" Pilate inquired. "Are You a Galilean?" he asked Jesus. With a sense of relief, Pilate realized that this was technically under the jurisdiction of Herod, the tetrarch of that northern province. Since Herod happened to be in Jerusalem at the time, Pilate had Jesus taken to him.

Herod relished the opportunity to finally meet Jesus. He had always wanted to watch Him do a miracle. Herod hammered Him with a barrage of questions, but Jesus would not answer or say a word. The chief priests and scribes threw in their vehement complaints, but Jesus stood silent. Herod and his body guard began to taunt Jesus, putting a royal robe over His shoulders and feigning honor to this would-be king. Then Herod sent Him back to Pilate.

Over the years, Herod and Pilate had been at odds with each other, but after this unusual charade they became friends.

Each year at this feast, the governor had a tradition of releasing to the Jews a prisoner of their choice. About this time, the crowd gathered to watch the proceedings. Chanting and shouting, they reminded Pilate that it was time to release the prisoner. He was pleased, thinking that this would relieve him of having to deal with Jesus. To make sure they would choose Jesus, he offered Barabbas as the alternative. This Barabbas had been a notorious criminal, leading insurrection against Rome and violently murdering any who stood in his way.

Pilate could tell that the chief priests had trumped up the charges against Jesus because they envied His popularity. He was certain the crowd would want Jesus released.

While all this was going on in the court, Pilate's wife had sent a messenger to him with a note, saying, "Don't have anything to do with that good Man. I've just had the worst nightmare about all this!"

Pilate called the accusers and declared, "You have brought this Man to me, claiming He is a trouble-maker. As you have seen this morning, I examined Him and found no cause for judgment. Besides, I sent Him to Herod and he, likewise, could find nothing deserving a death sentence. I will have my soldiers give Him a flogging, and He will be your released prisoner this year."

Immediately, the chief priests stirred up the crowd to demand that Barabbas be released instead. "Barabbas!" they shouted. "We want Barabbas!"

Pilate couldn't believe what he was hearing. "What? Who would you have me release to you?"

They cried out in unison, "Not this Man, but Barabbas!" "Take Him away and bring us Barabbas!" The din was deafening in the great stone courtyard.

Still looking for a way to get the crowd to choose Jesus instead, Pilate asked, "But what about your King? What shall I do with Jesus, your Messiah?"

It was too late; the leaders had prompted them to call for Jesus' crucifixion, and with one voice they shouted, "Let Him be crucified! Crucify! Crucify Him!"

Pilate refused to give up. "What has He done? I can't find anything as a charge against Him! I will scourge Him and let Him go!"

"No! He must be crucified!" the crowd demanded. "Crucify! Crucify! Crucify!" Their loud shouts echoed over and over until Pilate, beside himself with frustration, took a basin of water and washed his hands before the crowd in a symbolic gesture. "You are my witnesses," he announced, "that I am innocent of the blood of this upright Man."

The crowd was unshaken in their fervor. "His blood be upon us and our children then!"

Reluctantly, Pilate released Barabbas into the crowd and sent Jesus down to the whipping post to be prepared for crucifixion.

The whole garrison of soldiers gathered around Jesus as they stripped His robe from Him. Someone quickly fashioned a crown out of thorn branches and pressed it into Jesus' head. Another mockingly gave Him a reed of grass as a scepter. One by one the brazen officers bowed down to Him, saying, "Hail, King of the Jews!"

Relentlessly they beat Him with sharp whips, spit in His face, and cursed. Then, putting the robe back on Him, they sent Him up to Pilate and the waiting crowd.

Pilate announced Jesus' return, saying, "I present to you the One in whom I have found no fault." Hoping the crowd would be satisfied by the fierce scourging, he presented Jesus, dressed in the robe and wearing the crown of thorns. Pilate said, "Look at Him, the Man!"

But the moment they saw Jesus, the place erupted with cries of "Crucify Him! Crucify Him!"

Disgusted, Pilate shouted, "You take Him and crucify Him! I find no fault in Him!"

The Jews retorted, "But by our Law He must die! He declared Himself to be the Son of God!"

This made Pilate all the more troubled so he pulled Jesus aside and asked, "Where are You from?"

Jesus didn't answer him which only increased his anxiety. In frustration he challenged Jesus, "Are You not going to answer me? Don't You realize who I am? I have the power to crucify You and the power to release You."

That time Jesus did respond, saying, "Actually, you couldn't do anything against Me unless a higher Authority had given you the power. Those who delivered Me over to you have committed the greater sin."

From then on Pilate looked for any possible way to release Him, but the Jews shouted, "If you let this Man go free, you are no friend of Caesar! Anyone who calls Himself a king opposes Caesar."

This threat stripped away Pilate's resolve. He led Jesus to The Pavement where verdicts were read and final sentencing was announced. It was mid-morning, just hours before the start of Passover. Rising from the judgment seat, Pilate motioned toward Jesus and announced, "Behold your King!"

The crowd went wild with angry shouts of "Away with Him! Take Him away!" and "Crucify! Crucify! Crucify!"

Pilate screamed over the noisy uproar, "You want me to crucify your King?"

To which the chief priests replied, "We have no king but Caesar!"

Pilate had run out of options. He handed Jesus over to be cruci-fied. The soldiers ripped off the fancy robe and put His own cloak over the bruised and bleeding shoulders.

Taking up His cross, Jesus was led out of the judgment hall into the streets of Jerusalem. Somewhere along the way, the soldiers apprehended a bystander and made him carry Jesus' cross. His name was Simon. He was from Cyrene in northern Africa. He, along with his two sons, Alexander and Rufus, just happened to be passing through Jerusalem at that moment.

Crowds lined the narrow streets, pressing in to see the spectacle. Among them were many women who were weeping and crying out, distraught by the drama being played out before them.

Jesus gathered His strength and, turning to the women, stopped the procession long enough to say, "Oh, daughters of Jerusalem, don't weep over Me. Weep instead for what is going to happen to you and your children. Yes, a time is coming when you'll wish you had never had children, never had to watch them suffer. It will break your hearts to hear them begging the mountains and the hills to bury them rather than suffer at the hands of invading troops. Look, if they're willing to do this when the tree is alive and green, how much worse will it be when it is all just deadwood?"

The sobering death march continued to a crossroads just outside the city gates. Two criminals were facing execution along with Jesus on this fateful afternoon.

Rising up steeply beyond the road was a rocky hill. The small caves gave it the appearance of a huge skull, hence its name, "Skull Hill." There it stood, staring down on the grisly scene where soldiers prepared the three crosses.

The soldiers offered a strong drink for the condemned, something that would temporarily knock them out to minimize resistance as they secured them to the wooden stakes. Jesus would not drink it.

Midst cries of terror and cursing, the two criminals were cruci-fied and placed on either side of Jesus' cross. The prophet Isaiah had written, "And He was numbered with the transgressors."

As His cross was lifted up, Jesus said, "Father, forgive them. They don't know what they are doing."

Often the specific violation was written on a placard and nailed above the dying criminal. Pilate had personally made the placard for Jesus, writing in bold letters, "This is Jesus of Nazareth, the King of the Jews." He even printed it in the three dominant languages of the region: Greek, Latin, and Hebrew.

Because all this happened very near the city, nearly everyone could see it. When the chief priests saw what Pilate had written, they ran back to him insisting that he change it to read, "He claimed to be King of the Jews."

But Pilate was adamant, "What I have written, I have written."

It was only nine o'clock in the morning and the soldiers' only task was to keep an eye on their victims. They often made a sport of throwing dice to decide how to divide the dying man's valuables and clothing. Jesus' tunic was made without seams, so they decided not to tear it apart but to give it to whoever won the toss. His other garments were distributed evenly among the four soldiers. Even these details had been foretold in the Old Testament. David had written in Psalm 22, "They divided My garments among them, and for My clothing they cast lots."

Over the next couple of hours, streams of people passed by, some stopping to taunt the criminals, others cursing and mocking, wagging their heads in disgust as they shouted, "Ha! Destroy the temple and rebuild it in three days, will You? If You can do that, You certainly should be able to save Yourself! If You're really the Son of God, come down off that cross!"

The chief priests, scribes, and even the rulers chimed in, "He saved others but He can't save Himself!" "If He is the King of Israel," they sneered, "let Him come down from the cross. Then we'll believe in Him!"

"God's chosen Son? Why isn't God delivering Him? See, even God won't have anything to do with Him! Where is this God He trusted in, now that He needs Him?"

The soldiers weren't used to this much attention at a crucifixion. So they joined in after offering more sour wine, "If You are the King of the Jews, prove it! Save Yourself!"

Even one of the robbers picked up the taunt, saying, "Come on, Messiah. If You are who You say You are, save Yourself and save us while You're at it!"

The other robber, though, rebuked his friend, saying, "What are you doing? Do you not fear God, even just a little, seeing you're about to die? We deserve to die for what we've done, but this Man has done nothing wrong!"

Then he addressed Jesus, "Lord, remember me when You come into Your Kingdom."

Jesus promised him, "Today, this very day, you will be with Me in Paradise."

A small circle of mourners gathered near the cross: Mary, Jesus' mother; her sister; Mary, Clopas' wife; and Mary Magdalene; along with John, His beloved disciple. Concerned as the firstborn for His mother, He looked at her and said, "Dear woman, he (meaning John who was standing beside her) will be your son now."

Looking at John, He said, "Take care of her as your own mother." From that day on, John took care of her in his own home.

At noon, the sky suddenly became dark. It was as if someone had shut off the sun. The whole earth was under a shroud of darkness. It lasted for three hours.

Then, about three o'clock, Jesus raised His voice and said, "Eloi, Eloi, lama sabachtani?" which in English means, "My God, My God, why have You forsaken Me?"

Someone in the crowd said, "Hey! He's calling for Elijah!"

After this, in fulfillment of Scripture, Jesus, knowing that His work on earth was complete, said, "I'm thirsty!"

Someone grabbed the sponge tied to a stick and dipped it in the bucket of sour wine. Holding it up to Him, the man said, "Now let's see if Elijah comes to rescue Him!"

After Jesus had tasted the wine, He said, "Tetelestai!" meaning, "It is completed!"

One last time, Jesus took a deep breath and said in a loud voice, "Father, into Your hands I commit My spirit!" And having said this, He bowed His head, yielded up His spirit, and breathed His last.

At that moment the darkness lifted and the huge veil in the temple that hid the ark in the Holy of Holies was torn in two from top to bottom. The earth quaked, rocks were split, and graves burst open. These things shook up the crowd, especially the centurion assigned to guard Jesus. Fear gripped many and they beat their chests in despair. The soldier, having heard Jesus' words and seeing how He had died, remarked, "This Man was righteous!" Contemplating the phenomenon of darkness and earthquake, he went on to say, "Surely He was the Son of God!"

Slowly the crowd disbursed to attend to Passover preparations. The Jewish leaders, ever diligent to avoid defiling their holy days, asked if the criminals could be killed quickly so they wouldn't be a distraction during the feast. The leaders were asking the soldiers to break the legs of the crucified men so they could no longer push themselves up for breath.

When the soldiers came to Jesus and saw that He was already dead, they didn't break His legs. But to make sure He was dead, one of them pierced His side with a spear; blood and water gushed out. With that, two more prophecies were fulfilled: "Not one of His bones shall be broken," and "They shall look upon Him whom they pierced."

Several other women were watching the proceedings from a distance, including Mary Magdalene; Mary, the mother of James and Joses; and Salome, the mother of Zebedee's sons.

Evening was fast approaching, so a wealthy member of the Jewish council, Joseph from Arimathea, felt compelled to take care of Jesus' remains. He was an upright man who was looking for the Kingdom of God; he had been a follower of Jesus, but secretly for fear of what the other council members might say. He had not agreed with the Sanhedrin when they condemned Jesus. Knowing that it would expose his loyalty, Joseph gathered his courage and went to Pilate to request permission to take Jesus' body down and to attend to the burial.

When Pilate heard that Jesus was already dead, he was shocked. He summoned the centurion to verify Joseph's statement. Satisfied then that Jesus had died, he gave permission for the body to be turned over to Joseph.

On the way back to Skull Hill, Joseph purchased some linen to use as a wrap. Nicodemus, another council member, the one who had privately approached Jesus at night several years earlier, joined Joseph. He brought along nearly one hundred pounds of ointments and spices, including myrrh and aloes.

Carefully, they took Jesus' body and wrapped it in strips of linen, sprinkling the spices between the layers of cloth according to the custom of the Jews.

Close by the site where the crucifixion had taken place was a private garden owned by Joseph in which he had hewn out a small crypt for himself in the rocky hillside. They laid Jesus' body there and rolled a large stone over the entrance. The nearby location was convenient since the sun was setting and Passover candles were already being lit.

Two of the women mentioned earlier, Mary Magdalene and Mary, Joses' mother, followed the men and watched to see where the body was laid. They, along with Salome, had purchased spices and fragrant oils and planned to return as soon as Sabbath was over to give Jesus a proper burial.

Friday

Early the next morning, the chief priests and Pharisees called on Pilate. "Sir," they explained, "we remember that this Man, this imposter, claimed that He would rise after three days. We need you to secure the tomb. Otherwise His disciples might come and steal the body just so they can perpetuate the myth. If that were to happen, the last deception would be worse than the first."

"All right then, go," Pilate replied. "Take what you need to make it as secure as you can."

So they went and sealed up the tomb and posted guards.

Jesus' Resurrection and Beyond

Before daybreak on the Sunday morning after the Sabbath, Mary Magdalene, the other Mary, and Salome went to the tomb, bringing the spices they had bought. They were primarily concerned with who could help them roll the large stone away from the entrance.

About that time there was a great earthquake. An angel of the Lord had descended from heaven in blazing brightness and rolled the stone back exposing the tomb. In great fear the guards were stunned and fell down as though dead.

As the women approached the spot, they looked up and saw that the stone had already been rolled away; and sitting on top of the rock was the angel in his long white robe. The women were terrified and were about to run when the angel said, "Why are you looking for the living among the dead? Don't be afraid. I know you are looking for Jesus of Nazareth who was crucified. He is not here, for He has risen as He said.

"Remember how He explained all this to you back in Galilee, saying, 'The Son of Man must be delivered into the hands of sinful men, and be crucified, and the third day rise again.' Come, see the place where they laid Him. Then go quickly, find His disciples, especially Peter, and give them the good news!"

The women entered the tomb, completely bewildered as to what had happened. Suddenly a couple of angels stood beside them in shining garments. The women bowed low in fear. Another angel sat on the right side of the ledge where Jesus' body had lain. This angel, too, told them not to be alarmed, repeating the message that Jesus was alive, risen from the dead. "See, this is the place where they laid Him," the angel said. And indeed, there was no body there. They recalled what Jesus had told them and hurried as fast as they could to tell the disciples. Never in their lives had they felt such intense joy mixed with fear!

Now, while they were looking for the disciples, the guards were reporting to the chief priests what had just happened. Quickly the priests assembled with the elders and decided to bribe the soldiers into saying that they had fallen asleep and that Jesus' disciples had come during the night and stolen the body. Ordinarily this breach of duty would have meant certain death for careless guards; but the Pharisees assured them that if the governor ever heard about it, they would pay him off and there would be no reprisal.

The men took the money and spread their alibi so effectively that people today still believe the lie.

Mary Magdalene found Peter and John, the beloved disciple, and told them that the body was gone. Before she had time to tell the whole story, they started running for the tomb.

John got to the tomb first and could see the pile of linens, but he didn't go in. When Peter got there, he ran right in to investigate. He saw the pile of linens that had been wrapped around the body and, off to the side, the handkerchief that had been wrapped around Jesus' head. It had been carefully folded before being placed there. John followed him in and believed Jesus was alive even though he didn't yet understand from Scripture that He must rise from the dead.

The disciples returned to their homes, astonished and mystified.

By this time, Mary Magdalene had returned to the garden tomb. She looked inside and saw two angels inside, one at the head and the other at the foot of the ledge where the body of Jesus had been laid.

"Woman," they inquired, "why are you weeping?"

She answered them, "Because someone has taken away my Lord, and I don't know where they have laid Him."

Then, out of the corner of her eye, she saw someone coming up behind her. Assuming it was a gardener, she begged Him, "Sir, if you have carried Him away, tell me where you have laid Him and I will take care of the body."

Blinded by her tears and consumed with grief, she hadn't recognized that it was, in fact, Jesus she was speaking with. But then she heard His voice.

Jesus said to her, "Mary!"

She turned to look at Him more closely and exclaimed, "Rabboni!" (This is Aramaic for "Teacher.")

"Don't cling to Me," Jesus said. "Go tell My brothers that I am ascending to My Father and your Father, to My God and your God."

Mary met up with several of the other women and went to tell all the disciples what had happened. Along the way, Jesus appeared to them and said, "Yes, rejoice!"

The women fell at His feet and worshiped. Then Jesus said, "Don't be afraid. Tell My brethren I'll meet them in Galilee."

However, when the women had told the whole story to the disciples, they wouldn't believe them. It sounded like a fairy tale.

That afternoon, two of them were heading to their home in Emmaus, a village about seven miles from Jerusalem. They talked over the bizarre events of the week and tried to make sense of this new report from the women.

Jesus came up alongside them, but for some reason they didn't recognize Him. "What is all this I hear you talking about?" He asked. "And why are you so sad?"

One of the two, whose name was Cleopas, answered Him, "Have You not been around Jerusalem this weekend? Are You the only one who hasn't heard the news?"

"What news?" Jesus inquired.

So they poured out the details. "We're talking about Jesus of Nazareth, a tremendous prophet whose teachings and miracles were praised all over the country. We really thought He was going to be the One to deliver Israel from oppression, but the chief priests and our rulers had Him condemned to death. He was crucified just three days ago.

"But that's not all! Earlier today, some women we know went to the tomb; and, well, You're not going to believe this, but they said that some angels appeared and told them that Jesus was alive. A couple of the guys ran to check it out; and sure enough, the tomb was open and empty, but they never saw Jesus."

"Oh, you just don't get it, do you?" Jesus remarked. "You can't seem to wrap your minds around what the prophets have been saying down through history. Didn't they state clearly that the Messiah would first suffer and then enter His glory?"

For the next few miles, Jesus explained the Scriptures to them from Moses to Malachi, highlighting every passage which pointed to Him.

They were nearly home, and Jesus indicated that He would be traveling on. They begged Him to join them for dinner, saying, "Please, won't You stay with us? It is nearly evening already."

So Jesus accompanied them into the house. During the meal, He picked up the bread, blessed and broke it, and handed each of them a piece. At that moment their eyes were opened and they recognized that it was Him. In that same moment, He vanished from their sight.

"Unbelievable!" one exclaimed. "Did you feel what I felt along the road as He explained the Scriptures?"

"Yes, it was like my heart was on fire!"

They couldn't contain themselves. They hurried out and retraced their steps all the way back to Jerusalem to find the other disciples. Most of the disciples, plus a few others, were gathered together, doors tightly bolted shut for fear of what the Jewish leaders might do next.

The two from Emmaus were ushered in. They could hardly keep themselves from shouting, "It's true! The Lord is really alive! He appeared to Simon and now to us!" They went on to describe the remarkable conversation along the road and that amazing moment when they recognized Him in the breaking of the bread.

Suddenly, while they were all discussing these extraordinary reports, Jesus Himself entered the room, but not through the door. He just appeared in the middle of the room.

"Shalom!" He said. "Look, it is really Me!" He showed them the scars where the nails had penetrated His skin.

They were all terrified, thinking that it was a ghost or apparition.

"Really," Jesus assured them, "you can touch Me; I'm real. A spirit wouldn't have flesh and bones, would it?"

They couldn't believe their eyes. But they couldn't deny what they were seeing. Like the women at the tomb that morning, the disciples were filled with the conflicting emotions of joy and fear.

Then Jesus said, "Have you got anything to eat here?" They gave Him a piece of broiled fish and some honeycomb. He ate it and they watched in wonder at the sight. Then He rebuked the men for not believing the reports the women had brought earlier in the day.

Thomas, also called Didymus, wasn't at this gathering; and when the rest of them reported about Jesus' appearance, he stated categorically that he would not believe until he had personally put his finger through the nail prints in Jesus' hands and stuck his hand in the place where the spear had pierced Jesus' side. He was in for a surprise eight days later when they were all together again. Just like the last time, with the doors fastened securely, Jesus appeared right in the middle of the room.

He motioned to Thomas, "Come, friend. Put your finger here," He said, stretching out His hands. "Stick your hand in My side if you want to. Whatever it takes, be done with unbelief!"

Thomas melted. "My Lord and my God!" was all he could say.

Jesus addressed him again, saying, "Thomas, now that you can see for yourself, you believe. Blessed are all who believe even though they haven't seen what you've seen."

One day, a few of them, including Simon Peter, Thomas, Nathanael, the sons of Zebedee, and a couple others, were together when Peter said, "I'm going fishing!" The rest decided to go along.

They took out the boat and spent the whole night without any success at all. Early the next morning as they approached the shore, someone (they couldn't tell that it was Jesus) called out and asked, "Any fish?"

"Not a one!" was their answer.

"If you try once more and put the nets down on the right side, you'll find some!"

What did they have to lose? Hadn't this happened once before? They followed the suggestion and such a huge number of fish suddenly filled the net that they couldn't get it into the boat. John looked over at Peter and said, "It's the Lord!"

When Peter heard it was the Lord, he quickly put on his tunic, jumped overboard, and swam to meet Him. They were just a hundred yards or so from shore.

The rest of them slowly rowed toward land, dragging the heavy net. They were surprised to find a nice campfire with some fish already cooking and some bread. "Bring Me a few of those you just caught, men," Jesus said.

Peter helped them bring the net onto shore, and they just had to count this record-breaking catch — one hundred and fifty-three! There was more than one miracle that morning: even with such a huge catch, the net didn't break!

"Time to eat!" Jesus announced. Then He distributed the fresh-cooked fish and bread. This was the third time He had appeared to them since He had risen from the dead.

After breakfast, Jesus took Simon Peter aside. "Simon, son of Jonah, do you love Me more than these?"

"Yes, Lord, You know that I love You!" Peter answered.

"Then feed My lambs," Jesus told him.

"But are you sure that you love Me, Simon?" Jesus asked a second time.

"Yes, Lord, You know that I love You!" Peter replied.

"Take care of My sheep" was Jesus' instruction to him.

And then a third time Jesus asked, "Simon, son of Jonah, do you love Me as a friend?"

Peter was upset that Jesus had repeated the question a third time and answered, "Lord, You know all things; You know how much I love You."

Again, Jesus reiterated His directive for Peter, "Feed My sheep." Then Jesus added, "I want you to know this: as a young, independent man, you dress yourself and go wherever you want to; but when you are old, it won't be that way. You will stretch out your hands, and someone else will dress you and take you places you don't want to go." With these words, Jesus was indicating by what kind of death Peter would honor God. "Just keep following Me," Jesus said.

Peter turned and saw John nearby and asked Jesus what was going to happen to him.

Jesus smiled and said, "If I decide to keep him alive until I return, what difference will that make to you? You just keep following Me."

Later on, from that statement a rumor started circulating that John was not going to die, but that wasn't what Jesus had said. John did end up outliving the others and was one of the four who left us a reliable record of Jesus' life.

Sometime later Jesus sent the Eleven to a nearby mountain. When Jesus got there, they worshiped Him; but some still struggled with doubts.

"Shalom!" Jesus said. "God's peace to you! Receive the Holy Spirit." And He breathed on them, commissioning them, saying, "All authority in heaven and on earth has been given to Me. Just as the Father sent Me, now I am sending you. Go into the whole world proclaiming My message, making disciples, and baptizing all who believe into the name of the Father, and of the Son, and of the Holy Spirit. Teach them how to live this new life just as I have instructed you. Powerful signs will accompany your message. If you forgive the sins of any, they will be forgiven; if you retain the sins of any, they will be retained. Know that I am there with you every step of the way, right to the end of the age."

There were many other things Jesus did which were not included in this book. To attempt to describe them all would, I suppose, more than fill all the libraries of the world. These have been recorded to help convince you that Jesus is the true Messiah. And when you believe, you receive life in His name.

THE SEQUEL
(ACTS OF THE APOSTLES)

This New Testament book was Luke's record of events following the ascension of Jesus Christ. It chronicles the beginning stages of the church and describes the expansion from Jerusalem outward.

Luke had written an earlier record of the earthly life, death, and resurrection of Christ. Apparently an influential man by the name of Theophilus requested these journals of events that had changed the course of history.

Read it and imagine yourself in the scenes. The book of Acts ends rather abruptly, leading many to believe that it is an unfinished work, still being written today with the lives of ordinary people like you and me.

THE ASCENSION AND WAITING

Dear Theophilus,

I am compelled to offer you this historical supplement to my previous work which provided an orderly record of the life and teachings of Jesus. As you will soon see, His story continues.

After Jesus' suffering and death, He showed Himself to His followers, leaving no doubt in their minds that He had, in fact, risen from the dead. This was no one-time apparition. He appeared many times over the next forty days and discussed with them matters related to the Kingdom of God.

During one of their last meals together, Jesus specifically instructed His disciples to stay in Jerusalem and wait until the Holy Spirit came, initiating them into their new life. "Remember My Father's promise to you," He told them. "John used to baptize with water, but in a few days you will be baptized with the Holy Spirit."

The disciples, trying to figure out what that meant, asked, "Lord, does that mean You are ready to restore the Kingdom to Israel now?"

"I've told you before that only the Father knows when He plans to bring an end to the current era," Jesus explained. "The purpose for sending the Spirit is to empower you as My chosen witnesses. You will carry My message from here in Jerusalem, throughout Judea and Samaria, and then to the far corners of the earth."

Jesus had barely finished this commission when He began to ascend up into the clouds. The disciples stood staring up to where He had disappeared from sight. Suddenly someone was standing beside them on the Mount of Olives who asked, "Men of Galilee, why are you standing here looking up into the sky? This very Jesus who has been taken up from you into Heaven will come back in just the same way as you have seen Him go." They turned to see two men in dazzling white robes. Just as suddenly, they were gone.

What to do now? The eleven disciples, Peter, John, James, Andrew, Philip, Thomas, Bartholomew, Matthew, James the son of Alphaeus, Simon the Patriot, and Judas the son of James, returned the half-mile to Jerusalem and gathered in the upper room where they had been staying. Every day they met in the temple together with several of the women who had followed Jesus, and also Jesus' brothers and his mother Mary. For the next ten days they devoted themselves to waiting on the Lord in prayer.

At one point Peter stood to make a proposal. To the assembled company of one hundred twenty followers he said, "My brothers, we have witnessed the fulfillment of the prophecy of Scripture given through the Holy Spirit by the lips of David. Judas, who was counted as one of us and ministered alongside us, betrayed Jesus that night in the garden when he led the troops there to arrest Him. We know what happened to him: His own life ended in disgrace in the field bought with the blood money of betrayal. All of Jerusalem is aware of it and calls the place Akeldama or 'Field of Blood.'

"The psalmist also declared, 'Let his home be abandoned, so that no one lives there,' and 'Let someone else fill his position.' In light of that," Peter concluded, "we need to choose a successor. It has to be someone who has been alongside us faithfully the whole time, from the day the Lord Jesus was baptized right up to a few days ago when He was taken up from us. The man we choose must also be an eye-witness of the Lord's resurrection."

Two of the men present fit those qualifications; so they set before them Joseph, who was called Barsabbas by some and Justus by others, and Matthias. Then they prayed, "O Lord, You alone know the hearts of all. Show us which of these You have chosen to fill the role which Judas, the traitor, abandoned in order to go where he belongs." Then they cast lots and it fell to Matthias who from then on was counted among the apostles along with the original Eleven.

THE HOLY SPIRIT COMES UPON
THE JEWISH BELIEVERS

These prayer gatherings continued day after day. On Sunday morning, the day of Pentecost, they had met at the temple for prayer when suddenly the place was filled with the sound of a mighty rushing wind from heaven. Then, right before their eyes, a burning tongue-shaped flame of fire settled above the head of each person. They were all filled with the Holy Spirit, and He caused them to speak in different languages.

It just so happened that devout Jews from around the world were gathered there for the feast. Many hurried to the area where this phenomenon was occurring. As they listened, each heard the message of Jesus in their own mother tongue. They were shocked and filled with awe. There were folks from Mesopotamia, Judea, Cappadocia, Pontus, Asia, Phrygia, Pamphylia, Egypt and other parts of Africa. In the crowd were Parthians, Medes, and Elamites, as well as visitors from Rome, Crete, and Arabia. "Aren't those guys from Galilee? How is it possible that we are all hearing the same message about

God's mighty deeds yet in dozens of very different languages?" they asked in astonishment. "What on earth is going on here?"

Some onlookers suggested that the group had gotten drunk and were just blabbering; but Peter stood and spoke so all could hear, "Men of Judea, residents of Jerusalem, hear what I have to say! These men are not drunk. Why, it's only nine o'clock in the morning. What you are experiencing is nothing less than the fulfillment of Joel's prophecy.

"Hear the Word of the Lord: 'And it shall be in the last days that I will pour out My Spirit upon all mankind. Your sons and daughters will prophesy, your young men will see visions, and your old men will dream dreams. I will even pour My Spirit on slaves and servants, men and women alike, who also will prophesy.

"'Heaven and earth will erupt in signs and wonders: blood, fire, and smoke, the sun darkened and the moon turned blood-red. Then the magnificent Day of the Lord will come, and whoever calls on the name of the Lord will be rescued.'

"Now, people of Israel, hear me out! As you well know, Jesus of Nazareth lived among us and, with power given to Him by God, performed miracles, signs, and wonders. But you, using the arm of godless Rome, nailed Him to a cross and murdered Him. God knew you would do that; He had it all worked out in advance.

"God raised Him to life, defeating death in the process. David testifies in Psalm 16 that it was impossible for the Lord to be held in the grave: 'The Lord is always present with Me, even at My right hand, that I may not be shaken. That is why My heart rejoiced and My tongue sang for joy. My flesh can rest in hope, because You will not leave My soul in Hades, nor will You allow Your Holy One to see corruption. You lead Me into life; You make Me truly happy in Your presence.'

"Now, brethren, we all know that David was not speaking about his own body in these verses. We know where his grave is right here in Jerusalem. So to whom was he referring?

"The fact is that David was a prophet. He knew that God had promised a descendant of his who would reign forever, and in this psalm David spoke of the resurrection of that Messiah. This Messiah, who was not abandoned in death and whose body could not decay, is none other than Jesus. Yes, God raised Him up. Every one you see standing here is an eye-witness of that fact!

"Not only is He alive and well, but just as He promised, He has taken the place of honor at the right hand of the Father and poured out His Spirit on us this very day, which is what you are witnessing.

"Hear again the words of David, 'The Lord said to my Lord, "Sit at My right hand until I make Your enemies Your foot-stool."' Now David, as we know, never ascended to Heaven. He was, again, writing prophetically concerning the Messiah.

"What does all this mean? Listen, nation of Israel! Know beyond the shadow of a doubt that this same Jesus, whom you crucified, is our Messiah and has been declared by God to be Lord of all."

Peter's scathing exposé pierced their hearts and they cried out, "Brothers, now what do we do?"

Peter answered, "You must confess what you have done, turn away from your sin, and every one of you must be baptized in the name of Jesus Christ. Then your sins will be forgiven and you too will receive the gift of the Holy Spirit. This incredible promise is available to you and your children — yes, and for all who are far away, for as many as the Lord our God shall call to Himself!" Peter spoke at length and explained further, urging them to escape from their perverted generation.

The crowd received the message with open arms. Some three thousand were baptized and added to the number of Christ-followers that first day. They returned to the temple daily to learn more from the apostles and bonded deeply as they opened their homes to each other, sharing meals and praying together.

Everyone felt a deep sense of awe at what God was doing. In addition to the miracles being performed by the apostles, a new sense of community began to form as those with property or possessions sold them to meet the needs of others. Praising God for their new-found joy, they shared everything in common. These developments caught the attention of many others, and every day the Lord added more people to the ranks of the "saved."

One afternoon Peter and John were on their way to the temple for the three o'clock hour of prayer. Included in the crowd was a man who had been lame from birth. Every day his friends would carry him to a spot near the Beautiful Gate of the temple so that he could beg from the people as they went in. When he saw Peter and John passing by, he asked them for a donation.

Peter and John looked intently at the man and Peter said, "Look at us!" So he did, hoping to get a gift. "I know you're expecting us to hand you some money," Peter said to him, "but we don't have any. I can give you something, though. In the name of Jesus Christ of Nazareth, get up and walk!"

Peter took him by the right hand and helped him up. Immediately his feet and ankles were strengthened. He jumped to his feet, stood there for a moment, and then began walking and even leaping. Unable to contain himself, he accompanied Peter and John into the temple, shouting praises to God.

Everyone could see that this was the same beggar who used to sit at the Beautiful Gate. They were amazed by what had happened to him. While the man clung to Peter and John, a huge crowd gathered around them on Solomon's Portico.

Peter took advantage of the impromptu meeting and said:

> "Men of Israel, why are you so surprised at this, and why are you staring at us as though we possess some supernatural power or ability? No, the God of Abraham and Isaac and Jacob, the God of our fathers, is the One who has healed this man.

> "He did it to call your attention to His Servant, Jesus — yes, Jesus — whom you handed over to Pilate and disowned even while Pilate was anxious to release Him. You, brethren, turned your back on the Holy and Righteous One, preferring instead

the murderer Barabbas. You killed the Prince of Life; but God raised Him from the dead, a fact of which we are eye-witnesses.

"It is the name of this same Jesus that has cured this lame man because we believe the truth about Him. Do you understand? It is our trust in Christ that restored this man to perfect health as you can clearly see.

"Brothers, I realize that you had no idea what you were doing any more than your leaders did. But just as God had foretold through all His prophets, the Messiah had to suffer. It has all been fulfilled.

"Now you must repent of your willful rejection and turn to God so that your sins may be wiped out and your souls may enjoy rich times of refreshment that come down from the presence of God. Only then will He send back Jesus, your Messiah. For now, He must remain in Heaven until that universal restoration which God promised in ancient times through all His holy prophets.

"Moses, for instance, said, 'The Lord your God will raise up for you a Prophet like me from your brethren. You'd better listen to what He says because anyone who rejects Him will be destroyed.' And Moses was only the first of a long line of prophets through whom God foretold the events we've just experienced.

"Listen! Don't squander the incredible advantage you've been given: You are the very descendants of those prophets. You are heirs of the original agreement God made with our forefathers when He said to Abraham, 'In your seed will all the families of the earth be blessed.'

"God sent His servant Jesus to you first after He raised Him to life. God is now offering to rescue you from your evil ways."

While they were still talking to the people, the priests, the captain of the temple guard, and the Sadducees approached them. The Sadducees, who deny the concept of resurrection and life after death, were furious that Jesus' followers were teaching the masses about His resurrection. So they had them arrested and held in jail until the next morning.

That didn't stop the people from believing, however. In just a matter of days there were nearly five thousand who had embraced the message.

The next day Jesus' apostles were questioned by the leading members of the Council. The elders and scribes were there along with Annas the High Priest, Caiaphas, John, Alexander, and the whole of the High Priest's family. "Who gave you authority and where did you get the power to heal this man?" they asked.

Peter, filled with the Holy Spirit, responded by saying, "Leaders of the people and elders, apparently we are being interrogated today because of a kindness done to this handicapped man. You want to know how he was healed? Well, it is high time that all of you and the entire nation of Israel knew that it was done in the name of Jesus Christ of Nazareth — yes, the very One whom you crucified but whom God raised from the dead! It is by His power that this man stands here perfectly restored. Jesus Christ, the 'stone rejected by you builders, has become the Chief Cornerstone.' The fact is that He alone can rescue men from their helpless condition; in His name alone is there any hope of deliverance."

The Council was thrown off-guard by the boldness and competence of Peter and John, mere fishermen who were obviously uneducated and untrained. They recognized them as men who had traveled with Jesus. Because the man who had been cured was standing right there, they didn't know what to do. So they ordered them out of the Sanhedrin in order to discuss it among themselves.

"What are we going to do with these men?" they asked each other. "Everyone in Jerusalem knows that they've performed this miracle, and there's nothing we can do about it. But we've got to do something to prevent any more of this kind of thing. Let's warn them not to say anything more to anyone in this name or there will be severe consequences."

The disciples were called back in and commanded not to speak one more word about the name of Jesus, but Peter and John weren't about to be swayed by their threats. "You're going to have to decide," they answered, "whether it is right in the eyes of God for us to obey what you say rather than what He says. We cannot help talking about our experience!"

All that the Council could do at that point was to threaten them because the people were thrilled with the healing of this poor man who had suffered for over forty years. Everyone was praising God! Everyone, that is, except for the Jewish religious leaders.

Immediately upon being released, the two apostles went back to their friends and reported to them what the chief priests and elders had said. You might think that some would have been frightened, but just listen to what they did. Upon hearing the report, the believers raised their voices in prayer:

"Ah, Lord God, Maker of heaven and earth and the sea and all that is in them, You are not moved by the futile threats of men! You declared through Your servant David in Psalm 2, 'Why do the nations rage and the people waste their time with futile plans? The kings and rulers of the earth conspire together against the Lord and against His Christ.'

"Yes, that is what happened to Your holy servant Jesus whom You anointed. Herod and Pontius Pilate along with the Gentiles and the people of Israel all gathered together to accomplish precisely what Your hand and Your purpose determined beforehand had to be done.

"Now, Sovereign Lord, You have heard their threats. Would You give us, Your servants, fresh boldness to declare Your Word? Would You confirm the message by stretching out Your hand to heal? Grant that mighty signs and wonders may be done through the name of Your holy servant Jesus."

And God responded. When they finished praying, the meeting place was shaken; they were all filled with the Holy Spirit and spoke the Word of God fearlessly. The apostles testified forcefully as they proclaimed the resurrection of the Lord Jesus.

An extraordinary unity and love pervaded the large group of Christ-followers. They were so focused on one purpose that they willingly shared all their possessions in common. Such a spirit of generosity existed that no one experienced need. Any who owned property sold it and brought the proceeds to the apostles for them to distribute as needed.

One brother by the name of Barnabas sold his farm and brought the money to the apostles. Another couple, Ananias and Sapphira, wanting to give the impression that they were just as generous, sold their property but kept back part of the proceeds for their own use, pretending they were giving it all. However, when Ananias brought the money to Peter, Peter confronted him, saying, "Ananias, how is it that Satan has convinced you to cheat the Holy Spirit and keep back for yourself part of the price of the land? Before the land was sold, it was yours; and after the sale you were free to do whatever you pleased with the money. What has come over you? You have not lied to men, but to God!"

Upon hearing Peter's words, Ananias collapsed and died. Fear struck everyone in the room. Some young men got to their feet and after wrapping up his body carried him out and buried him. About three hours later Ananias' wife came in not knowing what had taken place. Peter spoke directly to her, "Tell me, did you sell your land for so much?"

"Yes," she answered, "that was the price."

Then Peter said to her, "How could the two of you have agreed to test the Spirit of the Lord like this? Listen, I hear the footsteps of the men who have just buried your husband coming back through the door. Now they will carry you out." Immediately she collapsed and died. When the young men came into the room, they saw her lying dead at Peter's feet. They carried her out and buried her beside her husband. The whole community of believers, indeed everyone who heard about it, was filled with holy fear.

What unforgettable days those were. There were so many gathering together that they decided to meet regularly in Solomon's Porch. They gained the respect of the public at large, but fear prevented casual onlookers from joining out of curiosity. Still, large numbers of men and women believed and the congregation multiplied.

With reports of ongoing miracles, many brought their sick into the streets and laid them down on mats so that Peter's shadow might fall upon some of them. A steady flow of people from outlying villages brought their sick or demonized loved ones, and they were all cured.

This was too much for the High Priest and the Sadducees. Jealous of the popularity of this new movement, they had the apostles arrested and put in jail.

But during the night an angel of the Lord opened the prison doors and led them out, saying, "Go, stand and speak in the temple. Tell the people the whole message about this new life!"

So early the next morning they entered the temple and began to teach. Meanwhile, the High Priest convened the Sanhedrin and the whole senate of the people of Israel. He then sent word to the jail to have the apostles brought in. Of course, when the officers arrived at the prison, they could not find them there. They came back with this report: "We found the prison securely locked and the guard standing on duty at the doors; but when we opened up, we found no one inside."

When the captain of the temple guard and the chief priests heard their report, they were extremely troubled and wondered what on earth would happen next. Just then someone arrived and reported to them, "Did you know that the men you put in jail are back in the temple teaching again?"

The captain and officers proceeded to the temple to apprehend them yet again. They knew they couldn't use force lest the masses should stone them. The apostles complied and willingly took their stand before the Sanhedrin. The High Priest addressed them, saying, "We gave you the strictest possible orders to stop teaching in this name. Now look what you've done — you have filled Jerusalem with your teaching, and we understand that you are saying we're responsible for this Man's blood!"

Peter and the apostles answered him, "We simply must obey God rather than men. We're talking about the same God whom our fathers worshiped. He raised Jesus to life after you murdered Him on that cross. Not only did God resurrect Him, He then gave Him the seat of honor as Prince and Conqueror at His right hand. He did all this to make it possible for His people Israel to repent and receive the forgiveness of their sins. We aren't making this up; we are eye-witnesses of the whole thing. God's Spirit, given to anyone who embraces the message, also bears witness to the truth of our testimony."

This mini-sermon didn't set well with the Council. In fact, they were so furious they wanted to kill the apostles on the spot. Gamaliel, a Pharisee and senior member of the Council, highly respected by all, ordered that the apostles be taken out of the room for a few minutes.

Then he addressed the assembly: "Men of Israel, be careful how you handle this! Let me remind you of a couple similar situations in recent years. Do you recall that fellow named Theudas who made some outlandish claims and succeeded in rallying about four hundred men to follow him? Once he was killed, all his followers dispersed and the movement came to nothing. After that, in the days of the census, a Galilean named Judas showed up and enticed a bunch of people to follow him. But he too died and his whole following scattered. That's why I think we should just leave this group alone. If their teaching or movement is merely human, it will dissolve in time; but if it should be from God, you can't stop them. What's worse, you might find that you've been fighting against God!"

The group agreed to his advice and called in the apostles. They had them flogged; and after commanding them not to speak in the name of Jesus, they let them go.

The apostles left the proceeding, rejoicing that they been given the privilege of suffering for "The Name." Every day they went to the temple and from house to house boldly proclaiming that Jesus was the Messiah.

As encouraging as the massive influx of new believers was, it created a challenge for the apostles as they attempted to meet the needs of so many. When a complaint surfaced that Jewish widows were being given preferential treatment while the Gentile widows were being slighted, the Twelve realized that they couldn't attend to all these needs and still keep up with their teaching opportunities. So they called the group together and said, "We're finding that managing the benevolence fund is keeping us from proclaiming the Word of God. Something has to be done. We'd like you to look around and pick out from among yourselves seven men of good reputation who are known for their wisdom and who are filled with God's Spirit. We will put them in charge of this matter. Then we'll be able to devote ourselves to prayer and the ministry of the Word."

The whole congregation agreed. After discussion, they chose Stephen, a man known for trusting God and walking in the power of the Holy Spirit; Philip; Prochurus; Nicanor; Timon; Parmenas; and Nicolas of Antioch, a former convert to the Jewish faith. They set these men before the apostles, who, after prayer, laid their hands upon them, commissioning them to this vital ministry.

The Word of God spread further and faster. A large number of priests accepted the message and the number of disciples in Jerusalem increased rapidly.

Stephen, one of the seven chosen to serve the poor, was given unusual power and insights; and he performed miracles among the people. A number of devout Jews, some from a synagogue known as the Libertines, some from synagogues in Cyrene and Alexandria, as well as some from Cilicia and Asia, tried to publicly debate Stephen; but they were no match for his wisdom nor the dominating presence of the Spirit. Desperate to silence Stephen, they bribed some men to testify against him by claiming that he was "blaspheming Moses and God." They also stirred up the religious leaders and some in the crowds, who took hold of him and forcibly dragged him to where the Sanhedrin had gathered.

The false witnesses stated their charges: "This man is constantly speaking against this Holy Place and the Law. We even heard him say that Jesus of Nazareth will destroy this place and change the customs which Moses handed down to us." As these claims were being made, everyone was staring at Stephen whose face had begun to radiate. Witnesses later said he took on the appearance of an angel.

Then the High Priest asked him, "Is what they're saying true?"

And Stephen answered:

"My brothers and my fathers, let me explain. As you know, our glorious God appeared to our forefather Abraham while he was in Mesopotamia before he ever came to live in Haran and said to him, 'Get out of your country, away from your relatives, and come to a land that I will show you.'

"That is why he left the land of the Chaldeans and settled in Haran. After his father's death, God brought him into this very land where you are living today. God promised him that one day his descendants would settle here. This promise was given before Abraham had any children of his own.

"God also explained to Abraham that his offspring would first live as strangers and slaves in a foreign country for four hundred years. 'Then I will judge that nation,' said the Lord, 'and I will lead them safely out to serve Me in this Promised Land.'

"To further distinguish this emerging nation, God introduced the covenant of circumcision; and that is why, when Isaac was born, Abraham circumcised him on the eighth day. Isaac became the father of Jacob; and Jacob, the father of the twelve patriarchs.

"Then began a pattern of Israel rejecting God's provision. You recall, don't you, that the patriarchs, in their jealousy of Joseph, sold him as a slave into Egypt; but God was with him and eventually delivered him from all his troubles, giving him unusual wisdom and favor in the eyes of Pharaoh the king of Egypt. Pharaoh made him governor of Egypt and put him in charge of his entire household.

"Then, when the famine struck the region and our forefathers could find no food, Jacob sent our forefathers into Egypt where there was grain to be had. Later, on their second visit to Egypt, Joseph revealed his identity to his brothers and introduced them to Pharaoh. At Joseph's invitation, Jacob and the entire clan of seventy-five moved to Egypt and lived out their days in that foreign land. When Jacob, and then later, Joseph died, their remains were brought back here to Shechem; they were laid in the tomb which Abraham had purchased from the sons of Hamor.

"As the time drew near for the fulfillment of God's promise to Abraham, our people grew more and more numerous in Egypt. Eventually another king came to the Egyptian throne who knew nothing of Joseph. This man plotted against our people, forcing our forefathers to abandon their infant sons so that the race would be exterminated.

"That was when Moses was born. God looked upon him with great delight. For three months he was cared for in his own home. Eventually his parents attempted to hide him, setting him out in the river in a basket. Pharaoh's daughter found him, adopted him, and brought him up as her own son. This gave Moses access to the finest education and training. He later gained a reputation as a compelling orator as well as a man of action.

"One day Moses, nearing forty years of age, decided it was time to visit his own brothers, the sons of Israel. When he saw one of them being treated harshly, he went to his defense and struck the Egyptian, killing him. In Moses' mind, he saw this as the first step in his role as 'God's chosen deliverer'; and he fully expected his Jewish brothers to rally behind his leadership. He was in for a rude awakening. The very next day, he went to break up a fight between two Jewish workers. 'Men, what are you doing?' he asked. 'No good can come of injuring each other; we need to work together.'

"But the man who was beating the other turned on Moses and pushed him away, saying, 'Who do you think you are? What gives you any right to tell us what to do? I suppose you're going to kill me like you did that Egyptian yesterday, aren't you?'

"That's when Moses realized he was in trouble, so he fled to the land of Midian. While living in exile there, he became the father of two sons.

"Forty years later, in the desert of Mount Sinai, an angel appeared to him in the flames of a burning bush, much to Moses' surprise. As he moved toward the bush to get a closer look, the voice of the Lord spoke to him, saying, 'I am the God of your fathers — the God of Abraham, the God of Isaac, and the God of Jacob.' Then Moses shook with fear; but the Lord spoke to him again and said, 'Take your sandals off your feet, for the place where you stand is holy ground. I have certainly seen the oppression of My people who are in Egypt; I have heard their groaning and have come down to deliver them. Come now, I am sending you to Egypt.'

"It was this Moses . . .

- who was rejected by his own people when they challenged him, saying, 'Who made you a ruler and a judge?'
- whom God had raised up to be their deliverer;
- to whom the angel of the Lord appeared in the bush;
- who performed mighty miracles in Egypt, at the Red Sea, and in the wilderness for forty years;
- who declared, 'The Lord your God will raise up for you a Prophet like me from among your brethren';
- who stood between the congregation and the angel who spoke with him on Mt. Sinai;
- to whom God gave life-giving instructions for His people.

"Yet it was our forefathers . . .

- who turned their backs on Moses and turned a deaf ear to the words from God;
- whose hearts had turned back to Egypt;
- who encouraged Aaron to make a god who could lead them since Moses, who had delivered them from Egypt, was gone so long on the mountain;
- who fashioned a golden calf out of their own possessions and celebrated their accomplishment by offering sacrifices to it;
- who worshiped the stars of heaven rather than worshiping the Creator;
- who were confronted by God through the prophet Amos: 'Was it to My tabernacle you brought all those sacrifices during the forty years in the wilderness? No, you were, in your hearts, offering them up to the tabernacle of Moloch and the star god, Remphan. Therefore I will take you away from this land into Babylon.'

"Even though they had the tabernacle of God . . .

- which was built according to the precise design which God had given to Moses,
- which was carried into this land by our forefathers as God drove out the Gentiles under Joshua,
- which was where Israel met with God right up to the time of David,
- which was replaced by Solomon's temple after David prayed that he might establish a permanent dwelling place for the God of Jacob. Of course, we know that the Most High cannot be contained in anything built by human hands as the prophet Isaiah recorded: 'Heaven is My throne and the earth is My footstool. What kind of house could you build to accommodate Me? Did I not make all these things with My own hands?'

"What is the point of all this? You stubborn people are every bit as bad as your fathers: you constantly resist God's Spirit, refusing to listen to Him or let Him change your hearts. Can you name any prophets whom your fathers didn't persecute? Indeed, they killed anyone who foretold the coming of the Messiah; and now you have betrayed and killed the Righteous One. You had God's Law handed to you by angels and look what you've done with it!"

These concluding remarks infuriated the Council, and they gnashed their teeth in anger. Stephen, however, being filled with the Holy Spirit, was given a vision of heaven as he gazed skyward. "Oh, look!" he exclaimed. "The heavens are open, and I can see the Son of Man standing at God's right hand!"

That was the last straw. The people, plugging their ears and shouting to drown out Stephen's words, grabbed him and dragged him outside the city walls where they began hurling stones upon him. One of the younger Pharisees, a man named Saul, was in hearty agreement with the proceedings. Many, hurrying to participate, left their outer garments in Saul's charge.

As the rocks flew, Stephen called out, "Lord Jesus, receive my spirit!" Then, falling to his knees, he cried out with a loud voice, "Lord, do not hold this sin against them!" Having said that, he collapsed in the sleep of death, the church's first martyr. A handful of devout believers took Stephen's body and buried it with much loud mourning and weeping.

This event touched off a wave of persecution against the church in Jerusalem. The believers, except for the apostles, were forced to flee to the outlying areas of Judea and Samaria. Saul, like a man possessed, ravaged the church as he went from house to house dragging out men and women and throwing them into prison.

The Holy Spirit Comes upon the Samaritans

All this did nothing to stop the message. All who had been scattered began spreading the Good News everywhere they went. Philip, another of the Seven chosen to help the apostles along with Stephen, traveled down to the city of Samaria. As he told the story of Jesus, large crowds listened and watched as evil spirits were cast out and the lame and paralyzed were cured. The whole city was buzzing with excitement.

One of the town's notorieties was a man named Simon, a sorcerer who had impressed the people with his magic acts. People called him "the Great Power of God." As the multitudes heard Philip's message about the Kingdom of God and saw what was done in the name of Jesus Christ, they embraced it and were baptized into the new faith. Simon too believed and was baptized. Then he stayed alongside Philip to see firsthand all the remarkable miracles. He was fascinated by it.

When the apostles in Jerusalem heard reports that Samaria had accepted the Word of God, they sent Peter and John down to check it out. The first thing they did upon arriving was to ask the Lord to pour out His Spirit on them as they had only been baptized in the name of the Lord Jesus. When the apostles laid their hands on the new believers, they received the Spirit. Simon, seeing this phenomenon, offered the apostles some money, saying, "I'd like to have the power you have to give the Holy Spirit to people by laying hands on them."

But Peter said to him, "What are you thinking? If you believe for a moment that you can buy God's gifts, you are in no position to be ministering to others. Your heart is in the wrong place; both you and your money will be destroyed. I can see that you are motivated by jealousy and are full of yourself. You'd better get your thinking turned around and beg God's forgiveness for this sin."

Simon answered humbly, "Oh, please pray to the Lord that this won't happen to me!"

The apostles and Philip spent some time explaining the message more fully before returning to Jerusalem. Along the way they presented the Good News to many Samaritan villages.

But an angel of the Lord said to Philip, "Get up and go down the road which runs from Jerusalem to Gaza out in the desert." So Philip headed south.

It so happened that an Ethiopian official was passing that way in his chariot. This man was the financial manager for Candace, queen of the Ethiopians, and he was on his way home after coming to Jerusalem to worship.

The Spirit said to Philip, "Run up alongside the chariot and listen."

As Philip ran forward, he heard the man reading from the prophet Isaiah. So he said to the Ethiopian, "Do you understand what you are reading?"

The man replied, "Not really. I need someone to explain it." Then he invited Philip to get up and sit beside him. The passage of Scripture he was reading was this: "He was led as a sheep to the slaughter, and like a lamb silent before its shearer, so He opened not His mouth. He was humiliated and denied justice. He was left with no descendants because they took His life."

The official turned to Philip and said, "Can you tell me what this is about? Is Isaiah talking about himself or someone else?"

Starting with these verses, Philip told him the story of Jesus. Before long they came to a place where there was some water and the man said, "Look, here is water. Is there any reason why I should not be baptized right now?"

He ordered the chariot to stop. The two of them went down to the water and Philip baptized him. When they came up out of the water, the Spirit of the Lord took Philip away suddenly; the man never saw him again. He proceeded on his journey, his heart full of joy.

Philip found himself at Azotus. As he passed through the countryside, he went on telling the Good News in all the cities until he came to Caesarea.

Meanwhile, back in Jerusalem, Saul continued his rampage against the Lord's disciples. Knowing that the message was spreading, he obtained letters from the High Priest authorizing him to investigate the synagogues in Damascus. His plan was to arrest any followers of The Way, men or women, and haul them back to Jerusalem as prisoners.

Somewhere along the way everything changed. They were not far from Damascus when a blinding light, like lightning, blazed around him and he fell to the ground. Then he heard a voice speaking to him, "Saul, Saul, why are you persecuting Me?"

"Who are You, Lord?" he asked.

"I am Jesus whom you are persecuting," was the reply. "But now stand up and go into the city. There you will be told what you must do."

The rest of the entourage stood there in stunned silence. They too had heard the voice but couldn't see who was speaking. Saul got up from the ground; but when he opened his eyes, he couldn't see anything. His companions took him by the hand and led him on into Damascus where he remained sightless for three days. During that time he fasted, having nothing to eat or drink.

One of Jesus' followers by the name of Ananias lived in Damascus. The Lord appeared to him in a dream and called him by name. "I am here, Lord," he replied.

Then the Lord said to him, "Get up and go down to Straight Street to the house of Judas. Ask there for a man named Saul from Tarsus.

Saul is praying; and I have given him a vision of a man by the name of Ananias coming into the house, placing his hands upon him, and restoring his sight."

But Ananias replied, "Lord, I have heard about him and all the trouble he has caused the believers in Jerusalem! We've heard that he has permission from the chief priests to arrest every one of us who call on Your name."

But the Lord said to him, "Go! I have chosen him to be the one who will take My name to the Gentiles and their kings, as well as to the sons of Israel. And I will show him how much suffering he will endure for My name's sake."

So Ananias made his way to Judas' house. There he laid his hands upon Saul, saying, "Brother Saul, the Lord Jesus, who appeared to you, has sent me here so that your sight may be restored and that you may be filled with the Holy Spirit."

Immediately something like scales fell from Saul's eyes and he could see again. He got to his feet and was baptized. After eating a meal, he regained his strength. Saul stayed in Damascus for some time, enjoying fellowship with the believers and preaching in all the synagogues that Jesus is the Son of God.

The Jewish congregation was dumbfounded, saying to one another, "Isn't this the guy who fought so hard against the Name in Jerusalem? Didn't he come here to arrest all who identify with Jesus and take them back to the chief priests?" But Saul became increasingly effective in proving that Jesus was the Messiah. The Jews living in Damascus could not refute his claim.

After several days of this the Jews plotted to kill Saul, but he got wind of it and made plans to leave. Guards watched the gates of the city day and night to prevent his escape; so in the middle of the night, he got some of his disciples to let him down through an opening in the wall, lowering him in a large basket.

Saul returned to Jerusalem and tried to join the disciples, but they were all afraid of him. They couldn't believe his claim to be a disciple. Barnabas, however, believed him and introduced him to the apostles. He spoke in Saul's defense, explaining that Saul had seen the Lord on his journey, that the Lord had spoken to him, and that he had spoken in Damascus with great boldness in the name of Jesus.

From that point on, Saul worked alongside them in Jerusalem, preaching fearlessly in the name of the Lord. He used to debate with the Greek-speaking Jews until they made several attempts on his life. Finally the threats prompted the brothers to take Saul to Caesarea and send him off to Tarsus.

Thus began a season of relative peace for the church as it became established throughout the region. The number of believers increased, and they continued in great reverence for the Lord and enjoyed the companionship of the Holy Spirit.

Now Peter, in the course of his travels, came to visit the believers in Lydda. There he found a man named Aeneas who had been paralyzed and bedridden for eight years. Peter said to him, "Aeneas, Jesus Christ heals you! Get up and roll up your bed."

He got to his feet at once. This miracle caused a major revival. Everyone living in Lydda and Sharon turned to the Lord when they heard about it.

Meanwhile in Joppa a disciple by the name of Tabitha became very sick and died. She was deeply loved, for her life had been fully devoted to serving others and helping the poor. They washed her body and laid her in an upper room. Now Lydda is quite near Joppa. So when the disciples heard that Peter was in Lydda, they sent two men to him and begged him, "Please come quickly!"

Peter hurried back with them. When he arrived in Joppa, they took him to the room where she lay. With much weeping, the gathered mourners showed Peter all the dresses and cloaks which she had made for them. Peter asked everyone to leave the room, and he knelt down and prayed. Then he turned to the body and said, "Tabitha, get up!"

She opened her eyes. As soon as she saw Peter, she sat up. He took her by the hand, helped her to her feet, and then called out to the believers and widows, presenting her to them alive. Here, as in Lydda, the miracle became known and many believed in the Lord. Peter himself remained there for some time, residing in the home of a tanner named Simon.

The Holy Spirit Comes upon the Gentiles

Some distance north of Joppa, in Caesarea, lived a man by the name of Cornelius, a centurion in what was called the Italian Regiment. He and his entire household were known for their devout reverence for God. He cared for the poor and was a real man of prayer. About three o'clock one afternoon an angel of God appeared to him in a vision. As the angel approached him, he called him by name, "Cornelius!"

Shaking with fear, Cornelius replied, "Yes, sir?"

The angel went on, "God has heard your prayers and seen your deeds of charity. Now send men to Joppa for a man called Simon, who is also known as Peter. He is staying as a guest with another Simon, a tanner, whose house is down by the sea."

Immediately, when the angel had gone, Cornelius called for two of his house servants and a devout soldier who was one of his personal attendants. He told them the whole story and then sent them off to Joppa.

On the following day as the group was nearing Joppa, Peter had gone up to the rooftop deck to pray. He became quite hungry and asked for some lunch. While it was being prepared, he fell into a trance and had a vision of the sky opening and a great sheet, held at its corners, descending to where he was. On the sheet were all manner of animals, reptiles, and birds. Then Peter heard a voice, saying, "Get up, Peter, kill and eat!"

It so happened that all the creatures on the sheet were things God's Law given in the Old Testament had forbidden His people to eat. Repulsed by the idea, Peter said, "Never, Lord! For not once in my life have I ever eaten anything common or unclean."

Then the voice spoke to him a second time, "You must not call unclean what God has cleansed."

Three times the vision was repeated before being taken back into Heaven. While Peter was still trying to figure out what the vision meant, the men sent by Cornelius had arrived and were standing at the very doorway of the house, calling out to inquire if Simon, sur-named Peter, was staying there. Peter was lost in his thoughts when the Spirit said to him, "Three men are here looking for you. Get up and go downstairs. Don't hesitate to go with them because I Myself have sent them to you."

So Peter went down to the men and said, "I believe you are look-ing for me. What can I do for you?"

They replied, "Cornelius the centurion, an upright and God-fearing man, who is loved and respected by all the Jews, was com-manded by a holy angel to send for you to come to his house that he might hear your message."

Peter invited them in and they spent the night there. Early the next morning, accompanied by some of the brothers from Joppa, Peter set out for Caesarea, arriving on the following day. Corne-lius was waiting anxiously for them and had gathered together all his relations and close friends. When Peter arrived at the house, Cornelius fell on his knees before him and began worshiping him. But Peter helped him to his feet and said, "Stand up, I am just a man like you!"

Upon entering the house, Peter found that a large number of people had assembled. He began by explaining, "You all know that it is forbidden for a Jew to associate with or enter the home of a non-Jew. But God has shown me plainly that no man must be called 'common' or 'unclean.' That is why I came here without hesitation. Now tell me your side of the story."

Cornelius said, "Four days ago, about this time, I was observing the afternoon hour of prayer in my house when suddenly a man in shining clothes stood before me and said, 'Cornelius, your prayer has been heard and your charitable gifts have been remembered before God. Now send to Joppa and invite here a man called Simon Peter. He is staying in the house of a tanner by the name of Simon, down by the sea.' So I sent to you without delay, and you have been most kind in coming. Now we are all here in the presence of God to listen to everything that the Lord has commanded you to say."

Then Peter began to speak, "This is most remarkable! God is showing us that He is no respecter of persons, but that He welcomes those from every nation who reverence Him and do what is right. Here is the message God sent first to the sons of Israel: the Good News of peace through Jesus Christ, who is Lord of us all. You have heard the story of Jesus of Nazareth, haven't you? Everyone around here has!

- It began in Galilee where He was baptized by John.
- Then God anointed Him with the power of the Holy Spirit.
- From there He went about doing good and healing all who were oppressed by the devil.
- God was clearly working through Him; and we were right there with Him, eyewitnesses of everything, from the villages to Jerusalem.
- But they murdered Him, hanging Him on a cross.
- On the third day God raised Him up, but not everyone could see Him. God caused Him to be visible to many of us whom He had chosen to be His witnesses.
- Indeed, we ate and drank with Him after His resurrection.
- Then Jesus instructed us to spread the Good News everywhere, explaining that He is the One whom God appointed as Judge of both the living and the dead.

- The prophets of old all pointed to Him, making it clear that everyone who believes in Him receives forgiveness of their sins through His name."

Even as Peter was saying these words, the Holy Spirit fell upon all who were listening to his message. The Jewish believers who had come with Peter were astonished that the gift of the Holy Spirit was being poured out on Gentiles also, for they heard them speaking in unusual tongues and glorifying God.

Then Peter exclaimed, "Well, since these men have received the Holy Spirit just as we ourselves did, what's to prevent us from baptizing them?" So he gave orders for them to be baptized in the name of Jesus Christ. At their request Peter stayed with them for several days.

News of Peter's interaction with Gentiles reached the group in Jerusalem, and the Jewish believers took issue with it. When Peter returned to Jerusalem, they confronted him, charging, "We hear that you actually shared a meal with uncircumcised men!"

Peter proceeded to explain the situation. "I was in the city of Joppa, praying," he said, "when in a trance I saw a vision — something like a great sheet coming down toward me, let down from Heaven by its four corners. It came right down to me. When I looked at it closely, I saw animals and wild beasts, reptiles and birds. Then I heard a voice say to me, 'Get up, Peter, kill and eat.' But I said, 'Never, Lord, for nothing common or unclean has ever passed my lips.'

"Then the voice from Heaven spoke a second time and said, 'You must not call unclean what God has cleansed.' This happened to me three times, and then the whole thing was taken up again into Heaven. The next instant, three men arrived at the house where we were staying, requesting that I return with them to Caesarea. The Spirit told me in no uncertain terms to go with these men and not to doubt His leading in this matter.

"These six brothers accompanied me and we went into the man's house. He told us how an angel had appeared in his house, saying, 'Send to Joppa and bring Simon, surnamed Peter. He will give you a message which will save both you and your whole household.' As I was beginning to tell them the message, the Holy Spirit fell upon them just as He had on us at the beginning. Immediately I recalled that our

Lord had told us, 'John indeed baptized with water, but you will be baptized with the Holy Spirit.' I figured that if God gave them exactly the same gift as He gave to us when we believed on the Lord Jesus Christ, who was I to get in the way of what God was doing?"

When they heard Peter's story, they were convinced; and they praised God, saying, "It's obvious that God has given Gentiles the gift of repentance which leads to life!"

Because of the persecution which began following Stephen's martyrdom in Jerusalem, the message spread out as far as Phoenicia, Cyprus, and Antioch, though exclusively among the Jews. However, some of the men, natives of Cyprus and Cyrene, shared the Good News of the Lord Jesus with Greeks in Antioch. The Lord blessed their efforts, and a large number turned to the Lord.

News of this reached the church in Jerusalem, so they sent Barnabas to check it out. When he arrived in Antioch and saw the amazing grace of God at work, he was thrilled. He encouraged them all to remain true to the Lord, for he was a good man who trusted God for everything and lived by the promptings and power of the Holy Spirit. As a result, even more people became followers of the Lord.

Barnabas recognized the need for mature believers to help in the work, so he went to Tarsus to find Saul. When he found him, he brought him back to Antioch where for the next year they taught the growing congregation. It was in Antioch that the disciples were first given the name of "Christians" (a derogatory term meaning "Little Christs").

Around this same time some prophets came down from Jerusalem to Antioch. One of them by the name of Agabus stood up and foretold by the Spirit that there would be a great worldwide famine. So the disciples arranged to send relief to the brothers in Judea, each according to their resources. They asked Barnabas and Saul to take the contribution to the elders in Jerusalem.

It was around this same time that King Herod, in an attempt to please the Jewish leaders, arrested several believers. He had James, the brother of John, executed with a sword. During the Feast of Unleavened Bread, he put Peter in prison, intending to deal with him after the Passover celebration. Herod assigned four squads of soldiers, a total of sixteen men, to guard him. The church, meanwhile, prayed fervently for Peter.

On the night before Herod was planning to bring him out, Peter was asleep between two soldiers, chained with double chains, with guards standing watch in the doorway of the prison. Suddenly an angel of the Lord appeared, and light filled the cell. He awakened Peter, tapping him on the side and said, "Quick! Get up!" The chains fell away and the angel said to him, "Get dressed and put on your sandals." Peter did so. Then the angel told him, "Put on your coat now, and follow me." Peter followed him out but thought it was all just a dream. They passed through the first and second guard-points and came to the iron gate that led out into the city. The gate opened for them automatically. When they got to the street, the angel disappeared.

By this point Peter realized he was very much awake and said to himself, "How about that! The Lord has sent His angel to rescue me from the power of Herod and from all that the people are expecting. Won't they be surprised!" He made his way to the house of Mary, John Mark's mother, where many had come together to pray. He knocked at the door, and a young maid named Rhoda came to answer it. As soon as she heard Peter's voice, she got so excited that she ran back to tell everyone and left him standing outside. The group told her she was out of her mind, but she insisted that it was really him. They concluded that it must be his angel, an indication that he had died.

Meanwhile Peter continued knocking. When they finally opened it and let him in, they were shocked. Peter motioned for them to be quiet and explained to them how the Lord had brought him out of prison. Then he said, "Go and tell James and the other brothers what has happened." After this he left them and went on to another place.

You can imagine the confusion and consternation at the prison the next morning. The soldiers couldn't imagine what happened to Peter. Herod had a search put out for him without success. He cross-examined the guards and then ordered their execution. After that, Herod left Judea and went down to Caesarea and stayed there.

While Herod was at his summer palace, representatives from Tyre and Sidon came to win his favor because, in his anger, he had been withholding food supplies from them. After much effort they convinced his personal assistant, Blastus, to schedule a meeting with the king. On the appointed day they met in the Coliseum.

When Herod arrived dressed in royal robes, he took his seat on the throne and addressed the crowd. The people, desperate to impress him, kept interrupting his speech with shouts of, "The voice of a god, the voice of a god, this is no mere man!" Herod relished the praise and didn't contradict their flattery. Because he failed to give glory to God, an angel of the Lord struck him with a terrible disease. He died a short time later, his insides eaten by worms.

But the message of the Lord prospered and multiplied. Barnabas and Saul returned to Antioch after taking the financial gift to Jerusalem, and they brought John Mark back with them.

Paul's First Missionary Journey

Included among the believers in the church at Antioch were a number of prophets and teachers: Barnabas; Simeon from Niger; Lucius from Cyrene; Manaen, the foster-brother of Herod Antipas; and Saul. While they were worshiping the Lord and fasting, the Holy Spirit spoke to them, saying, "Set Barnabas and Saul apart for Me for a task to which I have called them." After further fasting and prayer, they laid their hands on them and sent them on their way, John Mark accompanying them.

The Holy Spirit led them to the port city of Seleucia where they boarded a ship for the island of Cyprus. They explained God's message in the synagogues from Salamis to Paphos and throughout the island. In Paphos, the provincial capital, they made the acquaintance of Sergius Paulus, the governor, a man of considerable intellect. He summoned them, eager to hear what they had to say. Now a Jewish magician by the name of Elymas was a personal advisor to the governor. When he heard them explaining the Word of God, he tried hard to prevent the governor from taking hold of it.

Then the Holy Spirit filled Saul, who is also called Paul, with a rebuke for Elymas: "Why, you son of the devil! You're as devious and deceptive as the devil himself, the enemy of all that is right, forever twisting the simple ways of the Lord. May the Lord touch you with blindness since you refuse to see the truth and would hinder others." Instantly, something like a foggy mist came over Elymas; he had to get someone to lead him about. Witnessing this dramatic event convinced the governor of the truth of Paul's message.

From Paphos, Paul and the team sailed for Perga in Pamphylia on the mainland. John Mark turned back, however, and did not continue with them, returning instead to Jerusalem. After passing through Perga, they went on to Antioch in Pisidia. On the Sabbath they went to the local synagogue. After the reading of the Law and Prophets, the leaders of the synagogue invited them to speak, saying, "Men and brothers, if you have any message of encouragement for the people, by all means speak."

Paul stood up and proceeded to give them a brief history of God's dealings.

"Fellow Jews and all who fear God, listen to me. God chose our fathers and prospered the people of Israel while they were exiles in the land of Egypt. Then He demonstrated His power and led them out of that land, after which time He put up with them for forty years in the wilderness. He destroyed seven nations in the land of Canaan and gave them that land as their inheritance.

"For the next four hundred fifty years, He gave them judges until the time of the prophet Samuel. The people begged for a king; so God gave them Saul the son of Kish, a man of the tribe of Benjamin, to be their king for forty years. Saul was replaced by David, a man of whom God Himself said, 'I have found David, son of Jesse, a man after My own heart, who will do all My will.'

"And it is from the line of David that God, as He had promised, brought Jesus to Israel to be their Savior. Right before Jesus came, John the baptizer proclaimed the baptism of repentance for all the people of Israel. Toward the end of his ministry John said, 'Who do you think I am? I am not He. Behold, Someone comes after me whose shoelace I am not fit to untie!'

"Brothers, sons of Abraham, and all who fear God, hear me when I tell you that this message of salvation has now been sent to us! The people of Jerusalem and their rulers refused to recognize Him or to heed the prophets, which are read every Sabbath day. In condemning Him, they fulfilled these very prophecies!

"Even though they had no grounds for a death penalty, they begged Pilate to have Him executed. When they had carried out everything that was written about Him, they took Him down from the cross and laid Him in a tomb. But God raised Him from the dead. For many days He was seen by His followers from Galilee. These men are now His witnesses to the world.

"We have come to tell you the Good News that the promise made to our forefathers has come true. God has fulfilled it by raising up Jesus as He foretold in the second Psalm: 'You are My Son, today I have begotten You.' When He said, 'I will give You the sure mercies of David,' God was affirming that He would be raised up never to see death again, as He mentions in yet another Psalm, 'You will not allow Your Holy One to see corruption.'

"It could not have been referring to David, you know, because after he had completed God's plan for his life, he died and was laid with his ancestors. His body did experience decay, but this Man whom God raised up never saw corruption!

"The point of all this is that forgiveness of sins is available to you through this Man. Everyone who entrusts themselves to Him is freed from all those things from which the Law of Moses could never set him free. Only be careful that this saying of the prophets should never apply to you: 'Behold, you scoffers, marvel and perish; for I am doing something incredible in your day which you will by no means believe, even though it is explained to you.'"

As the people left the synagogue that day, they urged Paul to return the following Sabbath to share the message again. Many of the Jews and devout proselytes followed Paul and Barnabas, who spoke personally to them and urged them to put their trust in the grace of God.

On the next Sabbath almost the entire city gathered to hear the message of God; but when the Jews saw the crowds, they were filled with jealousy. They contradicted what Paul was saying and slandered him. Paul and Barnabas turned to the agitators and said, "We came to speak the message of God to you first; but since you reject it and evidently do not think yourselves worthy of eternal life, we will turn our attention to the Gentiles! In fact, the Lord commanded us to do so when He said: 'I have set you to be a light to the Gentiles, that you should take the message of salvation to the ends of the earth.'"

When the Gentiles heard this, they were overwhelmed with gratitude and responded wholeheartedly to the word of the Lord. All those who were destined for eternal life believed, and the Word of the Lord kept spreading throughout the region. But the offended Jews stirred up some of the prominent women and leading men who, in turn, started a wave of persecution against Paul and Barnabas, ultimately forcing them to leave the area. Shaking the dust from their feet in protest, they went on to Iconium. The disciples continued to be full of joy and the Holy Spirit.

Upon their arrival in Iconium, they went to the Jewish synagogue and spoke with such conviction that a very large number of both Jews and Greeks believed. But again, some unbelieving Jews stirred up some of the Gentiles and poisoned their minds against the brothers. Nevertheless, they remained there for a long time and spoke fearlessly for the Lord. He confirmed their testimony by granting power to perform signs and miracles.

The people of the city were divided in their opinions, some taking the side of the Jews and some, that of the apostles. Finally, when the apostles got wind of a conspiracy by both Gentiles and Jews in collaboration with the authorities to have them stoned, they fled to the nearby cities of Lystra and Derbe and continued to proclaim the message throughout the surrounding countryside.

At Lystra they encountered a lame man who had suffered this handicap since birth. He was listening to Paul speak; and Paul, looking him straight in the eye, perceived that he had the faith to be made well. So he said in a loud voice, "Stand straight up on your feet!" Immediately he sprang to his feet and began walking.

When the crowd saw what Paul had done, they shouted in the Lycaonian language, "The gods have come down to us in human form!" They began to call Barnabas "Zeus" and Paul "Hermes" since he was the spokesman. The next thing they knew, the high priest of the temple of Zeus had brought oxen to the gates and wanted to offer sacrifices to the two men.

As soon as Barnabas and Paul realized what was going on, they tore their clothes and rushed into the crowd, crying at the top of their voices, "Men, stop! Why are you carrying on like this? We are only human beings with feelings just like yours! We are here to tell you the Good News, that you should turn from these meaningless things to the Living God! He is the One who made heaven and earth, the sea and all that is in them. In the past He allowed all nations to go their own ways — not that He left you without evidence of Himself. In His kindness He sent you rain from heaven and fruitful seasons, providing you with food and making your hearts content."

It was all they could do to keep the crowd from making sacrifices to them — that is, until some Jews arrived from Antioch and Iconium, who turned the minds of the people against Paul so that they stoned him and dragged him out of the city, thinking he was dead. But while the disciples were gathered in a circle around him, Paul got up and walked back to the city. The next day he left there, taking Barnabas with him, and went to Derbe where they proclaimed the Good News and made many disciples.

From Derbe they retraced their steps back through Lystra, Iconium, and Antioch, encouraging the disciples along the way, urging them to stand firm in the faith, and reminding them that it is "through many difficulties that we must enter into the Kingdom of God." They appointed elders in each church and with prayer and fasting commended these men to the Lord in whom they had believed. They continued their journey through Pisidia to Pamphylia, on to Perga where they spoke the Word, and then down to Attalia.

Having finished their assignment, they sailed back to Antioch, to the church from which they had been commissioned to this special task by God's grace. When they arrived there, they called the church together and reported to them the amazing things God had done and how He had opened the door of faith for the Gentiles. They remained at Antioch with the disciples for a long time.

At one point, some men came down from Judea to Antioch and began teaching the Gentile believers that they had to submit to circumcision as prescribed by Moses in order to be truly saved. Paul and Barnabas argued and debated long and hard until finally the believers decided to send them to Jerusalem along with a few others to settle the issue with the apostles and elders there.

The church sent them on their way; and they headed down through Phoenicia and Samaria, telling the story of the conversion of the Gentiles as they went. All the brothers were overjoyed to hear about it. Upon their arrival at Jerusalem, they were welcomed by the church and by the apostles and elders. They reported all that God had done through them. But some members of the Pharisees' party who had become believers stood up and declared that it was absolutely essential that these new believers be told they must be circumcised and observe the Law of Moses.

The apostles and elders met to consider the matter. Finally, after much debate, Peter stood up and addressed the group: "Men and brothers, you know that in this matter of taking the message to the Gentiles, God chose me to be the first to carry it to them when He sent me to Cornelius. God, who knows the hearts of all, confirmed that He had cleansed their hearts when, just as He had with us, He gave them the Holy Spirit. He made no distinction between their faith and ours.

"So why would you further test God by putting a burden on the shoulders of these disciples which neither our fathers nor we were able to bear? There is no denying that it is by the grace of the Lord Jesus that we are saved by faith, just as they are!"

This quieted the crowd, and they listened as Barnabas and Paul gave a detailed account of the signs and wonders which God had worked through them among the Gentiles.

At the conclusion of their report, James spoke up, saying, "Men and brothers, listen to me. Peter has explained how God went about taking from among the Gentiles a people for His name. This is not a new concept. Even the prophets wrote as much in the Scripture, saying, '"After this I will return and will rebuild the tabernacle of David which has fallen down. I will rebuild its ruins, and I will set it up so that the rest of mankind may seek the Lord, even all the Gentiles who are called by My name," says the Lord who brings about things foretold long ago.'

"I do not believe that we should put any additional obstacles in the way of these Gentiles who are turning toward God. Instead, I think we should write to them, telling them to avoid anything polluted by idols, all forms of sexual immorality, eating the meat of strangled animals, or tasting blood. These regulations are commonly known since Moses has been read aloud in the synagogues every Sabbath day in every city."

Then it seemed good to the apostles, elders, and the whole church to choose representatives and send them to Antioch with Paul and Barnabas. Judas, surnamed Barsabbas, and Silas, both leading men of the brotherhood, were chosen to carry this letter:

"The apostles and elders send their greetings to our brothers who are Gentiles in Antioch, Syria, and Cilicia. Since we have heard that some of our number have caused you deep distress and have unsettled your minds by giving you a message which certainly did not originate from us, we are unanimously agreed to send you chosen representatives with our well-loved Barnabas and Paul, men who have risked their lives for the name of our Lord Jesus Christ. We have sent with them Judas and Silas who will give you the same message personally by word of mouth. For it has seemed right to the Holy Spirit and to us to lay no further burden upon you except what is absolutely essential, namely, that you avoid what has been sacrificed to idols, tasting blood, eating the meat of whatever has been strangled, and sexual immorality. Keep yourselves free of these things and you will make good progress. Farewell."

And so the group was sent to Antioch, carrying the letter. Upon their arrival the believers gathered and the letter was read, resulting in great rejoicing. Judas and Silas had much to say to the believers by way of encouragement and instruction. After some days they returned to Jerusalem. Paul and Barnabas stayed on in Antioch, teaching and preaching the Word of the Lord along with many others.

Some days later Paul spoke to Barnabas, "We should go back and visit the brothers in every city where we have proclaimed the Word of the Lord, to see how they are doing."

Barnabas agreed and wanted to again take John, surnamed Mark, as their companion. Paul refused to take along one who had deserted them in Pamphylia and who was not prepared to go the distance with them in their work. There was such a sharp disagreement that they parted ways. Barnabas ended up taking Mark and sailing to Cyprus.

PAUL'S SECOND MISSIONARY JOURNEY

Paul recruited Silas; and together they set out on their journey, commended to the grace of the Lord by the brothers in Antioch. They travelled through Syria and Cilicia, strengthening the churches, and from there they went on to Derbe and Lystra.

At Lystra there was a disciple by the name of Timothy whose mother was a Jewish believer, though his father was a Greek. Timothy was highly respected by all the brothers at Lystra and Iconium, and Paul wanted to take him on as his companion. Everybody knew his father was a Greek, so Paul had him circumcised because of the attitude of the Jews in that region. As they went from city to city, they shared the letter from the apostles and elders in Jerusalem, explaining the instructions. As a result the churches grew stronger and their numbers increased daily.

They continued on through Phrygia and Galatia, but the Holy Spirit prevented them from speaking God's message in Asia. When they came to Mysia and tried to enter Bithynia, again the Spirit of Jesus would not allow them. So they skirted Mysia and came down to Troas. While there, Paul had a vision of a man from Macedonia calling to him in these words: "Come over to Macedonia and help us!"

Paul, recognizing this as a call from God to take the Good News into Europe, immediately began making plans to sail from Troas. I, Luke, joined them there; and we put out to sea, sailing directly to Samothrace, then on to the port of Neapolis. From there we set off for Philippi, a Roman garrison town and the chief city in that part of Macedonia.

We spent several days in Philippi; and on the Sabbath day we went out of the city gate to the riverside, where we hoped to find a place for prayer. We joined the group of women who had assembled, among them a woman named Lydia who came from Thyatira and was a dealer in purple-dyed cloth. She was already a believer in God, and the Lord opened her heart to accept Paul's words. After she and her household had been baptized, she invited us to her home, saying, "If you accept that I am a true believer in the Lord, then come down to my house and stay there." She persisted until we had agreed.

Once, on our way to the place of prayer, we were met by a young girl who had a spirit of divination. This girl brought her owners a good deal of profit by foretelling the future. She kept following Paul and the rest of us, crying out, "These men serve the Most High God. They offer a way of salvation."

She kept it up for several days until Paul could take it no longer. He turned and spoke to the spirit in her, saying, "In the name of Jesus Christ, I command you to come out of her!" Immediately it left her.

When the girl's owners saw that their source of income was gone, they seized Paul and Silas and dragged them before the authorities in the market square. There they presented them to the chief magistrates, charging, "These Jews are causing great confusion in our city by proclaiming customs that are illegal for us as Roman citizens to accept or practice." The crowd joined in the attack. The magistrates had them stripped and ordered them to be beaten with rods. After giving them a severe beating, they threw them into prison, instructing the jailer to guard them closely. Assuming they were dangerous criminals, he took them into the inner jail and fastened their feet securely in the stocks.

About midnight Paul and Silas were praying and singing hymns to God. The other prisoners were listening to them when suddenly there was a great earthquake strong enough to shake the foundations of the prison. All the doors flew open and everyone's chains fell off. When the jailer woke and saw that the doors of the prison had been opened, he drew his sword and was about to kill himself; for he imagined that all the prisoners had escaped. But Paul called out to him in a loud voice, saying, "Don't hurt yourself; we are all here!"

Then the jailer called for lights and rushed in. Overcome with fear, he fell trembling at the feet of Paul and Silas. He led them outside, and said, "Sirs, what must I do to be saved?"

They replied, "Put your trust in the Lord Jesus and you will be saved, you and your household."

There, in the middle of the night, Paul and Silas explained to him and his family the Word of the Lord. The jailer washed their wounds, and he and his family were baptized right then. He then took them into his house for a meal. He and his whole household were overjoyed at finding faith in God.

When morning came, the magistrates sent officers with the message, "Let those men go."

The jailer reported this message to Paul, saying, "The magistrates have sent to have you released. So now you can leave this place and go on your way in peace."

But Paul said to the officers, "They beat us publicly without any kind of trial, and they threw us into prison despite the fact that we are Roman citizens. And now they think they can send us away quietly? Oh no, let them come and take us out themselves!"

When the officers reported to the magistrates that Paul and Silas were Roman citizens, they were extremely afraid and came in person to apologize to them. After taking them outside the prison, they asked them to leave the city. But upon their release from prison, Paul and Silas went to Lydia's house. Only after seeing the brothers and encouraging them did they depart from Philippi.

Their journey took them through Amphipolis and Apollonia and finally to Thessalonica where there was a Jewish synagogue. As was his custom, Paul attended each Sabbath, explaining from the Scriptures why the Messiah had to suffer and rise from the dead. "This Jesus whom I am proclaiming to you is God's Messiah!" he declared. Some of them were convinced and joined Paul and Silas, as did a large number of Greeks and leading women in the city.

But the Jews, motivated by jealousy, rallied a bunch of troublemakers in the marketplace to start a city-wide riot against Paul and Silas. They ransacked Jason's house looking for them. When they could not find them, they dragged Jason and some of the brothers before the civic authorities, shouting, "The men who have turned the world upside down have now come here, and Jason has welcomed them into his house. Besides that, they violate the decrees of Caesar by claiming that there is another king called Jesus!" This really unnerved the local authorities who would only release Jason and the others after they pledged to cooperate.

So Paul and Silas were sent off to Berea that night. When they went to the Jewish synagogue there, they enjoyed a much better reception than in Thessalonica. These folks listened to the message eagerly and studied the Scriptures every day to see if what they were now being told was true. Many of them became believers, as did a number of prominent Greek women and quite a few men.

When the Jews at Thessalonica found out that Paul was spreading the message in Berea, they came there to stir up the people. To avoid trouble, the brothers sent Paul down to the coast; but Silas and Timothy remained in Berea. The men who accompanied Paul took him as far as Athens and returned with instructions for Silas and Timothy to rejoin Paul as soon as possible.

While Paul was waiting in Athens for Silas and Timothy, he was overwhelmed with the large number of idols throughout the city. He talked about it with the Jews in the synagogue as well as the God-fearing Gentiles. He even argued daily with any who were in the marketplace. Athens was a popular gathering place for philosophers and tourists who were always on the lookout for some new idea or fad. Some Epicurean and Stoic devotees engaged Paul in conversation and invited him to present his novel teachings to the council at the Areopagus. They thought he was introducing new deities when he spoke of Jesus and the resurrection.

This was Paul's speech:

"Men of Athens, I see that you are an extremely religious people. In getting acquainted with your city, I even noticed a shrine 'TO THE UNKNOWN GOD.' It is this God, whom you acknowledge while admitting that you don't know Him, that I am here to proclaim to you. Your 'unknown' God is the One who made the world and all that is in it. He is the Supreme Ruler of both heaven and earth and does not live in temples made by human hands, nor could mere humans contribute anything to His well-being. Clearly, what could He need since He is the One who supplies life and breath and all that is needed to every living creature?

"Starting with the creation of one man, God has, through that bloodline, created every race of men and scattered them over the face of the whole earth. He determined when and where each should live, intending for them to search for God in the hope that they might reach out for Him and find Him — yes, even though He is not far from any one of us. Indeed, it is by Him that we live and move and have our being. Some of your own poets have said as much, 'For we are also His children.' If then, we are the children of God, we ought not to picture God in terms of gold or silver or stone, conceived and constructed by human art or ingenuity.

"It is true that God has overlooked man's ignorance for a long time. Today, however, He commands all men everywhere to repent. He has set a day on which He plans to judge the whole world by the perfect standard of the Man whom He has appointed. He has certified that Man's authority to judge by raising Him from the dead."

Now when the audience heard Paul talk about the resurrection from the dead, some of them laughed and mocked him, but others said, "We would like to hear you speak again on this subject." As Paul left the gathering, some did join him and took hold of the faith.

Among them were Dionysius, a member of the Areopagus; a woman by the name of Damaris; and a few others.

It wasn't long after this that Paul left Athens and went to Corinth where he found a Jew by the name of Aquila, a native of Pontus. He and his wife Priscilla had recently moved to Corinth from Italy because Claudius had ordered all Jews to leave Rome. Paul visited in their home; and because they were tent-makers as he was, he stayed with them and worked alongside them. Every Sabbath Paul used to speak in the synagogue trying to persuade both Jews and Greeks. When Silas and Timothy arrived from Macedonia, Paul devoted himself full-time to proclaiming the message, showing the Jews as clearly as he could that Jesus is the Messiah.

Here, as in the previous cities, the religious Jews turned against him and accused him of serving the devil. That was the last straw! He shook out his garments at them and said, "Your blood be on your own heads! From now on I go with a perfectly clear conscience to the Gentiles." So he left the synagogue and went next door to the home of a man named Titius Justus who feared God. Crispus, the leader of the synagogue, trusted in the Lord along with his household; and many of the Corinthians who heard the message believed and were baptized.

One night the Lord spoke to Paul in a vision, saying, "Do not be afraid, but go on speaking and don't let anyone stop you, for I Myself am with you; I won't let anyone harm you. I have many people in this city." So Paul settled down there for eighteen months and taught them God's message.

At one point a cadre of Jews apprehended Paul and took him to court. They set him before Gallio, the governor of Achaia, charging him with "brainwashing people to worship God in a way that is contrary to the Law." Just as Paul was about to defend himself, Gallio addressed the Jews, saying, "If you were bringing a violent criminal before me, I might put up with you Jews; but since it's just a squabble about words and names and your Law, take care of it yourselves. I don't have time for this." With that he had them ejected from the courtroom. In their pent-up frustration they grabbed Sosthenes, the synagogue leader, and beat him right in front of the courthouse, but Gallio still refused to take up their cause.

Paul remained in Corinth for a while after this incident and then sailed for Syria, taking Priscilla and Aquila with him. At Cenchrea he had his hair cut off, fulfilling a vow he had made. They all arrived at Ephesus where Paul once again went into the synagogue to debate with the Jews. They asked him to stay longer but he declined, saying, "If it is God's will, I will come back to you again." Leaving Aquila and Priscilla in Ephesus, he set sail for the port of Caesarea, traveled up to Jerusalem for a brief visit with the believers there, and then returned to the sending church in Antioch where he spent considerable time.

PAUL'S THIRD MISSIONARY JOURNEY

Finally, Paul launched a third mission excursion throughout Galatia and Phyrgia, encouraging the believers along the way.

Meanwhile a Jew by the name of Apollos, a native of Alexandria, a gifted communicator, and a man well-acquainted with the Scriptures, arrived at Ephesus. He had been instructed in the way of the Lord, and he was very effective in teaching about Jesus even though he only knew about the baptism of John. He was fearless in proclaiming the truth in the synagogue. When Priscilla and Aquila heard him, they took him aside and explained God's message to him more accurately.

When he decided to cross into Achaia, the brothers encouraged him and wrote a letter introducing him to the disciples there, asking them to make him welcome. Upon his arrival he proved a source of great strength to those who believed through grace. With a powerful defense he publicly refuted the Jews, showing from their Scriptures that Jesus was the promised Messiah.

While Apollos was in Corinth, Paul journeyed through the upper parts of the country, finally arriving at Ephesus. There he found a dozen disciples and asked if they had received the Holy Spirit when they believed. They indicated that they had never even heard of the Holy Spirit.

"How were you baptized?" Paul asked. So they explained that they had been baptized into John's baptism.

"John's baptism was a baptism to show a change of heart," Paul explained, "but he always made it clear that they must believe in the One who was coming after him, that is, in Jesus." When these men heard this, they were baptized in the name of the Lord Jesus. As Paul laid his hands on them, the Holy Spirit came upon them; and they began to speak with tongues and to prophesy.

Paul spent about three months in Ephesus. At first he reasoned with the Jews in the synagogue, explaining the Kingdom of God until, sensing a growing resistance to the message and some open hostility, he withdrew from there and continued his daily discussions in the lecture hall of Tyrannus. He carried on this work for two years, giving opportunity to all who lived in Asia, both Greeks and Jews, to hear the Lord's message.

God confirmed Paul's ministry with unusual demonstrations of power. People were being healed or delivered of evil spirits, at times through the laying on of Paul's hands, but sometimes just by touching handkerchiefs or aprons which had been in contact with his body.

Interestingly, there were some itinerant Jewish exorcists who attempted to invoke the name of the Lord Jesus when dealing with evil spirits. They got into the practice of saying, "I command you in the name of Jesus whom Paul preaches." Seven brothers, sons of a chief priest called Sceva, were among those doing this when one time the evil spirit answered, "Jesus I know, and I am acquainted with Paul, but who on earth are you?" Then the man in whom the evil spirit was living jumped on them and overpowered them all with such violence that they rushed out of that house wounded and naked, having had their clothes torn off by the man. Once this story became common knowledge, a great sense of awe came over all who were living in Ephesus; and the name of the Lord Jesus became highly respected.

A new openness and boldness was evident among those who had professed their faith. Many who had previously practiced magic gathered their occult books, which had a collective value of 50,000 silver coins (more than a million dollars by today's standards), and burned them publicly, and the Word of the Lord continued to grow irresistibly in power and influence.

Seeing the Word established in Ephesus, Paul determined in his spirit to travel on through Macedonia and Achaia, then to Jerusalem. "And after I have been there, I must see Rome as well," he confided. He sent Timothy and Erastus ahead to Macedonia while he remained a while longer in Asia.

Not everyone in Ephesus was pleased with the flourishing church, however. Those whose business depended on the worship of Diana saw profits plummeting. A prominent silversmith by the name of Demetrius called together the craftsmen in his trade and rallied them to take action, saying, "Men, you all know just how much our prosperity depends on this particular work. Why, reports from all of Asia show that this man Paul has persuaded great masses of people to join The Way by telling them that gods made by human hands are not gods at all.

"Do you understand what this could mean? Not only are our careers at risk, but the very temple of the great goddess Diana may also be neglected. Think of it: she whom all of Asia, yea, the whole world worships, dethroned from her place of honor!"

Demetrius' speech succeeded in stirring up the crowd who began chanting with angry fervor, "Great is Diana of the Ephesians!" It didn't take long for the whole city to take up the cause. They rushed into the coliseum dragging along Gaius and Aristarchus, two Macedonians who were Paul's travelling companions. Paul wanted to go in to address the crowd, but the disciples would not allow him to. Some high-ranking officials in the city who were Paul's friends also urged him not to risk his life by entering the theater.

As is often the case in mass protests, most of the people didn't even know why they had gathered. Some shouted one thing and some another. The whole assembly was in utter chaos. Finally, the Jewish contingent pushed Alexander to the front to make a speech; but when the crowd recognized him as being a Jew, they shouted him down, chanting for two hours straight, "Great is Diana of the Ephesians!"

When the town clerk was finally able to silence the crowd, he said, "Men of Ephesus, come now! Who in the world doesn't recognize that our great city of Ephesus is temple-guardian of the great Diana and of the image which fell down from Jupiter himself? Since these are undeniable facts, you ought to restrain yourselves and not do anything you might later regret.

"These men you have dragged in here aren't guilty of robbing the temple or blaspheming our goddess. If Demetrius and the rest of you have any charges to bring against anyone, the courts are open and there are judges ready to handle such cases; let them take legal action. If you want anything else, then bring it before the regular assembly. As it is, we are in danger of being charged with rioting over today's events especially since we have no good explanation to offer for all this commotion." And with these words he dismissed the assembly.

After this uproar subsided, Paul sent for the disciples to give final words of encouragement before departing on his way to Macedonia. Passing through the region, he exhorted the people and then went on to Greece where he stayed for three months.

Paul was about to sail for Syria when some Jews made a further plot against him, so he decided to make his way back through Macedonia instead. Part of the team, Sopater, a Berean, the son of Pyrrhus; two Thessalonians, Aristarchus and Secundus; Gaius from Derbe; Timothy; and two Asians, Tychicus and Trophimus, went ahead to Troas. The rest of us sailed from Philippi after the days of Unleavened Bread and joined them five days later at Troas, where we spent a week.

On the first day of the week, we assembled for the breaking of bread. Since Paul intended to leave on the following day, he began to speak to them and talked nearly till midnight. There were a great many lamps burning in the upper room where we met, and a young man called Eutychus, who was sitting on the window sill, fell asleep as Paul's address went on and on. Finally, completely overcome by sleep, he fell to the ground from the third story. When they got to him, he was dead; but Paul bent over him and embraced him. "Don't be alarmed," Paul said, "he is still alive."

They all went upstairs again; and when they had broken bread and eaten, they continued to talk together until daybreak. Paul then departed. As for the boy, he was taken home alive, much to the relief of all.

Meanwhile we had gone aboard the ship and sailed for Assos. Paul had arranged for us to pick him up there since he chose to go overland. After he boarded at Assos, we went on to Mitylene and then to the coast. We sailed from there and arrived off the coast of Chios the next day. From Chios we sailed to Samos and finally Miletus. Paul had decided not to visit Ephesus in order to save time so that he might reach Jerusalem in time for the day of Pentecost.

While we were in Miletus, he called for the elders of the church in Ephesus to come to him as he had a message on his heart for them.

"My life has been an open book among you ever since I first set foot in Asia. You are witnesses of how humbly I served the Lord and of the tears I shed because of the grievous trials I suffered at the hands of the Jews. You yourselves recall how I taught publicly and in your homes, always ready to proclaim whatever would be profitable for you. My message was the same whether to Jews or Greeks: repentance toward God and unwavering trust in our Lord Jesus.

"And now I am compelled by the Spirit to go to Jerusalem. I don't know what is going to happen to me there, except that the Holy Spirit keeps warning me that imprisonment and persecution lay ahead. Mind you, I'm not concerned for my own life as long as I can finish my course and complete the ministry the Lord Jesus has given me in declaring the Good News of the grace of God.

"I am painfully aware that not one of you to whom I preached the Kingdom of God will ever see my face again, which is why I wanted to meet with you one last time. My conscience is clear, for I have never shrunk from declaring to you the whole purpose of God.

"Let me urge you to be on your guard for yourselves and for the flock of which the Holy Spirit has made you guardians. You are to be shepherds of God's church, which our Lord Jesus won at the cost of His own blood. It won't be long before savage wolves will come in among you, having no mercy for the flock. Yes, and even from among your own group, men will arise speaking perversions of the truth, trying to draw away the disciples and make them followers of themselves.

"This is why I tell you to keep on the alert. When things get tough, remember my example, how for three years I never failed night and day to warn every one of you, often with tears. Now I commend you to the Lord and to the message of His grace which can strengthen you and secure your inheritance among all those who are consecrated to God.

"I have never coveted anybody's gold or silver or clothing. Instead, with my own hands I have provided for my needs and for those of my companions. I have demonstrated to you that through hard work we must help the weak, always bearing in mind the words of the Lord Jesus when He said, 'It is more blessed to give than to receive.'"

With these words he knelt down and prayed with all of them. There were plenty of tears as they reflected on the possibility of never seeing him again. Each of them embraced Paul with much affection before accompanying him down to the ship.

From Miletus we sailed to Cos, then on to Rhodes and Patara where we transferred to a ship bound for Phoenicia. We passed by Cyprus and arrived in Tyre where their cargo was to be unloaded.

We contacted the disciples there and stayed with them for a week. They felt led by the Spirit again and again to warn Paul not to set foot in Jerusalem; but when the time came, we left there and continued our journey. They all came out to see us off, bringing wives and children with them. We walked together down to the beach where we knelt down to pray, then said our farewells. Afterward we went aboard the ship while the disciples went back to their homes.

We sailed away from Tyre and arrived at Ptolemais where we fellowshipped with the brothers. On the following day we sailed to Caesarea where we met up with Philip the evangelist, one of the original seven deacons, and his four unmarried daughters, all of whom were gifted prophetesses. While we were there, a prophet by the name of Agabus came down from Judea. When he came to see us, he took Paul's belt and used it to tie his own hands and feet together, saying, "The Holy Spirit says this: 'The owner of this belt will be bound like this by the Jews in Jerusalem and handed over to the Gentiles!'"

Upon hearing this, those of us traveling with Paul, along with the believers in Caesarea, begged Paul not to go up to Jerusalem. Then Paul answered us, "You're breaking my heart with all your tears. Don't you know that I am ready not only to be bound but to die in Jerusalem for the sake of the name of the Lord Jesus."

Since there was nothing we could do to change his mind, we committed the situation to the Lord, saying, "May the Lord's will be done," and said no more. After this we made our preparations and went up to Jerusalem.

Imprisonment in Jerusalem

Some of the disciples from Caesarea went along with us. They brought us to the home of Mnason, where we stayed. He was a native of Cyprus and one of the earliest disciples. Upon our arrival at Jerusalem, the brothers were glad to see us. On the following day Paul went with us to visit James, and all the elders were present. After greeting them, he gave them a detailed account of all that God had done among the Gentiles through his ministry.

They praised God upon hearing the report and said to Paul, "You know, brother, how many thousands there are among the Jews who, though having become believers, still remain very zealous about upholding the Law. A rumor has spread among them that you teach all Jews who live among the Gentiles to disregard the Law of Moses, telling them not to circumcise their children nor observe the old customs. We're concerned about what may happen once they hear that you have arrived.

"We have an idea that may calm their fears. There are four men here who have made a vow. Why don't you join them and be purified with them? You might even pay their expenses so that they can get their hair cut. Then everyone will know there is no truth in the stories about you but that you also observe the Law.

"Mind you, we're not suggesting that any of this be imposed on the Gentiles who have believed. We have sent them a letter explaining that they should abstain from what has been offered to idols, from blood and from what has been strangled, and from sexual immorality."

So Paul joined the four men and on the following day, after being purified with them, went into the temple to give notice about the period of purification, when it would be finished, and what offering would be made on behalf of each one of them.

The seven days were almost over when some Jews from Asia saw Paul in the temple. They stirred up the whole crowd and shouted, "Men of Israel, help us! This is the man who is teaching everywhere against our people, our Law, and this temple. Besides, he has brought Greeks into the temple and has defiled this Holy Place!" This last accusation was because they had seen Trophimus the Ephesian with Paul in the city, and they assumed that Paul had brought him into the temple.

The whole city was stirred by their speech. They seized Paul and dragged him outside the temple, and the doors were slammed behind him.

They were about to kill him when a report reached the commander of the Roman cohort that the whole of Jerusalem was in an uproar. He immediately took soldiers and centurions and ran down into the crowd.

When the people saw the official and the soldiers, they stopped beating Paul. The commander took hold of Paul and arrested him, ordering that he be bound with two chains. Then he began asking who the man was and what he had been doing. Some of the crowd shouted one thing and some another. Since he could not be certain of the facts because of the shouting that was going on, he ordered Paul to be brought to the barracks. By the time they got to the steps, Paul had to be carried by the soldiers because of the violence of the mob. The crowd kept shouting furiously, "Away with him!"

As they were about to enter the barracks, Paul asked the commander, "May I say something to you?"

"What? Do you know Greek?" the tribune asked. "Aren't you that Egyptian who recently stirred up a revolt along with those four thousand assassins who escaped into the desert?"

"I am a Jew," replied Paul. "I am a man of Tarsus, a citizen of no insignificant city, I might add. I'd like a chance to address this crowd."

With permission, Paul stood on the steps and made a gesture with his hand to the people. The crowd quieted as he began, "My brothers and my fathers, listen to what I have to say in my own defense."

When they heard him addressing them in Hebrew, a profound silence came over the place.

"I myself am a Jew," Paul told them. "I was born in Tarsus in Cilicia, but I was brought up here in Jerusalem, having received my training at the feet of Gamaliel and being educated in the strictest observance of our fathers' Law. I was as much on fire with zeal for God as you all are today. You may not know it, but I am also the man who persecuted The Way vigorously, arresting both men and women, throwing them into prison, and killing many, as the High Priest and the whole council can readily testify. Indeed, it was after receiving letters from them that I was on my way to the synagogue in Damascus. I intended to arrest any followers of The Way I could find there to bring them back to Jerusalem for punishment.

"Then this happened to me: As I neared Damascus, about midday, a great light from Heaven suddenly blazed around me. I fell to the ground and heard a voice saying to me, 'Saul, Saul, why are you persecuting Me?' I replied, 'Who are You, Lord?' He said to me, 'I am Jesus of Nazareth whom you are persecuting.' Those traveling with me also saw the light, but they did not hear the voice of the One who was talking to me.

"'What do You want me to do, Lord?' I asked. The Lord told me, 'Get up and go to Damascus. There you will be told of all that has been determined for you to do.' The bright light had blinded me, so my companions had to lead me by the hand into Damascus.

"A man by the name of Ananias, a devout observer of the Law and one highly respected by all the Jews who lived there, came to visit me.

He stood by my side and said, 'Saul, brother, receive your sight!' And just like that, I looked and saw him. He went on to explain, 'The God of our fathers has chosen you to know His will, to see the Righteous One, to hear words from His own lips. He wants you to become His witness before all men of what you have seen and heard. There's no time to waste! Get up and be baptized! Let your sins be washed away as you call on His name.'

"Then it happened that when I returned to Jerusalem and was praying in the temple, I fell into a trance and saw Him, and He said to me, 'Quickly! Leave Jerusalem at once because they will not accept your testimony about Me.'

"'But, Lord,' I said, 'they know that I have gone from one synagogue after another, imprisoning and beating any who believe in You. And they know that when the blood of Your martyr Stephen was shed, I stood there giving my approval, even guarding the outer garments of those who killed him.'

"But He said to me, 'Go, for I will send you far away to the Gentiles.'"

They had listened intently to him until he said this, but now they raised their voices shouting, "Kill him, and rid the earth of such a man! He is not fit to live!"

As they were yelling and ripping their clothes and hurling dust into the air, the commander gave orders to bring Paul into the barracks and directed that he should be examined by scourging, so that he might discover the reason for such an uproar against him. But when they had strapped him up, Paul spoke to the centurion standing by, "Is it legal for you to flog a Roman citizen before he has had a trial?"

Troubled at hearing this, the centurion went in to the commander and reported, saying, "Do you realize what you were about to do? This man is a Roman citizen!"

Then the commander himself came up to Paul, and asked, "Tell me, are you a Roman citizen?"

And he said, "Yes."

"I had to pay a lot of money to obtain my citizenship," the commander remarked.

"Well, I was born a citizen," Paul replied.

Fear rippled through those who were about to examine him and they left quickly. The commander was especially alarmed when he realized that he had put a Roman citizen in chains.

Paul's Defense before the Sanhedrin

The next day Paul was released; and the commander, determined to get to the bottom of Paul's accusation by the Jews, ordered the chief priests and Sanhedrin to convene. Then he took Paul down and set him in front of them.

Paul looked intently at the Sanhedrin and said, "Men and brothers, I have lived my life with a perfectly clear conscience before God to this day." That's as far as he got before Ananias the High Priest ordered those who were standing near to slap him in the mouth.

Paul reacted and said to him, "God will strike you, you white-washed wall! There you sit pretending to judge me by the Law when you violate it by telling them to hit me!"

Tension mounted as a bystander challenged Paul, saying, "How dare you insult God's High Priest like that?"

But Paul quickly apologized and said, "My brothers, I didn't realize that he was the High Priest; as Scripture says: 'You shall not speak evil of the ruler of your people.'"

Then, as Paul realized that part of the Council were Sadducees and the rest were Pharisees, he spoke loudly for all to hear, "I am a Pharisee, the son of Pharisees, and it is because I believe in the resurrection of the dead that I am on trial!" Paul made this statement, knowing that it would distract the Council.

There was, in fact, a great uproar as the scribes of the Pharisees rose to Paul's defense against the Sadducees who don't believe in resurrection, angelic beings, or a non-physical spirit realm. "We find nothing wrong with this man!" they protested. "Suppose some angel or spirit has really spoken to him?"

By this point the Roman tribune feared that Paul might be torn to pieces. So he ordered the soldiers to come down and rescue him and bring him back to the barracks.

That night the Lord appeared at Paul's side and said to him, "Courage! You have witnessed boldly for Me here in Jerusalem, and you must give your witness for Me in Rome."

Early in the morning a group of about forty Jews formed a conspiracy and bound themselves by a solemn oath to neither eat nor drink until they had killed Paul. They approached the chief priests and elders and said, "We have bound ourselves by a solemn oath to let nothing pass our lips until we have killed Paul. Now you and the Council must ask the commander to bring Paul down to you, explaining that you want to examine his case more closely. While they are making their way here, we will kill him."

However, Paul's nephew got wind of this plot and hurried to the barracks to tell Paul about it. Paul called one of the centurions and said, "Take this young man to the commander. He has something to report to him."

So the centurion took him to the commander and said, "The prisoner Paul asked me to bring this young man to speak to you."

The commander took him by the hand, led him away from the others, and asked him privately, "What did you want to tell me?"

The boy replied, "The Jews have agreed to ask you to bring Paul down to the Sanhedrin tomorrow as though they were going to inquire more carefully into his case. But you mustn't let them persuade you because more than forty of them are waiting for him. They have sworn a solemn oath that they won't eat or drink until they have killed him. They have everything set in place and are waiting for you to give the order."

At this the man dismissed the boy, warning him, "Don't let anyone know that you have given me this information." Then he summoned two of his centurions and said, "Get two hundred soldiers ready to proceed to Caesarea along with seventy horsemen and two hundred spearmen by nine o'clock tonight." A horse was also to be provided for Paul so he could make it safely to Felix the governor.

The commander then wrote this letter of explanation to Felix:

"Claudius Lysias sends greetings to his Excellency Governor Felix. This man had been seized by the Jews and was on the point of being murdered by them. When I arrived with my troops and discovered that he was a Roman citizen, I rescued him. In my investigation of the charges against him, I had him appear before their Sanhedrin. That was where I discovered he was being accused regarding some of their laws and certainly nothing which deserved either death or imprisonment. Now, however, it has come to my attention that there is a plot against his life, so I have sent him to you without delay. At the same time, I have notified his accusers that they must make their charges against him in your presence."

Imprisonment in Caesarea

Paul's Defense Before Felix

So it was that the soldiers took Paul and, riding through that night, brought him down to Antipatris. The next day they returned to Jerusalem, leaving the horsemen to accompany him the rest of the way. The contingent proceeded to Caesarea; and after delivering the letter to the governor, they handed Paul over to him. Once Felix had read the letter, he asked Paul what province he came from. On learning that he came from Cilicia, the governor said, "I will hear your case as soon as your accusers arrive." Then he ordered him to be kept under guard in Herod's palace.

Five days later Ananias the High Priest arrived with some of the elders and an attorney by the name of Tertullus. They presented their case against Paul before the governor. When Paul had been summoned, Tertullus began his prosecution with these words:

"Most Excellent Felix, it is because of your outstanding leadership and reforms that our nation enjoys much peace and a greatly improved standard of living. At all times, and indeed in all places, we acknowledge all these things with the deepest gratitude.

"However, getting quickly to the point so as not to impose on you, we request this brief hearing. Quite simply, the issue is that we have found this man to be a pest, stirring up trouble among Jews all over the world. He is a ringleader of the sect known as the Nazarenes, and he was about to desecrate the temple when we apprehended him. I'm certain you will recognize the danger just as soon as you hear this man's own testimony."

While Tertullus was still speaking, the Jews kept butting in, confirming each detail. The governor looked toward Paul and called for his statement.

"Because you have been governor of this nation for many years, your Honor," Paul began, "I am pleased to present my defense before you. The facts show that it was just twelve days ago that I went up to worship at Jerusalem. Not once did I argue with anyone in the temple or start a riot, either in the synagogues or in public. What these men are claiming cannot be substantiated in the least.

"I will admit to you, however, that I do worship the God of our fathers according to The Way, which they call a heresy. My beliefs are based solidly on the authority of both the Law and the Prophets; and I have the same hope in God which they themselves hold, that there is to be a resurrection of both good men and bad. It is because of this belief that I do strive to live my whole life with a clear conscience before God and man.

"It is worth noting that I have been away from Jerusalem for several years and returned at this time to bring financial assistance to my own nation and to make my offerings. Indeed, I had completed purification rituals and was about to present my offering when I was accosted. There was neither mob nor disturbance until the Jews from Asia came, who, by the way, ought to be here bringing their accusations against me. Otherwise, let these men themselves speak out now and say what crime they found me guilty of when I stood before their Council — unless it was that one sentence that I shouted as I stood among them. All I said was this, 'It is about the resurrection of the dead that I am on trial before you this day.'"

Then Felix, who was well-acquainted with The Way, adjourned the matter and said, "As soon as Commander Lysias arrives, I will decide this case." Then he gave orders to the centurion to keep Paul in custody but to grant him reasonable liberty and to allow any of his personal friends to look after his needs.

Paul's Defense Before Festus

Some days later Felix along with his wife Drusilla, herself a Jewess, sent for Paul and enquired about the message of Christ Jesus. However, while Paul was talking about goodness, self-control, and the judgment to come, Felix became troubled and dismissed him, saying, "That will be enough for now. When I find time, I will send for you again." He was actually hoping that Paul would pay him money, which is why Paul was frequently summoned to come and talk with him. However, after two years had passed, Felix was succeeded by Porcius Festus; and as Festus wanted to curry favor with the Jews, he left Paul in prison.

Just three days after Festus had taken over his duties as governor, he went up from Caesarea to Jerusalem. While he was there, the chief priests and elders of the Jews informed him of the case against Paul and urged him to have Paul sent to Jerusalem. They had already made a plot to kill him on the way. But Festus replied that Paul was in custody in Caesarea, and that he himself was going there shortly.

"What you must do," he told them, "is to provide some competent men of your own to go down with me. They can present their charges against him there."

About ten days later Festus returned to Caesarea from Jerusalem. The very next day he took his seat on the bench and ordered Paul to be brought in. As soon as he arrived, the Jews from Jerusalem pressed in around him, bringing all kinds of serious accusations with no evidence whatsoever. Paul defended himself by simply stating, "I have committed no offence in any way against the Jewish Law, against the temple, or against Caesar."

But Festus, wishing to gain favor with the Jews, asked Paul, "Are you prepared to go up to Jerusalem and stand your trial over these matters in my presence there?"

Paul replied, "Here I stand in Caesar's tribunal, which is where I should be judged. I have done the Jews no harm, as you very well know. If I were proven to be a criminal and had committed some crime which deserved the death penalty, I would willingly accept the sentence of death. But since there is no truth in the accusations these men have made, I am not prepared to be used as a means of gaining their favor. I appeal to Caesar!"

Then Festus, after a brief meeting with his council, replied to Paul, "You have appealed to Caesar. Then to Caesar you shall go!"

Paul's Defense Before Agrippa

Some days later King Agrippa and Bernice arrived at Caesarea on a state visit to Festus. They prolonged their stay for some days and Festus spoke with him about Paul's case, saying, "I have here a man who was left a prisoner by Felix. Recently, while I was in Jerusalem, the chief priests and Jewish elders made allegations against him and demanded his conviction.

"I explained to them that the Romans were not in the habit of handing someone over to their accusers until they had been given the opportunity of defending themselves on the charges made against them. Since these Jews came back here with me, I wasted no time in pursuing the case. However, once the prosecution got up to speak, their charges weren't at all what I had expected.

"Their charges had to do with their religion and a certain Jesus who had died, but whom Paul claimed to be still alive. Since I did not feel qualified to adjudicate the matter, I asked the man if he would be willing to go to Jerusalem and stand trial there. It was at that point that he appealed to have his case reserved for the decision of the emperor himself. So I ordered him to be kept in custody until I could send him to Caesar."

Then Agrippa said to Festus, "I would like to hear this man myself."

"Then you shall hear him tomorrow," replied Festus.

The next day, Agrippa and Bernice proceeded to the audience chamber with great pomp and ceremony, which included an escort of military officers and prominent townsmen. Festus ordered Paul to be brought in and proceeded to address the gathering, "King Agrippa and all who are present, I present before you the man about whom the Jewish people both at Jerusalem and in this city have petitioned me. They keep insisting that he ought not to live any longer; but I, for my part, discovered nothing that he has done which deserves the death penalty.

"Now that he has appealed to Caesar, I must send him to Rome. I have nothing specific to write to the emperor about him and have therefore brought him forward before you all, and especially before you, King Agrippa. I trust that from your examination of him there may emerge some charge which I may put in writing. For it is embarrassing to me to send a prisoner before the emperor without indicating the charges against him."

Then Agrippa said to Paul, "You have our permission to speak for yourself."

So Paul, gesturing with his hand, began his defense:

"King Agrippa, in answering all the charges that the Jews have made against me, I consider it a privilege to be making my defense before you personally today. I know that you are thoroughly familiar with all the customs and disputes that exist among the Jews. Please bear with me as I present my case.

"It is known to all the Jews that I grew up from my youth among my own people in Jerusalem. If they would admit it, they know that I lived as a Pharisee according to the strictest sect of our religion.

"Even today I stand here on trial because of a hope that I hold in a promise God made to our forefathers, a promise for which our twelve tribes served God zealously day and night, hoping to see it fulfilled. It is because of this hope, your Majesty, that I am being accused by the Jews! I cannot understand why it should seem impossible to anyone here that God will raise the dead.

"There was a time when I felt it was my duty to oppose the name of Jesus of Nazareth. Right there in Jerusalem with the authorization of the chief priests, I had many of God's people imprisoned and on trial for their lives. I gave my vote against them. Time and again in all the synagogues, I had them punished; I did everything I could to get them to deny their Lord. I was mad with fury against them, and I hounded them to distant cities.

"Once, your Majesty, on my way to Damascus, armed with the full authority and commission of the chief priests, my journey was interrupted at high noon when a light from Heaven, far brighter than the sun, blazed around me and my companions. We all fell to the ground and I heard a voice saying to me in Hebrew, 'Saul, Saul, why are you persecuting Me? It's time for you to stop kicking against your own conscience.'

"'Who are You, Lord?' I asked. And the Lord said to me, 'I am Jesus whom you are persecuting. Now get up and stand on your feet for I have shown Myself to you for a reason. You are chosen to be My servant and a witness to what you have seen of Me today and of other visions of Myself which I will give you. I will keep you safe from both your own people and from the Gentiles to whom I now send you. I send you to open their eyes, to turn them from darkness to light, from the power of Satan to God Himself, so that they may know forgiveness of their sins and take their place with all those who are uniquely identified by their trust in Me.'

"So you see, King Agrippa, I could not disobey the heavenly vision. I proclaimed the message in Damascus and in Jerusalem, through the whole of Judea, and to the Gentiles. Everywhere I went, I preached that men should admit they've been living for themselves, should repent and turn to God, and should let Him change them from the inside out. This is why the Jews seized me in the temple and tried to kill me. God has been my help and I stand here as a witness to both rulers and peasants. My message is nothing more than what the prophets foretold should take place; that is, that the Messiah should suffer and that He should be first to rise from the dead. This is the message of light which I declare boldly both to our people and to the Gentiles!"

Festus wasn't buying any of this. He blurted out in the midst of Paul's statement, "You are crazy, Paul! All your learning has gone to your head!"

But Paul replied, "No, your Excellency, I am not out of my mind. I am speaking truth. The king here understands what I'm talking about because none of it has been done in secret." Addressing King Agrippa directly, Paul said, "You believe the Prophets, don't you? I'm sure you do."

"You keep this up, Paul," returned Agrippa, "and before long you will be making me a Christian!"

"O King," Paul replied, "whether it happens 'before long' or down the road, I would to God that both you and all who can hear me today might become what I am — except for these chains, of course."

Then the king and the other dignitaries stood up and excused themselves from the assembly. They discussed the matter among themselves and agreed, "This man is doing nothing to deserve either death or imprisonment." Agrippa commented to Festus, "He might easily have been released if he had not appealed to Caesar."

PAUL'S JOURNEY TO ROME

Once it was determined that we should set sail for Italy, Paul and some other prisoners were put under the charge of a centurion named Julius from the emperor's own regiment. We embarked on a ship hailing from Adramyttium, bound for the Asian ports, and set sail. Among our company was Aristarchus, a Macedonian from Thessalonica. On the following day we put in at Sidon, where Julius treated Paul most considerately by allowing him to visit his friends and to accept their hospitality. From Sidon we put out to sea again and sailed on the sheltered side of Cyprus since the wind was against us.

When we had crossed the gulf that lies off the coasts of Cilicia and Pamphylia, we arrived at Myra in Lycia. There the centurion found an Alexandrian ship bound for Italy and we boarded her. After several days of slow progress, we approached Cnidus; but since the wind was still blowing against us, we sailed under the shelter of Crete and rounded Cape Salmone. It was with much difficulty that we came to a place called Fair Havens, which is near the city of Lasea. We had by now lost a great deal of time, and sailing had become dangerous as it was so late in the year.

Paul warned them, saying, "Men, I can see that this voyage is likely to result in damage and considerable loss, not only of ship and cargo but even of our lives as well."

But Julius paid more attention to the pilot and the captain than to Paul's words of warning. Besides, since the harbor at Fair Haven is unsuitable for a ship to winter in, the majority were in favor of setting sail again in the hope of reaching Phoenix and wintering there. Phoenix is a harbor in Crete, facing both southwest and northwest.

So when a moderate breeze sprang up, thinking they had obtained just what they wanted, they weighed anchor and coasted along, hugging the shores of Crete. But we hadn't gone far before a terrific wind, which they call a northeaster, swept down upon us from the land. The ship was caught by it; and since she could not be brought up into the wind, we had to let it drive us. Running under the lee of a small island called Clauda, we managed with some difficulty to secure the ship's small landing boat. After hoisting it aboard, cables were used to reinforce the ship. To make matters worse, there was a risk of drifting onto the Syrtis banks, so the crew set the anchor and drifted. The next day, as we were still at the mercy of the violent storm, they began to throw cargo overboard. On the third day, with their own hands the sailors threw the ship's tackle over the side. After all that, we were still being whipped around mercilessly by the storm without seeing sun or stars for days. All hope of our being saved was lost.

Nobody had eaten anything for several days when Paul came forward among the men and said, "Men, if you would have listened to me and not set sail from Crete, we would not have suffered this damage and loss. However, now I beg you to take courage; for no one's life is going to be lost, though we shall lose the ship. I know this because last night the angel of the God to whom I belong and whom I serve stood by me and said, 'Don't be afraid, Paul! You must stand before Caesar. God has graciously extended His favor to preserve the lives of all those who are sailing with you.' Take courage then, men, for I believe God. I am convinced that everything will happen exactly as I have been told. But we shall have to run the ship ashore on some island."

On the fourteenth night of the storm as we were drifting in the Adriatic Sea, about midnight the sailors sensed that we were nearing land. When they measured, they found the water to be one hundred twenty feet deep. After sailing on only a little way, they measured again and it was just ninety feet. Fearing that we might crash against the rocks, they threw out four anchors from the stern and prayed for daylight.

Some of the sailors wanted to desert the ship. They got as far as letting down the landing boat into the sea, pretending that they were going to run out anchors from the bow. But Paul said to the centurion and the soldiers, "Unless these men stay aboard the ship, there is no hope of your being saved." At this the soldiers cut the ropes of the boat and let her fall away.

While everyone waited for the day to break, Paul urged them to take some food, saying, "For two weeks now you've had no food; you haven't eaten a bite while you've been on watch. Now take some food, please. You need it for your own well-being, for not a hair of anyone's head will be lost." When he had said this, he took some bread; and after thanking God before them all, he broke it and began to eat. This raised everybody's spirits and they began to take food themselves. There were about two hundred seventy-six of us aboard the ship. When we had eaten enough, they lightened the ship by throwing the remaining grain over the side.

When daylight came, no one recognized the land. In the dim light of dawn they could make out a bay with a sandy shore where they planned to beach the ship if they could. So they cut away the anchors and abandoned them in the sea. At the same time they cut the ropes which held the steering oars. Then they hoisted the foresail to catch the wind and made for the beach. But they struck a reef where the two seas converge and the ship ran aground. The bow stuck fast while the stern began to break up under the force of the waves.

The soldiers' plan had been to kill the prisoners in case any of them should try to swim to shore and escape. But the centurion, wanting to save Paul, stopped them and gave orders that all who could swim should jump overboard first and get to land; the rest should follow on planks and on the wreckage of the ship. In this way everyone reached the shore in safety.

Once we were safely on land, we discovered that the island was called Melita. The natives treated us with uncommon kindness. Because of the driving rain and cold, they lit a fire and made us all welcome.

Paul had collected a large bundle of sticks and was laying it on the fire when a viper, driven out by the heat, fastened itself on his hand. Seeing the creature hanging from his hand, the natives said to each other, "This man is obviously a murderer. He has escaped from the sea, but justice will not let him live." But Paul shook the viper off into the fire. Nothing happened to him. Naturally they expected him to swell up or suddenly fall down dead; but after waiting a long time and seeing nothing harmful happen to him, they changed their minds and began saying he was a god.

In that part of the island were estates belonging to the governor, whose name was Publius. He welcomed us and entertained us most generously for three days. Now it happened that Publius' father was lying ill with fever and dysentery. Paul visited him, prayed, laid his hands on him, and healed him. After that all the other sick people on the island came forward and were cured. Consequently they loaded us with presents; and when the time came for us to sail, they provided us with everything we needed.

However, it wasn't until three months later that we set sail in an Alexandrian ship which had wintered at the island, a ship that had the astronomical twins, Pollux and Castor, as her figurehead. We put in at Syracuse and stayed there three days; from there we tacked round to Rhegium. A day later a south wind sprang up and we sailed to Puteoli, reaching it in only two days. There we found some of the brothers and they begged us to stay with them. After spending a week there, we finally made our way to Rome.

The brothers there had heard about us and journeyed about thirty miles south of the city to meet us at the Market of Appius and the Three Inns. When Paul saw them, he thanked God and was encouraged. In Rome Paul was given permission to live on his own, accompanied by just one soldier.

Three days later Paul invited the leading Jews to meet him. When they arrived, he spoke to them, "Brethren, although I have done nothing against our people or the customs of our forefathers, I was handed over to the Romans as a prisoner in Jerusalem. They examined me and were prepared to release me since they found me guilty of nothing deserving the death penalty. But the objections of the Jews there forced me to appeal to Caesar — not that I had any accusation to make against my own nation. It is because of this accusation of the Jews that I have asked to see you and talk this over with you. The fact is that I am wearing these chains on account of the hope of Israel."

But they replied, "We have received no letters about you from Judea, nor have any of the brothers come here with complaints against you, officially or unofficially. We want to hear you state your views; although as far as this sect is concerned, we do know that serious objections have been raised to it everywhere."

When they had arranged a day for him, they came to his lodging in great numbers. From morning till evening he explained the Kingdom of God to them, giving his personal testimony, trying to persuade them about Jesus from the Law of Moses and the Prophets. As a result several of them were persuaded by his words, but others would not believe.

As they could not reach any agreement among themselves and began to go away, Paul added these final words, "The Holy Spirit nailed it when He spoke to your forefathers through the prophet Isaiah, saying, 'Go to the people and say, "Even though you hear, you won't understand; and even if I show you, you still won't see it. For the heart of this people has grown dull; their ears are hard of hearing, and their eyes they have closed, lest they should see with their eyes and hear with their ears; lest they should understand with their heart and turn, so that I should heal them."'

"From now on the message of salvation from our God has been sent to the Gentiles, at least they will listen to it!"

So Paul stayed for two full years in his own rented apartment, welcoming all who came to see him. He proclaimed to them all the Kingdom of God and gave them the teaching of the Lord Jesus Christ with complete freedom and without hindrance from anyone.

What an unusual way to end a "book" — especially since we know from other historical resources what happened next. Why this sudden "The End" in the middle of a page-turner about first-century world-changers? Aha! Maybe it wasn't intended to be The End. What we call "The Book of Acts" or "The Acts of the Apostles" was really never given an inspired title. If Part One of the *Trilogy* ("The Story of Jesus") was God presenting His plan and solution for bringing about the perfect Kingdom of God, then Part Two ("The Sequel") is the ongoing story of how the plan is taking shape in our lifetimes. Just maybe the Author wanted to pull the reader into the action in such a way that by the time they reach this page, they have become part of the story themselves! I hope you're "in."

THE FINALÉ
(REVELATION)

"The Finalé" is a presentation of the last book of the New Testament in which God portrays the consummation of His eternal plan. Midst all the mystery and metaphor, God moves human history toward His intended climax: a new realm in which He and His children live together forever in pure companionship with His Son Jesus at the center of all things.

EXPLANATION

Working through the complex images and metaphors of Revelation, my brain felt rather like a pretzel, all twisted and randomly connected . . . or not. But I just kept pushing forward, trying to visualize the scenes. In addition to adapting the grammar and structure to make the text more readable, I have organized and portrayed this unique portion of Scripture as a drama. In this drama, however, there are two stages visible simultaneously, one above the other. Some action occurs exclusively on the upper (heavenly) stage, but most of the scenes involve actions in the heavens whose consequences play out on the lower (earthly) stage. John, the apostle, plays the role of narrator throughout this drama. At times he may be seen seated in the audience observing from a distance, while occasionally he is drawn up onto the upper stage and provides live "on the scene" reports.

It wasn't until I was finished with it that I realized the best way (at least at first) to take in "The Finalé" is to experience it like a high-tech, Imax theater production. What do I mean? When you go to a theater to watch a cinematic thriller, you don't get a remote control to pause the presentation every time there's a character or plot twist you don't understand. No, you simply have to sit still and let the show go on from beginning to end. After all, the director of the project mainly wants you to come away so gripped with the overall impact that you have to go back time and again to fit the pieces together. That's what you need to do with this complex little "thriller." Read it through. Ask the Director what He mainly wants you to get from it the first time through. It is important that the reader not get dissuaded from finishing the complete presentation as the "loose ends" don't resolve until the final act. God, the original Author, chose not to make every detail readily understandable. He did leave no doubt, however, about how the Story ends. . . and begins anew.

And now, buckle your seatbelts; "The Finalé" is about to begin!

PROLOGUE

Narrator:

This is God's revelation of things to come, the Word from God regarding Jesus Christ. This message was delivered to God's bond-slave, John, by the Angel of the Lord.

A special blessing is promised to all who read these words, listen to them, and keep them. The time of fulfillment is very near.

I, John, am particularly addressing this to the seven churches in Asia. Grace to you and peace

- from Him
  - » Who is,
  - » Who was,
  - » Who is to come;
- from the seven Spirits before His throne;
- and from Jesus Christ
  - » The faithful Witness,
  - » Firstborn of the dead,
  - » Ruler of the kings of the earth.

Glory and never-ending dominion belong to Him
- Who loves us,
- Who has released us from our sins by His own blood,
- Who has made us into a Kingdom,
- Who has made us priests to His God and Father.

Look! He is coming through the clouds! Every eye will see Him, even those who pierced Him. The sight will bring every tribe on earth to its knees in bitter grief. Amen!

"I am the Beginning (Alpha) and the End (Omega)," declares the Lord God, "Who Is, Who Was, and Who Is to Come, the Supreme Almighty."

This Word came to me when I was exiled on Patmos for declaring God's Word and telling people about Jesus. We are brothers in Him, and in Him we share in suffering for the Kingdom and in patiently enduring all the difficulties we face, just as Jesus our Messiah did.

ACT 1: THE END IS NEAR: COUNSEL TO THE CHURCHES

SCENE 1: The Appearance of the Son of Man

It was the Day of the Lord, and I was in the Spirit when suddenly I heard a loud Voice from behind me. It shook me like a trumpet blast.

"Write down everything you see," the Voice said, "and send it to the churches: Ephesus, Smyrna, Pergamum, Thyatira, Sardis, Philadelphia, and Laodicea."

I turned around to see who was speaking; and there, standing among seven gold lampstands, was the Son of Man. He was wearing a kingly robe with a gold sash across His chest. His head and His hair were white like wool, as white as snow. His eyes blazed like they were on fire, and His feet were glowing like bronze just taken from the furnace. His voice thundered like a mighty waterfall.

In His right hand He was holding seven stars, and out of His mouth was a sharp two-edged sword. His face glowed like the sun shining in full strength.

Overcome by His majestic presence, I fell at His feet like I was dead. Then He laid His right hand on me and said, "Don't be afraid. I am the First and the Last, the Living One. I was dead, but look! I am alive forever and I hold the keys of death and the grave.

"So write down
- the things you have seen,
- the things that are going on right now,
- and the things that will be happening in the future.

"The seven lampstands represent the seven churches to whom I am addressing this revelation, and the stars you saw in My hand are the seven angels of the seven churches."

SCENE 2: Letters to the Seven Churches

EPHESUS

"To the Church in Ephesus I say,

"This message comes from the One who holds the seven stars in His right hand, and who walks among the seven golden lampstands.

"I know what you have done:
- how hard you have worked;
- what hardships you have endured;
- that you won't tolerate evil people;
- how you cross-examined self-proclaimed 'apostles,' proving them to be liars;
- how you have suffered for My name time after time without giving up;
- and that you hate the immoral deeds of the Compromisers (Nicolaitans) as I do.

"But I hold this against you: you have left your first love.

"Remember how it was when you first believed. Return to loving Me as you did then. If you don't do this, I will have to remove your lampstand.

"Let everyone listen to what the Spirit is saying to the churches:
Those who overcome will get to eat from the
Tree of Life which grows in the Paradise of God."

SMYRNA

"To the Church in Smyrna I say,

"This message comes from the First and the Last, who was dead and has come to life again.

"I know:

- the tribulation you go through,
- your poverty (though you are really rich),
- the slander you endure from those so-called Jews who are a synagogue of Satan.

"Don't fear what you will be suffering:

- the devil will be having some of you put in prison;
- your faith will be tested;
- the distress will last for ten days.

"Be faithful in the face of death and I will give you the crown of life.

"Let everyone listen to what the Spirit is saying to the churches:
Those who overcome will not be
the least bit affected by the second death."

PERGAMUM

"To the Church in Pergamum I say,

"This message comes from Him who has the sharp two-edged sword.

"I know:

- where you live — in Satan's headquarters;
- that you have stayed loyal to Me;
- that your trust in Me didn't waver even when Antipas, My faithful witness, was martyred before your eyes by Satan's cohorts.

"But these things must change:

- Some among you encourage moral compromise like Balaam did when he showed Balak how to seduce the children of Israel into doing evil.
- Others in your group are caught up in the deception of the Nicolaitans.

"These had better repent quickly or I will fight against them with the sword of my mouth.

"Let everyone listen to what the Spirit is saying to the churches:
To those who overcome I will give hidden manna
and a white stone with a new name written on it,
a name which only those who receive it
will understand."

THYATIRA

"To the Church in Thyatira I say,

"This message comes from the Son of God whose eyes blaze like fire and whose feet shine like pure bronze.

"I know:
- how much you have done for Me,
- that you have loved Me and stayed loyal to Me,
- how faithfully you have persevered in serving Me,
- that you are doing even more now than you did at first.

"But this I hold against you: you tolerate that pseudo-prophetess 'Jezebel' who deceives My servants with her seductive words, leading them into sexual immorality and fellowship with idolaters.

"I have given her time to repent, but she has no desire to change her ways. Watch! I will throw her and her children onto a sickbed, and they will suffer unto death unless they repent. Then all the churches will know that I see into the secret places of men's hearts and that I reward each one according to their deeds.

"For those of you who haven't fallen into her trap and learned 'the deep things of Satan,' I simply ask that you hold on to what you have until I come.

"Let everyone listen to what the Spirit is saying to the churches:
To those who overcome,
who steadfastly serve Me to the end,
I will give authority over the nations
just as the Father gave Me His authority.
They shall rule with a rod of iron,
breaking them to pieces like useless pottery;
and I will give them the morning star."

SARDIS

"To the Church in Sardis I say,

"This message comes from Him who holds in His hand the seven Spirits of God and the seven stars.

"I know about all your activity, which gives you a reputation as being alive when, in fact, you are quite dead.

"Wake up!

- Strengthen what little you have before it dies: you start so many things but never follow through.
- Think back to what you learned and received at first; take hold of those things and act on them.

"If you refuse to wake up, I will come to you like a thief; you'll be caught completely by surprise!

"I know the names of those few left in Sardis who have 'kept their garment clean.' They have earned the right to walk with Me in radiant glory.

"Let everyone listen to what the Spirit is saying to the churches:
Those who overcome
will receive glorious white garments
and I will never erase their names
from the Book of Life.
No, I will gladly declare their names
to My Father and His angels."

PHILADELPHIA

"To the Church in Philadelphia I say,

"This message comes from the One who is holy and true, who has the 'Key of David,' the One who opens doors so none can shut them and shuts doors so none can open them.

"I know how much you have accomplished. Look!

- Because you have been faithful to My message and not denied My name but have used what little you were given to do so much, I set before you a wide open door of opportunity that no one can close.

- Those liars who claim to be Jews but are really of Satan's synagogue will bow down before you and be forced to admit that I have loved you.
- Since you've obeyed Me so thoroughly, I will keep you safe from the deep trouble the rest of the world is about to face.

"I am coming back soon; hold on to what you have and don't let anyone steal your crown.

"Let everyone listen to what the Spirit is saying to the churches:
Those who overcome I will make pillars
in the temple of My God,
permanently established in His presence.
I will write upon him the name of My God
and the name of the city of My God,
the New Jerusalem which comes down
from Heaven from My God.
And I will write upon him My own new name."

LAODICEA

"To the Church in Laodicea I say,

"This message comes from the Amen, the Faithful and True Witness, the Founder of God's creation.

"I know all about your activities; they are neither hot nor cold. I wish you were cold or hot; but since you are lukewarm, I will spit you out of My mouth.

"You think of yourself as prosperous and quite successful. You're blind to the fact that you are actually wretched, miserable, poverty-stricken, blind, and naked.

"Here's My urgent advice to you:
- Buy from Me the gold that is purified in the furnace so you can be truly rich.
- Clothe yourselves with My white garments to cover your shameful nakedness.
- Ask Me for salve to heal your blind eyes.

"I always correct and discipline those whom I love. Shake off your complacency. Humble yourselves. Repent! I'm standing, knocking at the door. Listen! Do you hear My voice? Let Me into your life, and let us commune together.

"Let everyone listen to what the Spirit is saying to the churches:
Those who overcome
will have the privilege of sitting with Me
on My throne just as I have overcome
and sit beside My Father on His throne."

ACT 2: HEAVEN DECLARES WAR: SEVEN SEAL JUDGMENTS

SCENE 1: The Lamb Is Center Stage

After that I saw an open door leading into Heaven; and I heard that trumpet-like Voice again, this time saying, "Come up here so I can show you what will happen next."

Instantly I was in the Spirit participating in a heavenly scene, all focused on a marvelous throne. But what really caught my attention was the One sitting on the throne!

How can I describe the scene?

- He who sat on the throne radiated beauty like that of pure gems: jasper and carnelian, with an emerald-like rainbow encircling Him.
- Surrounding His throne were twenty-four more thrones with twenty-four elders upon them. They wore white garments and had gold crowns on their heads.
- Flashes of lightning and loud peals of thunder came from His throne.

THE Jesus TRILOGY

- There were seven lamps burning in front of the throne, the seven Spirits of God.
- Stretching out in front of the throne was a crystal lake, clear as glass.

Four unusual creatures were hovering about the throne, each with six wings and with eyes on all sides of their bodies:

- the first was like a lion,
- the second was like a calf,
- the third had a face like a man,
- the fourth was like a flying eagle.

Day and night these creatures declare, "Holy, holy, holy is the Lord God, the Almighty, Who Was and Who Is and Who Is to Come."

As they express this tribute to the One sitting on the throne, the twenty-four elders bow down before Him, lay their crowns at His feet, and add to the chorus of worship, saying,

"You are worthy, O Lord!
All glory, honor, and authority belongs to You
because You created all things
and everything exists for Your pleasure."

Then I noticed that the One seated on the throne held a scroll in His right hand. It had writing on both sides but was sealed up with seven seals.

A mighty angel boomed out, "Who is worthy to open the scroll and break the seals?"

But there was no one in heaven or on earth who qualified even to look into it. I began to weep over this until one of the elders said, "Wait! Stop your tears. Look, the Lion of the tribe of Judah, the Root of David, has overcome. He has authority to break the seals and open the scroll."

That's when I saw Him approach the throne — a Lamb, One that had obviously been sacrificed. He had seven horns and seven eyes which are the seven Spirits of God sent out into the whole earth. He came and took the scroll from the right hand of the One who sat on the throne.

As He took the scroll, the four creatures along with the twenty-four elders fell down before the Lamb. They each had a harp and golden bowls full of smoking incense, which are the prayers of the saints.

Then they began singing this new song:

> "You are worthy to take the scroll
> and to break its seals, for You were slain.
> With Your blood You have purchased for Your God
> men from every tribe and tongue
> and people and nation.
> You have made them kings and priests
> to minister to God,
> and they will reign upon the earth."

Joining them was the voice of countless angels, myriads upon myriads and thousands of thousands. Together with the creatures and the elders, they said with a loud voice,

> "Worthy is the Lamb that was slain
> to receive authority, riches, wisdom, strength,
> honor, glory, and blessing!"

Then I heard every creature in heaven, on earth, under the earth, and on the sea, every living thing everywhere, saying,

> "To Him who sits on the throne and to the Lamb,
> be blessing and honor and glory and dominion
> forever and ever."

The four living creatures kept saying, "Amen!" And the elders fell down and worshiped.

SCENE 2: The Scroll Is Opened

I saw the Lamb take the scroll and break open the first seal. Suddenly a voice thundered, "COME!" It was one of the four creatures who spoke, and a rider on a white horse sped past. The rider had a crown and took his bow to wage war on the earth.

When the second seal was broken, another of the four living creatures shouted, "COME!" Then I saw a rider on a red horse. He was carrying a great sword, and his job was to stir up conflict and remove all peace from the earth.

The third seal was broken. The third creature called for a rider on a black horse, who rode past holding a pair of scales. A voice in the midst of the creatures declared, "A loaf of bread for a whole day's wage, so also three loaves of barley. Do not touch the oil and the wine." He brought intense famine upon the whole earth.

As the fourth seal was broken and the fourth creature said, "COME!," a pale yellowish-green horse approached, whose rider was Death. The Grave followed close behind and they were given authority to wipe out one-fourth of the earth by means of sword, famine, pestilence, and wild beasts.

The fifth seal was very different. Beneath the altar I saw the souls of all who had been martyred because of their testimony and the offense of the Word of God. They cried out in unison, "How long, O Lord, Holy and True, will You hold back from avenging our blood on those who dwell on the earth?" Then I watched as each was given a white robe and told to wait just a little longer until more of their brethren joined them as martyrs.

When the Lamb broke the sixth seal,

- there was a great earthquake,
- the sun was darkened,
- the moon turned blood red,
- stars fell to the earth like ripe figs falling from trees in a windstorm,
- the sky was rolled up like a scroll,
- and the mountains and islands disappeared.

By this point terror swept over the earth. From the highest world leaders, the rich and famous, and military generals, to the lowest class slaves, everyone ran for the hills and hid wherever they could find cover. I heard them praying to the rocks around them, saying, "Fall on us! Don't let that One who sits on the throne see us! Hide us from the wrath of the Lamb! The dreaded Day of Their anger has arrived and who can stand up to Them?"

SCENE 3: Freeze Action on Earth: 144,000 Sealed

A little later I could see four angels standing at the four corners of the earth, holding back the winds so that they would not blow at all. Then another angel came up from the east carrying the seal of the Living God. He called out to the four angels who had power to destroy, "Don't touch the earth, the sea, or the trees until we have sealed the servants of our God upon their foreheads!" These angels went out and marked twelve thousand from each of the twelve tribes of Israel (Judah, Reuben, Gad, Asher, Naphtali, Manasseh, Simeon, Levi, Issachar, Zebulun, Joseph, and Benjamin), a total of 144,000.

Then suddenly a huge crowd was approaching the throne of the Lamb. They were dressed in dazzling white robes and held palm branches in their hands. I could tell that among the millions were people from every corner of the earth: every nation, every tribe, every language. In a thundering chorus they shouted, "Salvation belongs to our God who sits upon the throne and to the Lamb!"

I saw encircling the throne all the angels, the elders, and the four living creatures bowing down to the throne. Together they declared, "Amen! Blessing and glory and wisdom and thanksgiving and honor and authority and might belong to our God forever and ever!"

One of the twenty-four elders asked if I knew who this huge crowd dressed in white was or where they had come from. "No, sir," was my reply, "but surely you know."

"Yes," he answered, "they have just come out of the great tribulation. The white robes show that they have cleansed themselves in the blood of the Lamb. That is why they have been given the honor of serving before God's throne.

"Day and night as they minister to God, He will shelter them and be all that they need. Never again will they suffer hunger or thirst. The Lamb who sits front and center on the throne will shepherd them, leading them to springs of living water and shading them from the scorching heat of the sun. God Himself will wipe away every tear from their eyes."

Then, as the Lamb broke the seventh seal, there was total silence throughout Heaven for what seemed like half an hour.

ACT 3: THE BATTLE INTENSIFIES: SEVEN TRUMPET JUDGMENTS

SCENE 1: The Trumpets Are Blown

The seven angels who stand in the presence of God were each given a trumpet. Yet another angel approached the altar, carrying a smoking censer filled with much incense to offer up with the prayers of all the saints. As this was poured onto the altar, the smoke rose up before God, together with the prayers.

Then the angel took the censer, filled it with fire from the altar, and threw it down onto the earth. What an explosion that caused: thunderous noises, flashes of lightning, and a great earthquake. The seven angels raised their trumpets, ready to blow.

When the first angel blew his trumpet, hail and fire mingled with blood were hurled at the earth. One third of the earth was burnt up, including one-third of all the trees. Every bit of grass was scorched and withered.

The second angel blew his trumpet, and what looked like a huge mountain of fire was thrown into the ocean. A third of the waters turned to blood, a third of all sea creatures died, and a third of the world's shipping industry was destroyed.

Next, I watched as the third angel blew his trumpet. A star fell out of the sky, like a flaming meteor. It fell into a third of the rivers and fresh springs. The name of the star was Wormwood. A third of all fresh waters became poisonous; many people died after drinking it.

At the sound of the fourth trumpet, one-third of the sun, moon, and stars went dark, resulting in a third less light on the earth both day and night.

A great eagle appeared, flying through the heavens. "TERROR! TERROR! TERROR!" he cried out. "Woe to all who live on earth because of the judgments yet to come in the final three trumpets!"

The fifth trumpet sounded. Another star fell to the earth. This star had a key to the bottomless Pit; and when he opened it, smoke billowed out as from an enormous furnace. The smoke filled the sky, blocking out the light of the sun.

Gruesome locusts streamed out of the smoke:

- They could sting like scorpions.
- They were ordered not to bother plants or trees but only to afflict any humans who did not have the seal of God on their foreheads.
- They couldn't kill but could torture.
- They oppressed the earth for five months.
- Men wanted to die because of the horrendous pain, but they could not.

These locusts were unlike any creature I had ever seen before:

- They looked like horses ready for battle.
- Their faces looked human.
- They had long hair like women.
- On their heads were what appeared to be gold crowns.
- Their teeth were long and sharp like lion's teeth.
- Their chests looked like they were steel plates.
- As they flew, their wings made the sound of a vast army of chariots and horses charging into battle.
- Poisonous venom was in their tails like scorpions.

- This army of locusts was led by the king of the Pit whose name is The Destroyer. (In Hebrew his name is Abaddon; in Greek, Apollyon.)

The first terror is over but two more remain.

The sixth angel blew his trumpet, and a voice spoke from the midst of the altar which stands in the presence of God. The voice commanded the sixth angel to "release the four angels who are bound at the great river Euphrates!"

These four angels had been held back until just this moment. At this trumpet blast, they were released to kill one-third of all mankind. What I saw was an army of horsemen:

- There were two hundred million of them!
- The riders wore armor that gleamed fiery red, sky blue, and pulsing yellow like brimstone.
- The horses' heads looked more like lions.
- Their mouths spewed out fire, smoke, and sulfur so that a third of all mankind died just from that.
- Their powerful tails also caused harm and were like serpents with heads.

Believe it or not, after all this devastation, those who remained alive on earth still refused to repent of their self-worship, their idolatry, their murders, their sorceries, their sexual sins, and their many thefts.

SCENE 2: Freeze Action on Earth: The Mighty Angel

Before the seventh angel could blow his trumpet, I saw another powerful Angel coming down out of Heaven. This is what I saw:

- He was robed in clouds.
- A rainbow formed a halo over His head.
- His face was radiant like the glow of the sun.
- His legs flamed like pillars of fire.
- He had a little book lying open in His right hand.
- His right foot rested on the ocean and His left foot on the land.
- He shouted and His voice boomed like the roar of a great lion.
- When He shouted, seven thunders answered Him.

I picked up my pen to write down what the thunders had said but was interrupted by a voice from Heaven, saying, "You must not record what the thunders said. It is to remain a secret."

Then the Angel I just described raised His right hand to Heaven and declared an oath:

> "Thus says the Living One who lives forever, He who created the heavens, the earth, the seas, and all that is in them: 'No more delay! At the blast of the trumpet of the seventh angel, the mysterious plan of God will be completed precisely as He told His servants, the prophets of old.'"

Then the same voice that stopped me from writing commanded me to approach the mighty Angel and take the little book from His hand. I obeyed; and when I asked Him to give me the book, He said, "Take it; eat the whole thing. It will taste like honey in your mouth but will become bitter in your stomach."

I took the book and ate it. Just as the Angel had said, it tasted like honey at first but turned sour in my stomach. Then a voice said, "You must prophesy about many peoples, nations, languages, and kings."

After this I was given a measuring stick and instructed to measure the temple of God and to count the worshipers. "Don't measure the outer courtyard, though," I was told. "It has been turned over to the nations who will trample the holy city for three and one-half years."

SCENE 3: Time-lapse of Events on Earth

"During that period I will empower two witnesses who will proclaim My message for 1,260 days:

- They will be clothed in sackcloth.
- They are like the two olive trees and two lampstands that stand in the presence of the Lord of the whole earth.
- If anyone tries to hurt them, fire will come out of their mouths and consume them. Yes, all who attempt to do them harm will meet certain death during those days.
- They will have the authority to
  » stop it from raining,

» turn waters into blood,

» strike the earth with any plague as often as they wish."

At the end of those days, the Beast will emerge from the Pit and war against them. It will overcome and kill them; and their bodies will be left to lie on the streets of the great city, Jerusalem. Yes, the very city in which their Lord was crucified, the city which has become 'Sodom' and 'Egypt' to all who perceive with spiritual understanding.

For the next three-and-a-half days, people around the entire earth will be able to livestream the scene. It will be party time for the world. They will even exchange gifts to celebrate the end of the two witnesses who tormented them for over three years.

It happened after three-and-a-half days that God breathed life into the corpses, and they stood up in full view of all. Everyone watching was terrified. And a booming voice from Heaven commanded, "Come up here!" Then, as the stunned viewers watched, they rose up through the clouds and out of sight.

Immediately after the two witnesses left the earth, there was a great earthquake which destroyed a tenth of the city and killed seven thousand people. Everyone who didn't die was terrified and acknowledged the God of Heaven.

The second disaster is over and the third is about to begin.

ACT 4: THE PLOT THICKENS: WAR IN HEAVEN

SCENE 1: *The Proclamation of Final Victory*

The seventh angel blew his trumpet and I heard loud voices declaring: "The kingdoms of the world have become the Kingdom of our Lord and of His Messiah, and He will reign forever and ever."

Then the twenty-four elders who are seated on thrones in God's presence fell on their faces and worshiped God with these words:

> "Thank You, Lord God Almighty,
> Who Is, Who Was, and Who Is to Come!
> You have exerted Your authority and power
> and established Your reign.
> The nations shook their fists at You in anger,
> but Your wrath overcame them.
> The time has come to judge the dead.
> Now You will reward Your servants,
> the prophets and the saints,

yes, all who fear Your name, great or small.
The time has come to destroy those who destroy the earth."

Suddenly the innermost temple of God in Heaven was thrown open so that the Ark of the Covenant was clearly visible. There were flashes of lightning, loud blasts, peals of thunder, an earthquake, and a violent hailstorm.

SCENE 2: The Dragon and the Woman with Child

The image of a woman appeared in the sky:
- She was clothed with the sun.
- The moon was under her feet.
- She wore a crown with twelve stars on her head.
- She was pregnant and could be heard crying out in the labor pains of delivering her Child.
- Then another image appeared in the sky — a huge, blazing red dragon:
  » It had seven heads and ten horns.
  » A crown was on each of its heads.
  » With its tail it knocked one-third of the stars down from the heavens to the earth.
  » It crouched in front of the woman, ready to devour the Child as soon as it was born.

The moment the woman gave birth, her Son, who is to "shepherd the nations with a rod of iron," was snatched up to God and to His throne. Then the woman escaped to the wilderness where a hiding place had been prepared at God's command. She was fed there, secluded for 1,260 days.

SCENE 3: Freeze Action on Earth: The Angelic War

These events prompted a war in Heaven as Michael and his angels battled against the dragon. The dragon and his angels could not overpower Michael's hosts and were expelled from Heaven and thrown to the earth. I'm speaking of the same dragon, the serpent of ancient times, who is called the devil and Satan, the deceiver of the whole world. He and his angels were hurled to the earth.

A victory shout erupted in Heaven:

"Finally, the salvation and power and Kingdom of our God and the reign of His Messiah have come! The accuser of our brethren, who stood before God, accusing them day and night, has been thrown down. They conquered him through the blood of the Lamb and the word of their testimony. They did not love and grasp onto their own lives even in the face of death! Rejoice, O Heavens, and all who live in the heavens! But woe to you, earth and sea, for the devil has come down to you in a furious rage, knowing his time is short."

SCENE 4: More Trouble on Earth

As soon as the dragon was cast out of Heaven, he began to chase down the woman who had given birth to the male Child. However, she was able to escape with eagle's wings to the desert where she remained for three-and-a-half years, safe from the devil's vengeance.

The serpent spewed out a river of water from his mouth, attempting to drown the woman; but the earth opened its mouth and swallowed the water. Unable to overcome the woman, the devil made war with the rest of her children — all who walk in God's ways and openly confess their allegiance to Jesus.

As the dragon stood on the shore of the sea, I saw a strange beast come out of the water:

- It had seven heads and ten horns.
- There was a crown on each of the ten horns.
- Blasphemous names were tattooed on its heads.
- It looked like a leopard.
- Its feet were like those of a bear.
- Its mouth was that of a lion.

Then the dragon gave his throne, his authority, and his power to the beast:

- One of its seven heads appeared mortally wounded but then supernaturally healed.
- Everyone on earth was in awe of the creature and worshiped the dragon for giving it his powers.

273

- People everywhere called the beast "the Greatest ever" and dared any to stand up against its vast powers.
- The beast's blasphemies and wonders went on for three-and-a-half years.
- He blasphemed God, God's name, God's dwelling place, and all who live in Heaven.
- He was able to defeat the saints in battle.
- His rule extended over every tribe and people and language and nation.
- Everyone on earth worshiped it. Everyone, that is, whose name was not written in the Book of Life before the world was made, which belongs to the Lamb who was slain.

Pay close attention, reader, because everyone who has imprisoned others will himself go into captivity. All who kill with the sword must themselves be killed with the sword. Through all of this, the steadfast faith of the saints is revealed.

Next, I saw another creature rising not out of the sea but out of the earth.

- It had two horns like a lamb.
- Its voice was like that of a dragon.
- It acts with the authority of the first beast.
- It forces everyone on earth to worship the first beast, the one with the mortal wound that had been healed.
- It performs signs and wonders to deceive the people.
- It commands the people to erect a statue in honor of the beast that had been killed by the sword and then revived.
- It was given authority to give breath to the statue, enabling it to speak and condemn to death all who refuse to worship the statue.
- It commands every person on earth — rich or poor, small or great, free or slave — to receive a mark on their right hands or foreheads in order to buy or sell in the market. The number branded is the number of man: six hundred sixty-six.

SCENE 5: The Lamb and the 144,000

Then I looked and saw that the Lamb was standing on Mount Zion, accompanied by the 144,000:

- They have His name and the name of His Father written on their foreheads.
- They were singing before the throne and in the presence of the four living creatures and the elders.
- The song they were singing was a new song which no one could learn except for the 144,000 who had been redeemed from the earth.
- They are all celibate, never having married and having kept themselves pure.
- They follow the Lamb everywhere He goes.
- They were the first of many to be redeemed.
- They are men of integrity, above reproach in every way.

I heard a voice thundering out of Heaven. It sounded like a huge waterfall or loud thunder at first and then like the sound of harpists playing on their harps.

ACT 5: GOD'S WRATH COMPLETED: SEVEN BOWL JUDGMENTS

SCENE 1: *Heavenly Declarations*

Now an angel came flying through the skies. He was carrying the message of Good News for all the inhabitants of the earth. He called out loud and clear to every nation and tribe and language and people, "Fear God! Honor Him alone! The hour of judgment has come. Worship Him who made heaven and earth, the sea and the springs of water."

A second angel came behind the first, declaring, "At last! Babylon the Great has finally fallen! She made the nations drunk with her sensual pleasures."

Then a third angel followed, crying out, "Whoever has worshiped the beast and the statue, whoever has its mark on his forehead or hand, that person must drink the cup of God's angry judgment, the full extent of His wrath! In the presence of My holy angels and the Lamb, they will be tortured by fire and burning sulfur for endless ages. They will not escape! This is the fate of all who worship the beast and its statue and all who bear the mark of its name."

Through all of this, God's holy followers, those who follow His instructions and trust in Jesus, will stand strong to the end.

A voice called to me from Heaven, saying, "Write this: 'How blessed and happy will they be who die in the Lord!'"

"Yes," the Spirit echoed, "they are truly happy, for they rest from all their difficult struggles and their good deeds go with them."

SCENE 2: The Last Harvest

A remarkable scene unfolded before my eyes:

- There in front of me, sitting on a white cloud, was One who looked like the "Son of Man"; He had a sharp sickle in His hand.
- An angel came out of the temple and called to the One sitting on the cloud, "The harvest is ripe! Swing your sickle. The time of reaping has come!"
- The One sitting on the cloud swung His sickle and began to reap the harvest.
- Another angel bearing a sickle came out of the temple.
- Yet another angel, the one who has power over fire, came out of the altar and called to the angel with the sickle, "Go into the harvest! The grapes are fully ripe. Harvest the clusters from the vineyard of the earth."
- The angel swung his sickle upon the earth and brought in a vast harvest of grapes. The grapes were thrown into the great winepress of the wrath of God.
- As the grapes were crushed outside the city, a river of blood five feet deep flowed for two hundred miles.

Then, as if that weren't enough, I saw seven angels holding seven bowls, the last plagues, the final outpouring of God's wrath. Words cannot describe the awe I felt.

SCENE 3: Song of the Overcomers

Right in front of me was a crystal clear sea of glass mixed with fire. People were standing on it:

- They were the ones who had overcome the battle with the beast and had not worshiped the statue or taken its number.

- In their hands they were holding harps which God had given to them.
- They sang the song of Moses, the servant of God, and of the Lamb:

"Great and mighty are Your works,
Lord God Almighty!
Just and true are Your ways,
O King of the nations!
Who will not fear You
and honor Your name, O Lord?
For You alone are holy.
Let all the nations bow in worship before You,
for Your righteous actions have been revealed."

SCENE 4: Final Judgments from Heaven

After that I saw the temple in Heaven thrown open wide. Seven angels came out dressed in dazzling linen with gleaming golden sashes:

- One of the four living creatures gave a bowl to each of the seven angels, seven bowls filled with the wrath of the Everlasting God.
- The temple was filled with smoke from the power and glory of God so that no one could enter the temple until the seven angels had finished pouring out the seven bowls on the earth.

Then I heard a loud voice from the temple commanding the angels, "Go! Pour out over the earth the seven bowls of the wrath of God!"

When the first angel poured out his bowl, everyone on earth who had the mark of the beast and worshiped the statue broke out in painful, malignant sores.

The second angel poured his bowl into the sea, which turned the water into a deadly fluid like the blood of a corpse. Everything in the water died.

The third angel emptied his bowl into the rivers and springs, and they all turned to blood.

Then I heard the angel of the waters say, "You are right and just in this, O Lord, Who Is and Who Was and Who Is to Come. They have shed the innocent blood of saints and prophets, so You have given them blood to drink. They are reaping what is due them."

The altar called out in agreement, "Amen, Lord God Almighty, Your judgments are true and right!"

When the fourth angel poured out his bowl on the sun, it became intensely hot so that men were burned by its heat. They cursed God for bringing this on them, but they would not repent or give Him respect.

Then the fifth angel emptied his bowl on the throne of the beast, and its entire kingdom was plunged into darkness. The people gnawed their tongues because of all the pain they were going through, and they cursed the God of Heaven but refused to repent of all they had done against Him.

The sixth angel poured out his bowl into the great Euphrates River. It instantly dried up and became a highway for the kings of the east.

Next, I saw three demon-spirits appearing as frogs, coming out of the mouths of the dragon, the beast, and the false prophet. They were able to do supernatural feats, convincing the kings of the world to join together against God Almighty in the great battle. They gathered in the place called Armageddon.

INTERLUDE: Warning

"Watch! Be ready!
I will come as unexpectedly as a thief.
Happy are those who stay awake
and have their robes ready
so they won't be caught naked and ashamed."

SCENE 4 resumes

When the seventh angel poured his bowl into the air, a loud voice came out of the temple from the throne, saying, "The end has come!"

Chaos broke out:
- There were flashes of lightning.
- There was deafening thunder.

- The most intense earthquake ever experienced shook the earth.
- The great city split into three sections.
- The cities of all the nations fell in ruins.
- God forced Babylon to drink the cup of the wine of His furious wrath.
- Every island and mountain disappeared.
- Seventy-five pound hailstones fell from the sky with deadly force, causing men to blaspheme God.

ACT 6: THE FALL OF BABYLON: CIVIL WAR ON EARTH

SCENE 1: The Major Players

One of the seven angels carrying the bowls of judgment called to me, "Come here and I will show you what happens to the great prostitute. She is seated upon many waters; the kings of the earth are in bed with her. Indeed, everyone on earth got drunk on her sensual delights."

Then the angel carried me away in the Spirit into the desert where I saw the woman:

- She was riding a scarlet creature that was tattooed all over with blasphemous words. It had seven heads and ten horns.
- She was dressed in purple and scarlet and decked out with all kinds of jewelry, gold, and precious gems.
- She was carrying a cup full of all the perversions of the earth, along with her own foul passions.
- She had a name emblazoned on her forehead: "Babylon the Great, mother of all prostitutes and perversions."
- I could see that she was drunk — drunk on the blood of God's people and those martyred for Jesus.

The angel could tell that I was mystified by what I was seeing. "Why are you amazed by this?" he asked. "Let me explain the mystery of the woman and the animal with seven heads and ten horns on which she was riding:

- The animal she was riding lived long ago, is no more, but will rise out of the bottomless Pit before going to its final destruction.
- Everyone living on earth whose name is not included in the Book of Life (written down before the world began) will be stunned and impressed by the reappearance of the beast.

"Now understand the meaning of all this:

- The seven heads represent seven mountains on which the woman sits.
- The seven heads also signify seven kings:
  » Five of these king are history.
  » One of the seven is reigning now.
  » The seventh has not yet appeared; but when he does, his reign will be short-lived.
- The beast mentioned before is actually an eighth king. He was one of the seven. He passed off the scene but returns at the end only to face final destruction.
- The ten horns are ten more kings who have not yet begun their reign:
  » They will receive authority to be kings along with the beast, albeit very briefly.
  » They will go to war against the Lamb.
  » The Lamb, together with His called, chosen, and faithful followers, will overcome them all. He is the Lord of lords and King of kings.
- The woman we have described is the great city which dominates the kings of the earth.
- The waters on which she sits are the vast multitudes, people of every tribe and language.
- The ten horns and the beast despise her, ravage and strip her naked, and finally burn her with fire. These ten kings unite in bringing down Babylon because God has put it in their

hearts to do so, thus accomplishing His purposes and fulfilling His Word."

SCENE 2: Perspectives on Babylon's Demise

A majestic, powerful angel came down from Heaven; his radiance illuminated the whole earth, and he announced in a mighty shout:

"Babylon the great has fallen! Once the pride of kings and merchants who made themselves rich with her extravagant luxury and wasted themselves on her sensual pleasures, she lies in ruins, a cauldron of demons and evil spirits, a haunt of jackals and wild beasts, and a roosting place for buzzards and vultures."

Then another voice came from Heaven, saying, "Come away, My people! Escape lest you succumb to her enticements and share in her punishment. Behold, her sins have piled to the heavens and God has taken note of all her wickedness:

- Pay her in kind for what she has done. Yes, give her twice the misery she has caused. Mix up a double-strength cup of judgment.
- To the degree that she flaunted her luxury and pleasure, reward her with torment and suffering.
- In that she boasted of being 'on top of the world, queen of all, never to lack a lover,' let the plagues, pestilence, mourning, famine, and fire fall upon her in a single day.
- Let her know that the Lord God who judges her is powerful.

"The day of her downfall will bring rejoicing in Heaven, but on earth:

- The kings who indulged in her pleasures will stand back in horror at the sight as the smoke rises from her. They will cry out, 'How dreadful! Babylon the Great — to think that your judgment could happen in a single hour!'
- The merchants from around the world will lift up a wailing cry as their marketplace goes up in flames. All their commodities will suddenly be worth nothing — gold, silver, jewels, and pearls; fine linen, purple, silk, and scarlet; fine woods, vessels of ivory, bronze, iron, and marble; spices,

incense, myrrh, and frankincense; wine, oil, fine flour, and corn; cattle, sheep, and horses; chariots, slaves, and even the souls of men.

- The consumers and retailers who enjoyed all the riches will stand back and lament the devastation, 'Alas, our glorious city, so prosperous and abundant — how could all that wealth be gone in a single hour?'
- The captains and sailors aboard the mighty freighters, all whose business is on the ocean, will see the smoke of her burning from far off and cry out, 'Was there ever a city as great as that city?' Expressing their utter despair, they will throw dust on their heads and repeat, 'What has happened to our great city where all who had ships grew prosperous because of her? How could this possibly all be gone in a single hour?'

"But let all heaven rejoice! All God's holy ones, apostles and prophets, shout for joy! God has taken up your cause and pronounced final judgment against her!"

An angel, a very strong one, took up a stone the size of a millstone (nearly a thousand pounds) and threw it into the ocean. "That is Babylon the Great," the angel said, "thrown down never to be seen or heard from again!

- Gone are all your entertainments — harpists, singers, flutists, and trumpeters — never again to be heard.
- All your fine craftsmen along with their handiwork are gone.
- There is no sign of life whatsoever.
- Gone forever is the joyous sound of wedding bells.
- You sold your souls to the sorcery of material wealth and to those who enticed you with temporal prosperity.
- You filled your streets with the blood of prophets, of God's holy ones, indeed with all the innocent blood of all time."

SCENE 3: Celebration in Heaven

Then I heard the sound of a huge crowd, a mighty roar, as they exclaimed, "Alleluia! Salvation and glory and power belong to our God! He has judged the great prostitute who corrupted the earth and spilled the blood of His servants! His judgments are true and right!" This was followed by an echoing, "Alleluia! The smoke of her destruction rises forever and ever!"

The twenty-four elders and the four living creatures bowed low and worshiped God who is seated upon the throne, saying, "Amen! Alleluia! It is done!"

Then a commanding voice from the throne said, "Give praise to our God, all you who serve Him, small and great!"

The vast crowd erupted in praise. The heavens shook as with rolling thunder and with the deafening roar of a great waterfall as they declared:

> "Alleluia! For the Lord our God,
> the All-powerful One, reigns supreme!
> Let us celebrate with wholehearted joy and exalt Him;
> for the wedding day of the Lamb has finally arrived,
> and His bride has made herself ready."

To His bride was given a gown of spotless, glistening fine linen, all her God-birthed acts woven into a glorious garment.

The angel instructed me to write this pronouncement as the very oracle from God:

> "Blessed are those invited to share
> in the marriage supper of the Lamb."

Overwhelmed by the majesty and glory of the moment, I fell at the feet of the angel to worship him; but he stopped me, saying, "No, do not worship me. Worship God alone! I am but a fellow servant of yours and of your brothers whose testimony is all about Jesus. Yes, the unfolding of all prophecy points ultimately to Jesus."

ACT 7: THE FINAL BATTLES: RESURRECTIONS AND JUDGMENT

SCENE 1: Confrontation with the Kings of the Earth

Then the heavens opened like a stage curtain and a magnificent white horse stood before me. The One who sat upon the horse was absolutely breathtaking:

- He is called Faithful and True — His every act of judgment is flawless; every act of war, justified.
- His eyes are flames of fire.
- His head is covered in jeweled crowns.
- There is a name written on Him which only He knows.
- His robe is dipped in blood.
- He is called the Word of God.
- Out of His mouth extends a sharp sword to strike the nations. As it is written, "He will rule them with a rod of iron."
- Singlehandedly He will tread the winepress of the furious wrath of God Almighty.

- Emblazoned across His robe and on His thigh is the title King of kings and Lord of lords.
- The armies of Heaven follow Him, riding on white horses and dressed in spotless, white linen.

I saw another angel standing right in the blazing light of the sun. He called out to all the vultures, saying, "Come! Gather together at God's great feast! Enjoy a banquet of rich meat as you feast on the flesh of kings and generals, warriors, horses and their riders, slaves and free, small and great!"

Meanwhile, on earth, I could see the beast along with the kings of the earth and their armies all converging in the valley of Armageddon. The next thing I knew, the beast and his false prophet, who, by his miracles, had deceived the world into taking the mark and worshiping the statue, were captured and thrown alive into the lake of fire which burns with sulfur. The remaining armies of the earth were wiped out by the sword that came from the mouth of the Rider on the white horse. The birds of prey had the feast of their lives!

Next, I noticed an angel descending from Heaven, carrying a key and a huge chain. He grabbed the dragon, the serpent of ancient days who is also called the devil and Satan, and bound him with the chain. Then he hurled the devil into the Pit and locked it shut for one thousand years so that he could have no access to the nations until the thousand years were over. Only then would he be temporarily released.

SCENE 2: The First Resurrection: The Saints Who Reign

After that, thrones were set up; and all the saints who had been martyred for proclaiming God's message and the story of Jesus (these were the ones who had refused to worship the statue and had not accepted its mark on their foreheads or hands) were resurrected and set on the thrones to reign with Christ for one thousand years. Uniquely blessed are those who get in on the first resurrection. They can never be touched by the second death. Instead, they get to serve God and Christ personally and reign alongside Christ for the thousand years. The rest of the dead won't come to life until after the thousand years.

SCENE 3: The Last Battle

At the end of the thousand years, Satan will be given one last chance to deceive the nations. He will gather them, numerous as the sand of the seashore, from all corners of the earth and rally them to surround the Beloved City. But fire will come down from the sky and consume them completely. Then the devil who deceived them will himself be thrown into the lake of fire and burning sulfur to join the beast and the false prophet. There they will face never-ending torture with no possibility of escape.

SCENE 4: The Second Resurrection

Then I saw a great white throne. The One seated upon it was so terrifyingly glorious it made you want to run and hide, but there was nowhere to go from His presence. The sea gave up its dead; death and the grave released the dead who were in them. A sea of humanity, great and small, stood before the throne.

Books were opened. Most were books containing the life history of each person. People were judged according to all that they had done. Also the Book of Life was opened.

Death itself was the first to be thrown into the lake of fire. No more death! Any whose names were not found written in the Book of Life were thrown into the lake of fire.

ACT 8: ALL THINGS NEW: NEW HEAVENS AND NEW EARTH

SCENE 1: The New Jerusalem

Suddenly before me was a brand new heaven and a brand new earth. The first heaven and earth as well as the seas had all disappeared.

Then, what looked like a city, a New Jerusalem, came floating down from God out of Heaven. It somehow looked like a bride coming down the aisle to meet her beloved.

Next, a voice from the throne announced: "Look, everyone! God now lives among His people — the Home He has always wanted. Now God will be your companion and will wipe every tear from your eyes. Never again death! No more pain! No more sorrow or sadness! Gone forever are your troubles!"

The One seated upon the throne added, "Yes! Everything is new! Count on it! Trust Me! I am setting everything right." Then He turned to me and said, "My plan is complete! I am Alpha and Omega; I began it all and I will wrap it up just as I planned:

- All who are thirsty can drink from My fountain of life at no cost.

- All this is for the overcomers. I will be their God, and they will be My sons.
- The cowards, perverts, unbelieving, idolatrous, murderers, and liars get what's coming to them, too: an inheritance of eternal death, the second death, in the lake which burns with fire and sulfur."

He then carried me away in the Spirit to the top of a tall mountain. He pointed toward that city I had seen descending from Heaven, radiant with the glory of God, the holy Jerusalem:

- She sparkled like a precious jewel, crystal clear, made of the purest gold.
- A massive wall surrounded the city with twelve gates guarded by twelve angels:
  - » The wall itself was built of translucent stone.
  - » There were three gateways on each side of the city: each gate was made of a single pearl.
  - » The wall was set on twelve massive foundation stones:
    - * On each stone was engraved the name of one of the twelve apostles of the Lamb.
    - * Each was fashioned out of precious stone: jasper, sapphire, agate, emerald, onyx, cornelian, goldstone, beryl, topaz, green goldstone, zircon, and amethyst.

I watched as He measured the city with a golden measuring rod:

- It formed a perfect cube whose length, width, and height were each 1,400 miles in length.
- The walls around the city were 216 feet thick.

Inside the city I saw even greater splendor:

- There was no temple or place of worship in the city because the Lord, Almighty God, and the Lamb are the temple.
- I saw no external light sources, sun or moon. God's glory illuminates everything and the Lamb is the light.
- The nations of the earth will operate in the light coming from the city, and they will bring their treasures and tributes into it.

- The city's gates will always be open since there is never night in the city.
- Nothing unclean, no one dealing in dishonesty, nor any kind of evil can enter at any time.
- Only those whose names are written in the Lamb's Book of Life are allowed in.
- I saw the river of the water of life, sparkling like crystal as it flowed from the throne of God and of the Lamb. It flowed right through the middle of the city.
- Planted along the banks of the river was the Tree of Life:
  » It bore twelve different fruits, producing a different kind each month.
  » Its leaves provided healing for all peoples.

No longer was there any evidence of the curse. As noted earlier, the throne of God and of the Lamb are within the City. God's servants will gaze on His face, His name engraved on their foreheads; and they will worship Him. There will be no more night and no need for artificial or external light because the Lord God will shed His light upon them, and they will reign together for timeless ages.

Then an angel said to me, "Know that everything you have seen and heard is utterly true! The Lord God, who inspired the prophets, has sent His angel to show His servants what is about to happen. You can rely on it!"

"Watch! I am coming soon! Those who pay close attention to the words written here will be blessed."

SCENE 2: Final Exhortation

As I, John, wrote these things down, I was again overwhelmed and fell at the feet of the angel who was explaining it all to me. "No!" he said to me, "I am just your servant and the messenger to your brothers, to the prophets, and to all who take hold of the words of this book. Worship God! And see that you do not hide this book," he added. "Everything written here will come to pass soon. Those who are bent on wickedness can carry on in it; those devoted to doing what is right should steadfastly carry on living good lives."

"See, I come quickly! I am bringing My reward with Me. Everyone will be rewarded according to what he has done. I am Alpha and Omega, the First and the Last, the Beginning and the End. Those who wash their robes are the truly blessed, for they have the right to the Tree of Life and freedom to come and go through the gates of the City. Shut out from the City shall be the depraved, the sorcerers, the impure, the murderers, the idolaters, and everyone who loves and practices a lie!

"I, Jesus, have sent My angel to you with this message for the churches. I am the One who created David, and I am his descendant who has now inherited his throne. I am the bright Morning Star!"

The Spirit and the bride say, "Come!"

Let everyone who hears this also say, "Come!"

Let the thirsty ones and all who desire the water of life come and receive it as a gift.

In closing, let me solemnly warn the reader and all who hear the words of this book:

- If anyone adds to these words, God will add to him the disasters described in this book.
- If anyone takes away from the words written here, God will take away from him his share in the Tree of Life and in the holy City which are described in this book.

He who is behind all of this says, "Yes, I am coming very quickly!" Amen! Come, Lord Jesus.

The grace of the Lord Jesus be with all His people. So be it.

APPENDIX A

The Earthly Lineage of Jesus Christ (from the Gospel of Matthew)

Jesus' genealogy through Joseph:

Jesus' lineage proves that He is both the Son of David and the Son of Abraham, which fulfilled important prophecies concerning the Messiah.

Abraham was the father of Isaac.
Isaac was the father of Jacob.
Jacob was the father of Judah and his brothers.
Judah was the father of Perez and Zerah
  (whose mother was Tamar).
Perez was the father of Hezron.
Hezron was the father of Ram.
Ram was the father of Amminadab.
Amminadab was the father of Nahshon.
Nahshon was the father of Salmon.
Salmon was the father of Boaz
  (whose mother was Rahab).
Boaz was the father of Obed
  (whose mother was Ruth).
Obed was the father of Jesse.
Jesse was the father of King David.
David was the father of Solomon
  (whose mother was Bathsheba, the widow of Uriah).
Solomon was the father of Rehoboam.
Rehoboam was the father of Abijah.
Abijah was the father of Asa.
Asa was the father of Jehoshaphat.

Jehoshaphat was the father of Jehoram.
Jehoram was the father of Uzziah.
Uzziah was the father of Jotham.
Jotham was the father of Ahaz.
Ahaz was the father of Hezekiah.
Hezekiah was the father of Manasseh.
Manasseh was the father of Amon.
Amon was the father of Josiah.
Josiah was the father of Jehoiachin and his brothers
(born at the time of the exile to Babylon).

After the Babylonian exile:

Jehoiachin was the father of Shealtiel.
Shealtiel was the father of Zerubbabel.
Zerubbabel was the father of Abiud.
Abiud was the father of Eliakim.
Eliakim was the father of Azor.
Azor was the father of Zadok.
Zadok was the father of Akim.
Akim was the father of Eliud.
Eliud was the father of Eleazar.
Eleazar was the father of Matthan.
Matthan was the father of Jacob.
Jacob was the father of Joseph, the husband of Mary.
Mary gave birth to Jesus, who is called the Messiah.

You'll note that there are almost the same number of generations from Abraham to David, David to the Babylonian exile, and from the Babylonian exile to the Messiah.

Appendix B

The Earthly Lineage of Jesus Christ (from the Gospel of Luke)

Jesus' genealogy through Mary:

Jesus started His ministry when He was about thirty years old. It was supposed that He was the son of Joseph.

> [Mary was the daughter] of Heli.
> Heli was the son of Matthat.
> Matthat was the son of Levi.
> Levi was the son of Melchi.
> Melchi was the son of Janna.
> Janna was the son of Joseph.
> Joseph was the son of Mattathiah.
> Mattathiah was the son of Amos.
> Amos was the son of Nahum.
> Nahum was the son of Esli.
> Esli was the son of Naggai.
> Naggai was the son of Maath.
> Maath was the son of Mattathiah.
> Mattathiah was the son of Semei.
> Semei was the son of Joseph.
> Joseph was the son of Judah.
> Judah was the son of Joannas.
> Joannas was the son of Rhesa.
> Rhesa was the son of Zerubbabel.
> Zerubbabel was the son of Shealtiel.
> Shealtiel was the son of Neri.
> Neri was the son of Melchi.
> Melchi was the son of Addi.

Addi was the son of Cosam.
Cosam was the son of Elmodam.
Elmodam was the son of Er.
Er was the son of Jose.
Jose was the son of Eliezer.
Eliezer was the son of Jorim.
Jorim was the son of Matthat.
Matthat was the son of Levi.
Levi was the son of Simeon.
Simeon was the son of Judah.
Judah was the son of Joseph.
Joseph was the son of Jonan.
Jonan was the son of Eliakim.
Eliakim was the son of Melea.
Melea was the son of Menan.
Menan was the son of Mattathah.
Mattathah was the son of Nathan.
Nathan was the son of David.
David was the son of Jesse.
Jesse was the son of Obed.
Obed was the son of Boaz.
Boaz was the son of Salmon.
Salmon was the son of Nahshon.
Nahshon was the son of Amminadab.
Amminadab was the son of Ram.
Ram was the son of Hezron.
Hezron was the son of Perez.
Perez was the son of Judah.
Judah was the son of Jacob.
Jacob was the son of Isaac.
Isaac was the son of Abraham.
Abraham was the son of Terah.
Terah was the son of Nahor.
Nahor was the son of Serug.
Serug was the son of Reu.
Reu was the son of Peleg.

Peleg was the son of Eber.
Eber was the son of Shelah.
Shelah was the son of Cainan.
Cainan was the son of Arphaxad.
Arphaxad was the son of Shem.
Shem was the son of Noah.
Noah was the son of Lamech.
Lamech was the son of Methuselah.
Methuselah was the son of Enoch.
Enoch was the son of Jared.
Jared was the son of Mahalalel.
Mahalalel was the son of Cainan.
Cainan was the son of Enosh.
Enosh was the son of Seth.
Seth was the son of Adam.
Adam was the son of God.

13457763R00197

Made in the USA
San Bernardino, CA
22 December 2018